Leveraging Technology as a Response to the COVID Pandemic

In 2019, the world was struck with the Coronavirus (COVID-19) infecting major portions of the world's population. There were no vaccines or treatments available to help mitigate the disease or offer a cure. The world's health systems were inundated with massive numbers of patients with varying ranges of symptoms, acuity, and levels of criticality. The world's healthcare organizations soon found themselves in an unmanageable situation, directly impacting the ability to manage patients across the entire healthcare environment. Most healthcare institutions had plans for emergency preparedness and procedures to deal with temporary crises, none of which were effective against the impact of COVID-19. COVID-19 was a highly contagious disease, resulting in high volumes of admissions with long lengths of stay. The virus quickly overwhelmed institutions with large patient volumes, resulting in shortages of patient beds, medical equipment, personal protective devices, cleaning agents, and other critical supplies. Hospital operations were further impacted by staff shortages due to exposure, resulting contagion, the shutdown of transit systems, and responsibilities at home due to school and business closures.

This timely and important book describes the impact on the hospital ability to provide patient care and how healthcare institutions leveraged diverse technology solutions to combat the impact of COVID-19 on providing patient care. The authors also discuss the implementation of these technology solutions and the many lessons learned of how healthcare institutions can enhance their emergency preparedness in the future from the COVID experience.

The authors would like to acknowledge, thank, and dedicate this book to the hundreds of thousands of healthcare workers around the world who spent countless hours and put their own lives and families lives at risk to help patients through this pandemic.

Leveraging Technology as a Response to the COVID Pandemic

Adapting Diverse Technologies, Workflow, and Processes to Optimize Integrated Clinical Management

Paul H. Frisch, PhD and
Harry P. Pappas

First published 2023
by Routledge
605 Third Avenue, New York, NY 10158

and by Routledge
4 Park Square, Milton Park, Abingdon, Oxon, OX14 4RN

Routledge is an imprint of the Taylor & Francis Group, an informa business

ISBN: 9780367769338 (hbk)
ISBN: 9780367769307 (pbk)
ISBN: 9781003352297 (ebk)

DOI: 10.4324/b23264

Typeset in Garamond
by codeMantra

To my wife, Susan and our children and their spouses, Paul & Katie, Lauren & Tom, and Daniel & Gabby and our grandchildren, Reagan, Mia, Austin, Zoey, and Landon, thank you for all the support which I needed to do my share and help deal with the impacts of the COVID pandemic. I hope you will all benefit from lessons learned from dealing with virus and will never need to deal with this type of virus again.

Paul H. Frisch

I would like to thank and dedicate this book to Dr. Paul H. Frisch, my longtime friend and a TOP healthcare technology professional. And to all of the front line healthcare givers who gave to save others. May the Creator grant them a long and healthy life.

I would also like to thank and acknowledge the hidden contributions that my wife, Linda, has made on this project and many others, along with my children Mark Pappas and Maria Pappas Sparling; my daughter in law, Giorgia Meseti Pappas; my son-in law Steve Sparling; along with my grandchildren, Penelope and Giada Pappas for their support as I worked on this book so that others may learn and unlearn about COVID-19.

Harry P. Pappas

Contents

About the Intelligent Health Book Series

IHA's COVID Book

The Intelligent Health Association (IHA) is pleased to be publishing a series of educational books under the name of the: "Intelligent Health" series in cooperation with our publisher, Taylor & Francis, a division of Informa a publicly traded London based, global events corporation.

The IHA advisory board and the IHA Educational committee have identified experts in many areas of health and wellness and have formed several committees, comprised of healthcare professionals and technology thought leaders for the purpose of publishing a set of technology centric books for the health and wellness community.

This book will be targeted to health and wellness professionals and clinicians who were involved in the recent COVID pandemic, designers, and manufacturers of medical devices and medical instruments, as well as healthcare and government administrators.

We organized a team of pandemic experts to both authors and edit chapters in this book.

The publication of this book and others will be available online via Barnes and Noble, Amazon, etc. Content from the books will also be repurposed into audio books, podcasts, webinars, and conferences in cooperation with its editors and authors.

Prior books sponsored under IHA's leadership, and its partners have been well received and circulated internationally. For an example:

https://www.amazon.com/Voice-Technology-Healthcare-Leveraging-Experiences/dp/0367403862/ref=sr_1_1?crid=3U7A0ZQY9YPGA&dchild=1&keywords=voice+technology+in+healthcare&qid=1599062738&sprefix=Voice+technologies+in+healthcare%2Caps%2C165&sr=8-1

This and other books in the Intelligent Health Series will be marketed through future conferences promoted by IHA and their partners, through Wikipedia, LinkedIn, and various industry and training events worldwide where IHA participates.

Let's educate the global health and wellness community together.

Thank you.

Harry P. Pappas, Founder and CEO

Paul H. Frisch, PhD, President IHA
Intelligent Health Association

Acknowledgments

Dedication to the Front-Line Healthcare Workers:

This book is dedicated to the many front-line healthcare workers who worked endless hours to manage and provide medical care to the millions of COVID patients seeking help and treatment in the world's healthcare organizations and systems. These medical workers placed themselves and their families at significant risk to continue to do their jobs and provide healthcare services at all levels within the hospitals, clinics, remote care facilities, and even in the home.

These workers not only made the difficult commute to their institutions but also worked multiple shifts performing a variety of diverse functions for long and endless days. Many fellow workers became ill and some succumbed to their contagion.

These healthcare workers along with many other critical workers, law enforcement, fire men and women, workers providing critical services and manufacturing are all to be recognized by the editors and authors of this book.

As a worldwide society their sacrifices need to be recognized and should not be wasted. The world needs to learn from this experience and move toward a unified alliance to address the world's medical, environmental, and politically driven crisis that can occur.

Paul H. Frisch, PhD

Attending Department of Medical Physics

Chief of Biomedical Engineering

Memorial Sloan Kettering Cancer Center

Harry P. Pappas

Founder and CEO, Intelligent Health Association

About the Authors/Editors

Paul H. Frisch is currently an Attending in the Department of Medical Physics and the Chief of Biomedical Engineering at Memorial Sloan Kettering Cancer Center. He currently serves on technical advisory boards of IEEE Counsel on RFID, ECRI Institute and serves as the Chief Technical Officer for the RFID in Healthcare Consortium and President of the Intelligent Health Association.

Paul's responsibility focuses on the investigation of new and evolving technologies, their potential integration into clinical applications, and operations to enhance patient outcomes, care, and safety. This includes management of Technology and Medical equipment to ensure device integrity, patient safety, and regulatory compliance. Current areas of investigation focus on clinical 3D imaging and printing, robotics, medical device development, and cybersecurity.

Previous experiences include research in electromagnetic field-induced gene expression focused on targeted gene therapy, human robotic application in pharmaceutical development, and biodynamic response resulting from transitory acceleration such as crash-impact and aircraft ejection.

Paul H. Frisch has a Doctoral degree in Biomedical Engineering from the State University of New York at Binghamton (2008) and Master's and Bachelor's degrees in Electrical Engineering from the State University of New York at Stony Brook (1975, 1976).

Harry P. Pappas is a successful, High Tech., Serial Entrepreneur with a strong focus on the health technology sector. He is a strong believer in applying technology to transform the health and wellness community in today's "Continuum of care" from-the-hospital, to the primary care giver, and to the patient's Smart Home. Pappas firmly believes that the world of digital health is being driven by the adoption of technology and therefore the need for Quality, ON-GOING education.

Harry is a global thought leader and has been a tech geek since the age of 12. He is a speaker at many Health and Wellness conferences and trade shows around the world.

He and his team are the producers of the award-winning "Intelligent Health Pavilion™" a technology centric, Digital Hospital that you may have visited at many trade shows around the world, including at HIMSS over the last ten years.

Pappas is the Founder and CEO of the Intelligent Health Association, a global, Social Purpose, educational, technology centric organization dedicated to helping educate members of the healthcare community on the adoption of new technologies, new software, smart drugs, apply digital therapeutics, and APPS that can improve patient care, patient outcomes, and patient safety, while driving down the cost of healthcare.

Harry is also the creator of the (i-HOME™), an "In Context" concept that demonstrates a plethora of health and wellness technologies placed in a Digital Smart Home setting. Harry was developing the concept of the "Smart Home" utilizing Steve Jobs, original Apple "NEWTON" PDA device many years ago.

He is clearly an "out of the box thinker" and a long-term strategic player in the world of health technologies for the Digital Hospital and for today's Smart Home.

Harry is unique in that he has "hands-on" experience with a wide variety of technology and software development projects as they relate to the health and wellness industries. He has been ahead of the technology curve most of his life and was developing data-driven e-commerce websites back in 1994.

Harry is an internationally recognized thought leader with auto-ID, BLE, NFC, RFID, RTLS, Sensors, Voice, Robotics, and Wireless technologies. He has been presenting educational programs around the world since 2001.

Harry's Goal: To help educate the healthcare community on on-going bases, so that it may adopt new technology, software, APPS, Voice, 5G, Blockchain, and AI that can have a dramatic impact on the delivery of improved health.

Mantra: "Help Others", Do "SOCIAL GOOD".

List of Contributors

Jim Beinlich's experience includes large, complex health systems in the areas of data and analytics, project and program management, strategic planning, process redesign, IoT, and operations improvement. Jim has consulted for large private health systems and academic medical centers as well as the US Department of Defense and the National Institutes of Health. He has held numerous senior leadership positions in large healthcare systems and was most recently the Chief Data Information Office at a large academic health system. Jim currently has adjunct faculty appointments at Temple University's College of Public Health and Widener University's Graduate School of Business.

Paul Booth, MS, is currently the Section Head of Biomedical Systems in the Biomedical Engineering Group of the Department of Medical Physics at Memorial Sloan Kettering Cancer Center. In this role, he is part of the team that is tasked with identifying and implementing new and evolving technologies into healthcare operations. Paul is also heavily involved in the Medical Device Initiative where he works alongside physicians and researchers and is the technical lead in the engineering and business development of new medical devices. He is also involved in the Biomedical Engineering internship program where several students each summer have the opportunity to work alongside medical professionals on engineering projects.

Paul has several patents for the devices and systems he has worked on and has peer-reviewed publications on technology implementations within healthcare.

Paul received a BS in Electrical Engineering from Bucknell University, MS in Electrical Engineering from Stevens Institute of Technology, MS in Finance from Texas Tech University, MS in Computer Science from Stevens Institute of Technology, and is currently in the PhD program for Technology Management from the Stevens Institute of Technology.

Elena Cyrus, PhD, MPH, is an Assistant Professor in the Department of Population Health Sciences, College of Medicine, University of Central Florida. Dr. Cyrus is an infectious disease epidemiologist with research experience in sub-Saharan Africa, Southeast Asia, and the Latin American and Caribbean region. Her research focuses on investigating social determinants of health contributing toward health inequities among vulnerable populations globally.

Tim Germann has spent more than 30 years building life science and healthcare businesses. He was a sales person and manager, consultant, and now a C-level executive responsible for all customer and industry-facing functions of Carterra, one of the world's most innovative and enabling life sciences companies. Tim has logged a career traveling the globe in pursuit of customers and partnerships of novel technology while hiring and inspiring dozens of commercial professionals along the way. He has lived all over the USA and twice overseas but hails from his beloved San Antonio, Texas. Tim graduated from the Marriott School of Management at Brigham Young University and is an annual guest lecturer at Princeton University where he coaches engineering students on how to start technology businesses. Tim currently lives in Salt Lake City, Utah, with his wife of 33 years, Joy; they have five children and seven grandchildren.

Dexter Hadley, MD/PhD, has expertise in translating big data into precision medicine and digital health. His research generates, annotates, and ultimately reasons over large multi-modal data stores to develop clinical intelligence and identify novel biomarkers and potential therapeutics for disease. His research is supported by grant funding for developing deep-learning methods in medicine including over $5M from the National Institutes of Health, and his contributions have yielded well over 60 peer-reviewed publications. Dr. Hadley is the Founding Chief of AI at UCF College of Medicine where his team is building a community of patients, clinicians, and data scientists that is needed to make this concept of community-driven AI a reality.

Samuel Hellman, PhD, Manager of Mechanical Engineering, is a mechanical engineer with a background in experimental fluid dynamics, thermodynamics, instrumentation, mechanical design, scientific imaging, and optics. In addition to his position at MSKCC, he holds an appointment as an Adjunct Assistant Professor of Mechanical Engineering at the University of North Carolina–Charlotte (UNCC). He has experience designing a broad range of mechanical systems and instrumentation for use in research and production environments. These projects span medical, aerospace, manufacturing, and energy-production sectors with academic, government, and industrial collaborations. His personal research has been related to experimental laser-measurement systems for flow-structure interactions.

Jennifer Nedimyer Horner is a medical student at UCF College of Medicine. Her research experience is in cell and molecular biology, and her clinical interests are in obstetrics and gynecology. As a non-traditional medical student with a previous career in editing for non-profit organizations and small publishing companies, she maintains a love for communication and literature. She currently serves as president of the UCF College of Medicine Literature Club.

Ashley Jackson is the Manager of the Health Technology Management Group at Memorial Sloan Kettering Cancer Center (MSK). She manages a team of over 25 engineers and technicians, with varied specialties (Clinical Engineering, Radiological Engineering, Service Coordination, Project Management), responsible for the maintenance and support of more than 36,000 medical devices across MSK.

Ashley is passionate about implementing technology-driven solutions to optimize operations within the hospital, ranging from small deployments of new technologies to large, institution-wide, medical equipment rollouts. She strives to find new and innovative ways to utilize technology to enhance patient care.

Ashley is an active member of numerous hospital committees, including the Clinical Device Product Evaluation Committee (CDPEC), Executive Safety Council, and the Alarm Management Committee. As part of the Alarm Management Committee, she has presented at events including but not limited to the Voalte VUE Conference, the Comprehensive Cancer Consortium for Quality Improvement (C4QI), and the 2019 MSKCC Joint Commission Opening Ceremony.

Ashley holds a Master's degree in Electrical Engineering with a concentration in Wireless Communication and a Bachelor's degree in the same subject.

Mary Jagim, MSN, RN, CEN, FAEN, Principal Consultant at CenTrak, is an experienced leader in healthcare consulting with an expertise in real-time location systems, emergency nursing, healthcare operations, and public policy. In 2001, she served as the national president of the Emergency Nurses Association (ENA) and led the development of ENA's Key Concepts in ED Management Course and Guidelines in Emergency Department Staffing Tool. She was also a member of the Institute of Medicine (IOM) Study on the Future of Emergency Care and the National Quality Forum ED Consensus Standards Committee. As the Principal Consultant for CenTrak, Mary works with healthcare organizations to leverage real-time technologies coupled with process enhancements to improve the patient experience, patient and staff safety, and workflow efficiency. Having implemented hundreds of real-time location system projects in the last 15 years, Mary is one of the most experienced clinical leaders and implementers in Healthcare RTLS in the world and developed the "Jagim Lean RTLS Model for Healthcare". She also currently serves as a member of the IoT Community, Healthcare Advisory Board.

Vinay Joshi is an entrepreneur with two decades of experience in the medical device industry. In addition to managing early stage startup companies, Vinay held senior roles with GE Healthcare and Hill-Rom where his responsibilities were focused on respiratory health products in the disciplines of product development and marketing. At GE Healthcare, he worked on diagnostic imaging and life support systems like ICU ventilation. At Hill-Rom, he worked on their airway clearance product portfolio. He is CEO of ABM Respiratory Care.

Vinay has a degree in Engineering from IIT Delhi and MBA from IIM Bangalore.

Matus Knoblich was born in former Czechoslovakia, a political refugee who escaped communism with his family in 1987. Growing up in New York and Florida, he attended the University of Virginia where he attained a Bachelor of Science degree in Chemistry with a special focus in Biochemistry.

Matus has focused on global business development, sales, and marketing since 2005, with an international assignment in Geneva, Switzerland for six years, conducting business in over 100 countries. During this time, Matus focused on company restructuring and building. In 2016, he assumed management of Med-Stat Consulting Services Inc., a medical device service company with specific focus on hospital bed repair. At this time, he also founded Glo-Med Networks Inc., with a focus on sales and distribution of new and novel medical devices and consumables. In 2019, Glo-Med began global distribution of the Orbel personal hand sanitizer, with many new and exciting products about to enter distribution as development is completed in the coming months and years. Matus opened a European office in Switzerland in 2020 to support Europe, Middle East, and Africa via founding of Glo-Med Networks AG.

Matus has continued his work in the sector, opening support businesses such as medical logistics facilities in the greater New York area and western Florida, along with a transport company, counting some of the largest and most respected healthcare facilities in the USA as his clients. With a devotion to family and staff, interests in snowboarding and boating, Matus looks to the future of healthcare and how he can have a direct impact for positive change.

Arthur Kreitenberg, MD FACS, is a Board-Certified Orthopaedic Surgeon and award-winning Clinical Professor at the University of California, Irvine School of Medicine. He has published numerous peer-reviewed studies and has served as a reviewer for peer-reviewed journals.

His interest in UVC disinfection technology dates back to 2009 H1N1 outbreak when he developed a device to disinfect volleyballs and basketballs that was used by Team USA in the 2010 London games. He co-founded Dimer UV and serves as the Chief Innovation and Technical Officer and has developed UVC products for aviation, spaceflight, farming, healthcare, education, athletics, and building environments.

The GermFalcon for aviation was named the best travel innovation in 2018 by the BBC and by the Global Business Travel Association. This UVC aircraft disinfecting robot, together with the GermRover, a robotic zero-gravity drone for disinfecting spacecraft, received top honors at a NASA iTech competition. In 2020, Dimer entered into a strategic partnership with Honeywell to commercialize the GermFalcon.

The UVHammer for healthcare has won industry awards for its novel design that overcomes inherent challenges of UV exposure including distance, shadowing, and angles of incidence. Dr. Kreitenberg and Dr. Martinello of Yale University coauthored a paper recommending tough standards for UVC devices to protect patients.

He is a member of the Association of Professionals in Infection Control and the American Institute of Aeronautics and Astronautics, an Associate Fellow of the Aerospace Medical Association, and a Fellow of the American

Academy of Orthopedic Surgeons. He was a two-time NASA Astronaut Selection finalist.

Cynthia Kyin is a medical student at the University of Central Florida, College of Medicine. She holds a Bachelor of Arts degree in Health and Human Biology from Brown University where she focused her studies on the social context of health and disease. Her research interests include the use of blockchain technology in healthcare and the application of machine learning for medical imaging interpretation.

Chris Landon, MD, is the Director of Pediatrics at Ventura County Medical Center, CEO of Landon Pediatric Foundation, and the Technology Development Center. He is currently a member of FathomWerx and serves as an advisor to Bodimetrics, Vironix, ABM Respiratory Care, and Bentley Biomedical.

Chris' interests focus on the investigation of new and evolving technologies, their potential integration into clinical applications and operations to enhance patient outcomes, care, and safety to promote global health. Chris focuses on airway clearance, remote patient monitoring, population management of COPD and asthma, artificial intelligence, and blockchain in healthcare.

Previous experiences include sponsored research in telemedicine and education in multiple sclerosis, asthma, and COPD through the USDA Rural Utility Services Distance Learning and Telemedicine grants, CMS Innovations grant, American Academy of Pediatrics, and pharmaceutical and device company support.

Chris Landon has a BS in Psychobiology from UC Riverside, MD from USC Keck School of Medicine, internship and residency at Stanford University, Allergy Immunology Respiratory Fellowship at Children's Hospital at Stanford, and certificate in Global Health from Harvard University.

Jennifer Larbi is a Project Management Team Lead at Memorial Sloan Kettering Cancer Center. She graduated from the Boston University College of Engineering with a Bachelor of Science in Biomedical Engineering Concentrating in Technology Innovation. She continued her education and received a Master of Science in Management Studies through the Questrom School of Business at Boston University. With her current role, she leads a team that manages medical equipment onboarding, customizing integrated system, and optimizing workflows. She also collaborates with the clinical team to select the best medical devices to utilize in the institution.

Jennifer is visionary who is driven to enhance how clinical engineering's role in the hospital can be utilized to help the future of hospital construction and their operations. She believes that patient care is the mission; innovation is the answer.

Tom Lawry serves as the National Director of AI for Health and Life Sciences at Microsoft and previously served as Director of Worldwide Health. Tom works with providers, payors, and life science organizations in planning and implementing innovative solutions that improve the quality and efficiency of health services delivered around the globe.

Tom focuses on strategies for digital transformation applied to performance optimization including artificial intelligence (AI), machine learning (ML), and Cognitive Services. He previously served as Director of Organizational Performance for Microsoft's health incubator (Health Solutions Group).

Prior to Microsoft, Tom served as Senior Director at GE Healthcare with global responsibilities for revenue cycle analytics and operational performance solutions.

Lawry was founder and CEO of Verus, a healthcare software company named as one of the Top 100 Fastest Growing Washington Companies for three consecutive years and to the Deloitte Fast 500 Technologies list.

For 12 years, Lawry served in various executive management roles in hospitals and integrated delivery networks. He has published numerous articles on using technology to innovate healthcare. His last book, *Artificial Intelligence in Healthcare: A Leader's Guide to Winning in the New Age of Intelligent Health Systems,* was a HIMSS 2020 Bestseller. His new book coming in May is *Hacking Healthcare – How AI and the Intelligence Revolution Will Reboot an Ailing System* (Taylor & Francis Publishing).

David Metcalf, PhD, has more than 20 years' experience in the design and research of web-based and mobile technologies converging to enable learning and healthcare. Dr. Metcalf is the Director of the Mixed Emerging Technology Integration Lab (METIL) at UCF's Institute for Simulation and Training. His research interests span simulation, mobilization, mobile patient records and medical decision support systems, visualization systems, scalability models, secure mobile data communications, gaming, innovation management, and operational excellence. His team has built mHealth solutions, simulations, games, eLearning, mobile, and enterprise IT systems for Google, J&J, VA, US military, and UCF's College of Medicine among others. Dr. Metcalf frequently presents at industry and research events shaping business strategy and use of technology to improve learning, health, and human performance.

Dr. Alisa L. Niksch, MD, is a pediatric cardiologist and electrophysiologist and currently serves as a Senior Director of Medical Affairs at Owlet Baby Care, Inc. She has lent her experience to the digital health, medical device, and remote patient monitoring fields since starting her practice at Tufts Medical Center in 2010. Dr. Niksch was Chief Medical Officer of Genetesis, Inc., a company which created a novel cloud-connected and AI-powered cardiac diagnostics and imaging platform where she led pivotal clinical trials and managed medical affairs initiatives. She has been an advisor and researcher for multiple healthcare companies like AliveCor, Cohere Health, Ometri, PraxSim VR, Medaica, Mindchild Medical, Zephyr Technologies, and Sproutling. She continues to be a startup mentor with programs at Northeastern University and MassChallenge HealthTech. She has authored a book chapter and articles in peer-reviewed journals on digital health and wearable technologies and has spoken on the applications of AI in medicine and the role and design of wearable technologies in clinical practice. She is a graduate of the University of Virginia School of Medicine and completed her cardiology and electrophysiology fellowship training at Morgan Stanley Children's Hospital at Columbia University Medical Center and Stanford/UCSF Medical Centers, respectively.

Rachna Sannegowda was born and raised in Orlando, Florida and is currently a medical student at the University of Central Florida. She graduated with high honors in Biomedical Engineering from the University of Florida. Her research interests are focused on mental health and include chronic pain perception, substance use in youth, and participant motivations toward community-driven AI.

Joanna Wyganowska, MBA, PMP, is a Senior Director of Commercial Marketing at CenTrak. Joanna Wyganowska works with progressive healthcare organizations to leverage real-time location solutions (RTLS) to reduce costs and improve patient and staff safety and experience. She has been sharing RTLS best practices through the RTLS in Healthcare Community. Joanna is a certified Project Management Professional, Lean Master, and a UAV Pilot.

Introduction—About the Book

In 2019, the world was struck with the Coronavirus (COVID-19) infecting major portions of the world's population. There were no vaccines or treatments to help mitigate the disease or offer a cure. The world's health systems were inundated with massive numbers of patients with varying ranges of symptoms, acuity, and levels of criticality. The world's health organizations found themselves in an unmanageable situation, impacting healthcare operations across all parts of the institutions. Most healthcare institutions had plans for emergency preparedness with procedures to help these organizations deal through these temporary crises, none of which were effective against the impact of COVID-19. COVID-19 was a contagious and long-lasting illness which overwhelmed institutions with large patient volumes, resulting in shortages of beds, medical equipment, personal protective devices, cleaning agents, and other critical supplies.

At many hospitals and healthcare institutions, technology leaders coordinated with administration to unify and focus on the various institutional technology groups including Biomedical Engineering, Information Technology, and Facilities to support the clinical departments' operational requirements targeting the needs of the patient and clinical staff (physicians, nursing, and all care providers) to deliver the much-needed patient care. Though all healthcare systems were significantly impacted by this pandemic, each institution approached the issues in alternative ways depending on the specific size and capabilities of the institution.

The focus of this book is to summarize and detail the many solutions that were implemented across a broad base of healthcare systems, including research institutions, large healthcare systems, and small regional patient care centers. The topics discussed in this book cover a broad spectrum of diverse topics, all focused on providing enhanced patient care during a very difficult and strained time. The topics cover areas including

- Shortages of patient beds, medical equipment, and devices
- Medical equipment management
- Facility expansion to enable larger patient volume
- Reconfiguration of medical devices and system to support increased patient capacity optimize staff safety
- Manage the lack of personal protective devices
- New technologies applied to infection control
- Patient management, remote patient care, and telemedicine
- Development of new medical devices and personal protective systems
- New data processing, analytics, and management tools
- New antibiotic discovery technologies

The importance of this book focuses not only on how diverse technologies were leveraged to combat the virus, but more importantly on the lessons learned from dealing with the pandemic. These lessons need to help identify and define the future requirements of healthcare's emergency preparedness. Any incident that drives a high patient volume presenting at our healthcare systems, including major storms (hurricanes, floods, etc.), terrorist attack, or other biological events, requires our healthcare institutions to be increasingly prepared to care, treat, and manage patients. If one good thing that can come out of the COVID pandemic is that it provided healthcare institutions the knowledge and experience to establish a methodology of dealing with future catastrophic events. Let's take advantage of what we have experienced and learned. Our objectives as a healthcare professional need to focus on education to drive and develop emergency preparedness solutions at all healthcare systems and organizations.

Paul H. Frisch, PhD, FHIMSS

Attending, Department of Medical Physics,
Chief of Biomedical Engineering,
Memorial Sloan Kettering Cancer Center,
New York, NY

Harry P. Pappas

Founder and CEO, Intelligent Health Association

Chapter 1

COVID-19—What We Learned from a Global Health Crisis

Tom Lawry

Contents

> *Stop using your phones and laptops as toys*
> *and use them to start a revolution.*
>
> —*Van Jones*

It arrived without warning. No announcements preceded it. No scientific papers were presented before it came crashing into our lives. The COVID-19 (COVID) pandemic was simply there when the day before it was not. We recognized it when our family, friends, and co-workers started getting sick and dying in numbers not seen since the beginning of the last century. Like something out of a bad science fiction novel, the human versus virus battle was on.

Healthcare has always been steeped in emergency preparedness, but nothing prepared it for what was to come. Intensive care units (ICUs) were quickly overrun by critically ill patients. As COVID patients were highly infectious, treatments for other medical needs came to a grinding halt. The lack of common items such as ventilators and personal protective equipment (PPE) became a matter of life and death.

DOI: 10.4324/b23264-1

Frontline caregivers worked around the clock. When systems were pressed to the brink, resourceful people stepped in to bolster, bridge, and fix what wasn't working. Makeshift ICUs were created. Ventilators were MacGyvered back into service.

Doctors and nurses displayed near superpowers. In the end, they were still human. What was already a problem of clinician burnout became an epidemic in its own right. It still is as I write this.

For some health providers, it was simply too much. Hospitals with no beds put critically ill COVID patients in planes, helicopters, and ambulances, sending them hundreds of miles away from family for treatment.[1] Refrigerator trucks served as makeshift morgues. People with other pressing medical conditions waited. And the sick and infected kept coming.

In the world of drug discovery, the race was on. As infection rates and death tolls climbed at a mind-blowing rate, we woke up to the fact that getting new drugs or a vaccine from the lab to the pharmacy historically took an average of 12 years at a cost of $2.6 billion.[2]

Almost overnight, consumers became legitimately fearful of premature death *en masse*. COVID cut to the core of what we universally care about the most. Our health. Our loved ones. Our jobs and financial security. In a matter of months, this singular issue forced everyone to change their daily living activities and to see their life priorities in a different light.

The world was seemingly descending into darkness never seen by those walking the planet today. Just when it felt like the bad news would never end, something happened. As humans always do, we learned. We adapted. We began to prevail.

People led the fight. The Intelligence Revolution gave them the tools to win.

AI and Digital to the Rescue

Early in the pandemic, health leaders discovered a body of knowledge on coronaviruses, but it was of little use as it was scattered around the world in disparate locations and formats. To solve this problem, the Allen Institute for AI, the National Institute of Health (NIH), and others leveraged something known as Natural Language Processing (NLP) and created the COVID-19 Open Research Dataset (CORD-19) which fused together 47,000 scholarly articles and studies in a matter of weeks.[3]

CORD-19 gave researchers, drug developers, and public health leaders open access to a unified body of knowledge that was fully searchable and readily sharable for collaborations worldwide, thus saving them precious time.

As pandemic pandemonium set in among citizens, Microsoft created a COVID bot and made it freely available to health organizations like the Centers for Disease Control (CDC). The bot walked anxious citizens through a series of questions, then provided guidance by intelligently mapping their specific situations to clinical guidelines. Forty million people used it to get accurate information and gain a sense of comfort.[4]

Because COVID was highly infectious, clinicians and health organizations turned to telehealth. Virtual visits became the centerpiece of adapting to keep consumers and providers connected. Before the pandemic, only 43% of health centers could provide telemedicine services. By the end of the first phase of the outbreak, 95% of health centers were using it. With this quick pivot, nearly one-third of all health visits in the summer of 2020 were conducted using telehealth.[5] At its peak, growth in telemedicine and virtual care shot up 38× from pre-pandemic levels.[6]

Telehealth facilitated patient triage and reconnected consumers to care providers. This reduced the effects of patient surges on care facilities. It also helped address limitations to healthcare access, conserved PPE, and reduced disease transmission.

Meanwhile, pharma and biotech companies faced impossible odds to compress the time to get a vaccine from the lab into the arms of consumers. AI evened those odds by improving the precision and speed of drug development while de-risking the process.

Intelligence tools were used to evaluate whether existing drugs could be repurposed for COVID. Researchers used AI to take ideas and progress them into actionable research accomplishing that in hours instead of months or years. It was used to interrogate massive data sets such as population-wide COVID infection rates and decades of accumulated research papers to spot valuable clues and trends for vaccine development.

AI expedited clinical trial simulations. As vaccines were approved and made available, AI tools ingested social determinants and other demographic data to identify and prioritize vulnerable and underserved populations to ensure equitable distribution.

Just as healthcare providers and pharma organizations were adapting through AI and digital technologies, so too were consumers in taking control of health issues that mattered most to them, using their smartphones, connected devices, and AI-driven apps to understand and manage their health and medical concerns.

In the first six months of the pandemic, downloads of mental health apps rose 200%. Diet and weight loss app usage climbed by 1,294%, while downloads to help manage diabetes jumped by 482%.[7] Mental health, diabetes, and cardiovascular disease apps account for almost half of disease-specific apps. Most are powered in some way by AI.[8]

In 2020 alone, more than 90,000 new consumer digital health apps hit the market. There are currently over 350,000 consumer health apps and that number is growing rapidly.[9]

Never Let a Good Crisis Go to Waste— Three Things We Learned

The pandemic challenged and changed all of us. It rearranged our priorities. It also taught us three valuable lessons:

- When individuals and populations are healthy, everything works better. When they are not, the interconnectedness of health to the economy, job security, and family safety becomes painfully and dangerously obvious.
- Health systems and health leaders are capable of agile transformation when faced with a big challenge. An industry previously known for changing at glacial speed suddenly began moving at warp speed. If we can do this for COVID, we can do this to tackle other big challenges.
- AI, digital and intelligent health work. These tools and solutions deliver a rapid time-to-value for providers and consumers alike when properly curated and applied.

The speed and effectiveness of our response to COVID were made possible by strong leadership. Clinical, health, and business leaders led from the front. They assessed long-standing work methods and then quickly adapted to address the current problem before them. You'll hear about some of these innovative breakthroughs in upcoming chapters.

Humans fought the COVID battle, but the increased use of AI, digital and other technologies allowed us to turn the tide in our favor quickly. It enabled and empowered clinicians and consumers alike to adapt at a much greater velocity.

Leveraging various intelligent tools, leaders rethought how to deliver care and services. Intelligent solutions were creatively put into service to make things smarter and faster. Without their use, the story would have been dramatically different.

In my last book, *AI in Health—A Leader's Guide to Winning in the New Age of Intelligent Health*, I put forward the concept of Intelligent Health Systems. Unlike Traditional Health Systems, Intelligent Health Systems are emerging as entities that leverage data, AI, the cloud, and digital tools to create strategic advantages and better outcomes. And while all health systems may lay claim to doing some of this, there is a difference in the approach taken by Traditional Health Systems compared to those on the path to becoming Intelligent Health Systems.

Both models recognize the inherent power of using data and AI to improve the delivery of health services. The approach of Traditional Health Systems is to use AI and digital tools to improve current service delivery models.

Intelligent Health Systems are taking this to the next level. They are using the Intelligent Health Revolution to rethink the entire delivery model. Their focus is on leveraging AI to efficiently provide health and medical services *across all touchpoints, experiences, and channels.*

Before the pandemic, we saw the slow but steady movement of traditional health providers and new entrants interested in becoming Intelligent Health Systems. The pandemic became a forcing function. It accelerated our thinking and willingness to change. It tested our ability to harness the power of the Intelligence Revolution to do good.

Satya Nadella, CEO of Microsoft, said it best at the beginning of the pandemic, *"We've seen two years' worth of digital transformation in two months."*[10]

Intelligent Health Systems are taking new approaches to overcome the age-old challenges of improving access, quality, and effectiveness, while lowering the costs of health services. In the future, they will become the health systems of choice as connected health consumers become the new norm.

This book is about understanding and applying what we learned from fighting a planetary health crisis. It's about using our newfound knowledge to tackle many other big challenges facing healthcare. Most importantly, it's about restoring power to clinicians and consumers alike by creating a system that is better aligned with our goals and balanced with available human and financial resources.

We had already started down the path of the Intelligent Health Revolution. Nature came along and gave us the impetus to go faster. The days of slow progress are over. We know what can be done. It's time to apply our learnings and experiences to tackle healthcare's other significant challenges.

We have an unprecedented opportunity to take what we've learned and make healthcare better for all. To create a system that empowers citizens to be healthier while providing better ways to care for them when they are not. To harness the power of the most highly trained health workforce on the planet.

Thomas Jefferson said, *"Every generation needs a revolution."* Let the Intelligent Health Revolution be our charge to improve the health of our people, our nation, and the planet.

Notes

1. Heather Hollingsworth, Jim Salter, With no beds, hospitals ship patients to far-off cities, AP News, August 18, 2021, https://apnews.com/article/health-coronavirus-pandemic-0ba6aa292483a89d52ab44b5f5434815.
2. FDA Drug Approval Process, Drug.com, April 13, 2020, https://www.drugs.com/fda-approval-process.html FDA.
3. Cliff Saran, Microsoft and Google join forces on COVID-19 dataset, Computer Weekly, March 17, 2020, https://www.computerweekly.com/news/252480156/Microsoft-and-Google-join-forces-on-Covid-19-dataset.
4. Delivering information and eliminating bottlenecks with CDC's COVID-19 assessment bot, March 20, 2020, Microsoft Official Blog, https://blogs.microsoft.com/blog/2020/03/20/delivering-information-and-eliminating-bottlenecks-with-cdcs-covid-19-assessment-bot/.
5. Trends in use of telehealth among health centers during the COVID-19 pandemic—United States, June 26–November 6, 2020, Centers for Disease Control, February 9, 2021, https://www.cdc.gov/mmwr/volumes/70/wr/mm7007a3.htm.
6. Oleg Bestsennyy, Greg Gilbert, Alex Harris, Jennifer Rost, Telehealth: A quartertrillion-dollar postCOVID-19 reality? McKinsey and Company, 2021, https://www.mckinsey.com/industries/healthcare-systems-and-services/our-insights/telehealth-a-quarter-trillion-dollar-post-covid-19-reality.
7. COVID-19: Digital Health Trends and Opportunities for 2021, The Organization for the Review of Care and Health Applications (ORCHA), January 2021.
8. Chloe Kent, Digital health app market booming, finds IQVIA report, Medical Device Network, August 2021, https://www.medicaldevice-network.com/news/digital-health-apps/.
9. Chloe Kent, Digital health app market booming, finds IQVIA report, Medical Device Network, August 2021, https://www.medicaldevice-network.com/news/digital-health-apps/.
10. CIO.com, April 30, 2020, https://cio.economictimes.indiatimes.com/news/corporate-news/we-saw-2-years-of-digital-transformation-in-2-months-satya-nadella/75471759.

Chapter 2

COVID-19 Healthcare System Impact and Hospital Response

Paul H. Frisch

Contents

DOI: 10.4324/b23264-2

Introduction

Starting in December 2019, a novel coronavirus, designated SARS-CoV-2, caused an international outbreak of respiratory disease identified as the novel, COrona VIrus Disease 2019 or COVID-19 [1]. On February 11, 2020, the World Health Organization (WHO) declared the disease a pandemic [2]. By April 2020, more than 1.2 million cases were reported worldwide, resulting in greater than 72,000 deaths [3]. As a result in early 2020 the world healthcare systems were experiencing a global pandemic event, which over the course of 2020 and continuing through 2021 spread across the globe, quickly impacting all healthcare systems which were unprepared to deal with this type of large-scale event. Over the course of the pandemic the world has experienced multiple peaks in the number of infections or transmission cases of the disease resulting 276 million cases (Figure 2.1) and 5.34 million deaths (Figure 2.2) worldwide as of March 22, 2022 [3]. The resulting influx of patients presenting at hospitals coupled with the large volume of admissions and subsequent patient deaths rapidly exceeded the capacity of hospitals and the overall healthcare systems capacities in terms of available beds, medical equipment, protective devices, supplies, overall resources, and staffing.

Coronavirus (COVID-19)

Coronavirus (COVID-19) is a novel virus, which means that humans do not have a natural immunity or ability to fight it off with their immune systems. The first known case was identified in Wuhan, China in December 2019 [4]. COVID-19 is a highly contagious airborne virus primarily entering the body through the eyes, nose, or mouth and progressing into the lungs, causing severe acute respiratory syndrome. Transmission occurs when people are exposed to and breathe air contaminated by droplets and small airborne particles. The risk of breathing in these particles is highest when people are in close proximity, but they can also be inhaled over longer distances, especially indoors. People can remain contagious for up to 20 days; however, experts believe that the time from exposure

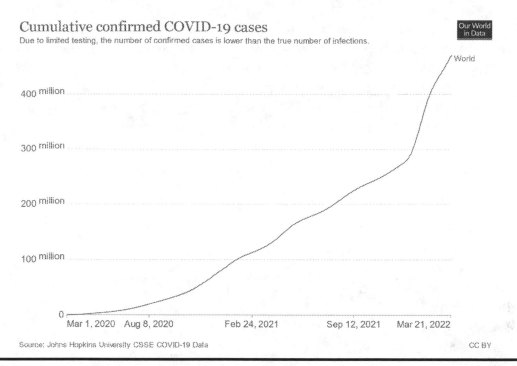

Figure 2.1   Cumulative confirmed COVID-19 cases worldwide 2020–2022. https://ourworldindata.org/coronavirus-data.

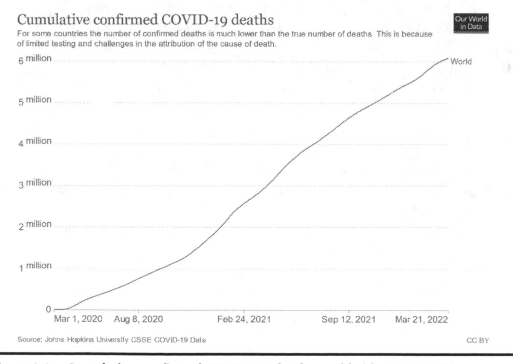

Figure 2.2   Cumulative confirmed COVID-19 deaths worldwide 2020–2022.

to symptom onset, also known as the incubation period, is 2–14 days. However, symptoms typically appear within 4–5 days of exposure [5]. It is important to note that not all cases exhibit symptoms and that the virus can be spread even if a person does not develop any symptoms [6].

People diagnosed with COVID-19 can exhibit a wide range of symptoms as outlined below, ranging from mild symptoms to severe illness which may appear 2–14 days after exposure to the virus.

The following symptoms are commonly associated with COVID-19 [7–9]:

- Fever or chills
- Cough
- Shortness of breath or difficulty breathing
- Fatigue
- Muscle or body aches
- Headache
- New loss of taste or smell
- Sore throat
- Congestion or runny nose
- Nausea or vomiting
- Diarrhea

At least a third of people who are infected do not develop noticeable symptoms [10]. Of those people who develop symptoms approximately 81% develop mild to moderate symptoms which frequently include mild pneumonia. Approximately 14% develop severe symptoms (dyspnea, hypoxia with greater than 50% having lung involvement as determined via imaging, and 5% suffer critical symptoms resulting in respiratory failure, shock, or multi-organ dysfunction [11]. Older people typically greater than 60 years of age and people with underlining medical conditions like heart or lung disease or diabetes are at a much higher risk of developing severe symptoms requiring hospitalization and result in potential death. Some people continue to experience a range of effects post-COVID for months after recovery, with observed damage to organs [12].

Preventive measures were quickly recommended by the CDC and other healthcare agencies to minimize the onset rate of the virus which included:

- Wearing face masks and coverings
- Avoiding crowded indoor spaces
- Ventilation

- Frequent handwashing and hygiene
- Social distancing
- Surface cleaning
- Self-isolation
- International travel-related control measures

COVID-19 Surges

To understand the impact on healthcare systems, it is important to establish metrics on the rapid onset and spread of the virus. Review of the statistics and data associated with surges provides a clear visualization of the stress on hospitals and healthcare organizations. The following section summarizes and highlights the data in terms of the world, United States, New York State, and New York City. There are many sources of statistical information which are available from a variety of government agencies, universities, the CDC, WHO, etc. Many of these sources provide data download capability enabling the COVID data to be analyzed from many perspectives [3, 13, 14, 15]. The impact of the virus to date (as of March 22, 2022) can be summarized as follows:

Country (Locations)	Total Number of Cases	Deaths
World	470,737,068	6,077,582
United States	79,734,788	972,361
New York State	4,948,160	67,203
New York City	2,290,000	40,020

In addition to the raw data identifying the magnitude of the infections and consequent deaths, the data needs to be examined associating the surge numbers in terms of impact on hospital resources. For this review and analysis, let's examine the impact of the initial patient spike or surge which resulted in an unprecedented large number of patients presenting at hospitals for testing, diagnostics, treatment, and admission.

Figure 2.3 illustrates an overview of the number of daily admissions or hospitalizations in the New York City over the course of the pandemic (February 2020–June 2021).

Similarly, Figure 2.4 details the resulting number of daily deaths due to COVID-19 over the same time period. As shown, the initial spike occurred in the end of February through the May 2020 time frame followed by a

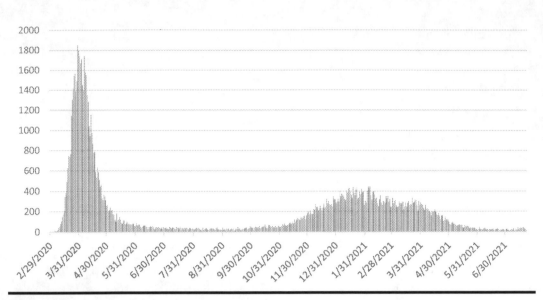

Figure 2.3   Daily hospital admissions in the New York City metropolitan area.

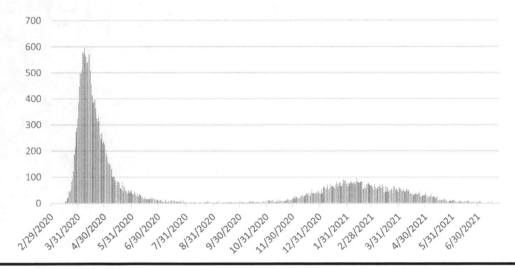

Figure 2.4   Daily COVID-19-related deaths in New York City metropolitan area.

secondary lower level, but longer duration peak starting in the fall of 2020 and continuing through the spring of 2021. In the first quarter of 2020, New York City became the epicenter of the coronavirus pandemic in the United States, putting historic pressure on the City's world-renowned healthcare institutions as the number of confirmed cases in the area grew exponentially. New York became the model of what other cities and areas of the United States would experience as the virus spread across the country.

As we examine the impact of the hospitalizations based on the data gathered of the initial surge, we can review the statistics and extrapolate key trends creating the overload conditions within the health systems. COVID-19 patients exhibited lengthy hospital stays with a median length of stay (LOS) ranging from 4 to 21 days with 4–19 days typical for intensive care unit (ICU) patients [16]. As reported by the US News based on a dataset published in the *Lancer Journal* on May 19, 2020, NYC patient hospitalizations resulted in 22% of all admissions requiring critical care within an ICU setting of which 79% of these ICU admissions required ventilation [17].

These factors directly contributed to the increasing need and urgency for ICU or critical care level facilities. These facilities include critical care beds, isolation areas, advanced medical devices, and systems, including physiological monitoring, ventilation, and infusion systems. Based on the statistic that 22% of all the admissions required critical care, we can then project the daily demand for ICU beds as represented in Figure 2.5, indicating that at the peak approximately 400 additional ICU beds are required daily to support the admissions.

Impacts on Bed and ICU Capacity

According to the American Hospital Association (AHA), there are a total of 6,146 hospital beds housed in 62 hospitals located throughout the New York City Metro area with a combined capacity of 15,659 beds which includes 2,111 ICU level beds [18]. To fully understand the impact of the COVID patient demand for beds, especially ICU level beds, one needs to examine the typical ICU bed availability and the LOS or utilization of the ICU beds. For most level 1 trauma centers and tertiary care facilities, ICUs typically operate at 80%–90% capacity even before the COVID-19 pandemic hit [19].

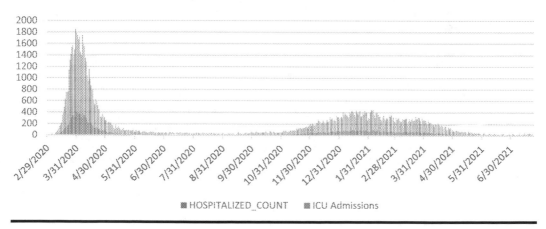

Figure 2.5   ICU admission as a function of admission.

As reported by FOX News on December 31, 2020 summarizing a *New York Times* report, highlighting a study published by the Society of Critical Care Medicine supported the statistics confirming typical ICU occupancy ranged from 57.4% to 82.1% [20, 21].

If one examines bed utilization as a function of patient LOS to determine bed availability, we can develop a broader view of how resources quickly diminish as a function of the increased LOS associated with COVID patients. Patient LOS varies as a function of the type or acuity of the illness and treatment protocols and procedures. The average LOS in a hospital is commonly used as a measure or gauge of the efficiency of a healthcare facility. The national average for a hospital stay is 4.5 days, according to the Agency for Healthcare Research and Quality [22]. The average ICU LOS is 3.3 days, and for every day spent in an ICU bed, the average patient spends an additional 1.5 days in a non-ICU bed [23]. In the case of COVID-19 patients' hospitalization, mean LOS is estimated to be between 15.8 and 20.1 days [24]. The impact of the increased LOS limits a hospitals bed turn-around rate rapidly reducing bed availability as the number of COVID patients requiring increase hospital stays.

The combined impact of the increased number of patients requiring ICU levels bed coupled with the increased LOS quickly impacts and exceeds the capabilities of most hospitals. Figure 2.6 illustrates the dynamics of this combined effect as a function of LOS, using the surge data observed in the New York City area.

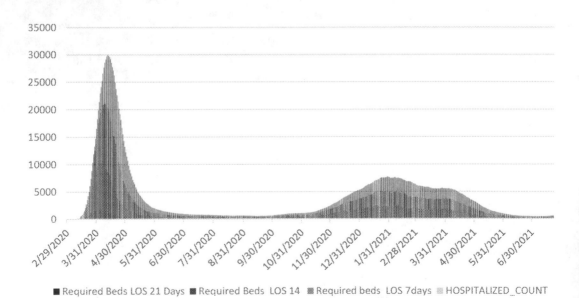

■ Required Beds LOS 21 Days ■ Required Beds LOS 14 ▓ Required beds LOS 7days ▒ HOSPITALIZED_COUNT

Figure 2.6   Increasing bed demand *as* function of LOS.

Hospital Impact and Expansions Efforts

In response to this magnitude of patients' admissions, Hospitals across New York started to erect temporary facilities, tents, rework spaces, and doubling up rooms where possible, in an effort to add beds and increase bed availability to support the increasing number of confirmed coronavirus cases. In March of 2020, Governor Andrew Cuomo issued Executive Order No. 202.5, which allows the state to rapidly increase hospital capacity to prepare the NYS healthcare system to handle the potential influx of patients suffering from COVID-19. To accommodate the anticipated increase in admissions, Governor Cuomo mandated the NYS Department of Health to suspend and relax certain regulations to allow existing hospitals to rapidly increase space and capacity [25]. In effect all New York's hospitals were ordered to put together plans to increase bed capacity by at least 50%, with a projected target to double overall bed capacity from 53,000 to 140,000. This order becomes one of the hospital's primary objectives to manage COVID patients. In New York Government officials and hospital executives worked to expand finding space for more beds, deploying the Army Corps of Engineers to convert the Javits Center into a hospital and bringing up a Navy hospital ship, the USNS Comfort, to handle non-virus overflow cases.

The initial surge of 2020 demonstrated hospital unpreparedness for this mass influx of patients. The impact was felt across all patient care areas including the Emergency Departments, in-inpatient beds ambulatory beds and all operations across the entire healthcare system. The pandemic required institutions to quickly expand and redefine the operational areas of hospital expanding bed capacity, add medical inventory with the expectation and requirement that the patient standard of care would not be impacted, and regulatory standards maintained. This required that fundamental systems such as nurse calls, EMR integration, and physiological monitoring coupled with supporting communications, to provide data delivery, process acknowledgment, and documentation continued to be in place and operational in all expansion areas.

Specific impacts varied from hospital to hospital, however, all healthcare institutions were severely impacted and had to come to grips of dealing with the issues outlined below:

■ Management of Large Patient Volumes
■ Insufficient Patient Bed Capacity
■ Insufficient Acute Care/ICU Level Beds
■ Limited Patient Isolation Capability

■ Shortages of Medical Devices Equipment
  – Ventilators
  – Patient Monitoring
  – Air Filtering Systems

■ Infection Control Issues
■ Shortages of Staff and Patient Personal Protection
  – Personal Protective Device (PPE)
    • Face Masks and Shields
    • Gowns and Shields

■ Shortages in Staffing and Availability due to
  – Contagion
  – Child Care Responsibilities
  – Transportation Limitations

■ Shortages of General Supplies
  – Medical Supplies
  – Cleaning Supplies

Technology-Driven Solutions

To attack these objectives, hospitals rapidly formulated collaborative inter-department working committees and groups to address the many issues facing the hospitals. In most cases, solutions utilized a diverse set of technology solutions, coordinated across all the many clinical areas of the hospital, requiring expertise from a broad range clinical and technical staff. Hospitals attempted to expand and reconfigure the patient environment of care to maximize bed availability and provide the necessary medical devices to maintain the required standard of care.

At most hospitals OR platforms were shut down for surgical procedures and converted as one of the critical care (ICU) expansion areas which effectively doubled the critical bed capacity. Similarly, other locations such as the Surgical Acute Care Unit (step down area), provided additional expansion and overflow capability which fortunately already supported many of the required clinical systems and medical devices such as physiological monitoring, telemetry, and advanced communications.

To support the increased bed/patient capacity, expanding medical equipment requirements were analyzed and correlated with the existing inventory to identify the specific equipment which needed to be acquired (purchased or rented).

In today's intelligent hospital environment medical devices are not simply standard-alone devices, but are complex medical systems that operate, communicate and pass information via the hospitals network and wireless infrastructure integrating with other medical devices and clinical applications. These complex medical data systems enable a seamless data environment, providing connectivity, data archival, and alarm delivery to the point of care and ensure data integrity and association to the patient. Deploying medical equipment without this connectivity and associated integrations impacts both patient care and operational workflow. With all hospitals simultaneously attempting to obtain medical devices and supporting equipment, obtaining the appropriate devices supporting the necessary capabilities was challenging and frequently not possible. This required institutions to quickly alter, adjust and update their patient care model and workflows, and utilize their technology groups to develop and establish temporary solutions and workarounds.

To achieve these objectives, large quantities of medical devices and systems were redistributed, on-boarded, networked, and configured throughout the institution. It was critical that all devices were networked into the hospital infrastructure to maintain as seamless of data environment as possible. Since many hospitals in New York City utilize a common complement of medical equipment this quickly resulted in shortages as outlined below:

Increasing Medical Equipment Inventory Requirements

■ Ventilators
■ Physiological Monitoring
  – Continuous
  – Vital Signs Intermittent
  – Telemetry

■ Infusion Systems
■ Feeding Pumps
■ Air Quality Filtering Systems
  – Hepa Filters

Management of Medial Equipment and Supporting Inventory Processes

During the pandemic the acuity of patients rapidly changed between various patient care areas. It was critical that equipment be rapidly on-boarded, identified, acceptance tested, and device status determined and distributed as patients' distributions changed with environment of care. With the shortages of medical equipment and the influx of large quantity devices and systems, which included new purchases, and temporary devices such as loaners, and rentals the precise management of this inventory was vital to manage and support the continuing needs of the institution and patients, The hospitals centralized medical equipment database or archive needed to be accurately updated to provide detailed information of devices, availability, and location to all clinical areas. Even under pandemic conditions each medical device needed to follow the regulatory standards, including acceptance testing, and inspection by Biomedical Engineering prior to deployment. From a cybersecurity perspective, devices also needed be assessed in terms of risk and vulnerability. All mobile and critical devices were also tagged with active radio frequency identification technology to enable device real-time location and tracking. The inventory needed to be globally visualized and available to all departments, staff, and users throughout the organization regardless of site or location.

The database enabled visualization via real-time location system (RTLS) technology which enhanced the management and distribution of medical equipment resulting from the fluctuations in COVID patient surges. Institutions which were RFID /RTLS enabled were able to capitalize on these enhanced inventory management processes. Memorial Sloan Kettering Cancer Center has utilized active RFID-based systems operating on the hospitals robust Wi-Fi infrastructure for many years enabling the optimization of inventory management processes and workflow. Prior to the pandemic the hospitals 60,000+ medical device inventory had 25% of the device's RFID enabled.

During the pandemic the influx of critical devices, such as heap filters and ventilators were required to be RFID tagged as part of the on-boarding process to ensure rentals, loaner and government provided inventory was easily tracked, visible and recoverable within the institution.

Minimizing Staff Exposure

During this period of patient overload with a high volume of patients requiring critical care, medical staff was also dealing with shortages of personal protective equipment and devices. With the closure of schools and transition to remote learning, childcare became a major issue for many younger parents and staff. In addition, public transportation systems were shut down resulting in the lack of subway and bus transportation limiting the ability for staff to travel back and forth to work. As the surge continued many staff members also became infected or exposed resulting in absence and quarantine of vital and critical staff. As the number of staff members unable to report to work increased, it quickly became clear that all clinical staff especially clinical patient facing staff needed to be protected as much as possible to minimize the growing staff shortage. As part of the patient care environment reconfiguring and expansion several innovative steps were developed and implemented to minimize staff exposure by limiting the amount of times staff needed to enter the patient room to review the patients' physiological parameters or handle equipment. To minimize this exposure the following solutions were implemented within the patient care areas:

- Position Monitoring Systems Closer to Door Proximity
- Mount Monitoring Systems Outside the Room (where possible)
- Use of Remote Applications to Display Physiological Parameters outside the room
- Install Extended Remotes
- Maximize the Use of Central Monitoring Stations and Slave displays

These mobile and configurable solutions were deployed providing alarm and critical parameter delivery to the institutional EMR, data archives as well as delivery to remote workstation (Figure 2.7) and handheld devices at the point of care.

Infection Control and Personal Protection Equipment/Devices

With high demand for personal protection equipment, dwindling supplies of this PPE continued to grow. MSK implemented a methodology of managing the distribution PPE to staff, while simultaneously investigating and preparing methods of reprocessing PPE and other devices. Biomedical Engineering investigated the combined use of UV and hydrogen peroxide vapor sterilization (HPO) processes to reprocess various types of PPE. The Hospital worked with Central Processing Department (CPD), Nursing, Infection Control, and Environmental Safety to develop the process of managing the collection, association of PPE to specific staff, and redistributing

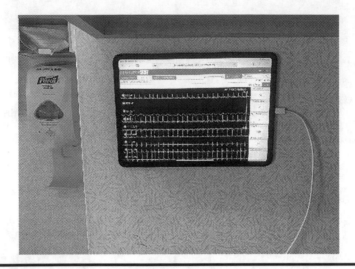

Figure 2.7   Remote monitoring to minimize staff exposure.

the reprocessed PPE. In parallel the hospital was designing and developing a dedicated reprocessing facility. The facility was designed and configured for both UV and HPO technologies and systems and was operationally setup to start a daily reprocessing. Significant workflow was designed for collection and redistribution of PPE maximizing staff safety and ensuring that all PPE was handled, reprocessed, and returned to the original users of the PPE. This facility was ready for operation as the shortages started to lift and PPE started to become increasingly available. The unit remains ready should future conditions warrant its use, with staff continuing to investigate and evaluate the effectiveness of the reprocessing methods.

The shortages also extended to supplies, where hospitals had limited access to disinfectants and hand sterilizing solutions. Novel approaches which included internal preparation of hand sanitizer in our laboratories, ensured sufficient quantities of hand sanitizer for our patients and staff. MSK also deployed a novel personal hand sanitizer product worn by the clinical staff, as illustrated in Figure 2.8. This product complimented our traditional use of sanitizers and enabled staff to enhance compliance with our infection control policies and standards.

Drivers for Change

Telemedicine

The COVID-19 pandemic highlighted the limitations and vulnerabilities of the standard healthcare model. Over the years innovators have developed

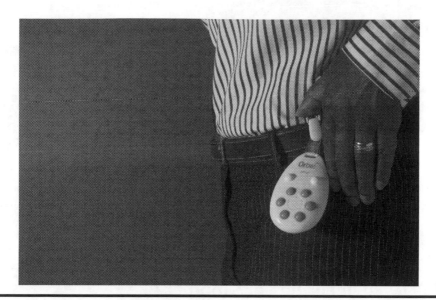

Figure 2.8   Personal hand sanitizer solution.

new telehealth models and practices. With the limitations being experienced in the hospital systems and patient reluctance to come to large healthcare organizations, exploiting home health possibilities became a driver for treating patients remotely in their home. The evolution of home-based networks and wireless capabilities like Wi-Fi and Bluetooth have enabled an assortment of medical devices to be used at home communicating back to hospitals over these networks. This enabled hospitals to manage patients remotely limiting the number of patients requiring follow-up at the hospital offsetting the patient load already being experienced in the Emergency departments and critical care units.

Data Analytics

The COVID-19 pandemic also heightened the importance and use of healthcare data and analytics in a way that has not been seen before. Accurate, reliable data and information played a critical role in providing healthcare executives and caregivers with the tools needed to make critical decisions. Unlike the normal operations of a health system and the associated information flow, which is very predictable based on seasonality, service volume norms. As Hospitals and health systems struggled to understand what might happen with COVID-19 hospitalizations continued to grow at an alarming rate. Inpatient census in the United States for COVID-19 patients exploded in just 26 days from March 26 to April 21, according to statistics from the COVID Tracking Project [26]. Healthcare administrators scrambled to plan for unknown surges in hospitalizations, ICU admissions, ventilators, and other medical device needs.

COVID-19 forced healthcare systems to utilize real-time data coming from other countries as information from which to make key decisions. This data was the only reliable historical data that could be used to start projecting future cases, hospitalization, etc. This data became the fundamental source for analytic prediction and decision support. This demonstrated the importance and value of analytic tools utilizing real-time data sources to drive administrative decisions and clinical care solutions.

COVID-19 Engineering Development

In traditional hospitals, Biomedical Engineering's role is primarily focused on Health Technology Management or Clinical Engineering emphasizing medical equipment management, service support, maintenance, and preventative maintenance ensuring regulatory compliance and addressing the environment of care initiatives of CMS and Joint Commission. As was previously discussed this expertise played a significant role in equipment expansion and management during the pandemic. However, at MSK Biomedical Engineering with a strong focus on the investigation of new and evolving technologies, was able to exploit these resources to impact patient care, enhance outcomes and ensure improved patient safety and satisfaction. At MSK, Biomedical Engineering supporting strong synergies and affiliations with IT and clinical departments focused its resources to provide analytic, design, and development capabilities exploiting and implementing new technologies and innovations. Biomedical Engineering was augmented to include electromechanical and software application development and production capabilities which included a Mechanical Engineering and Biomedical Systems groups providing capabilities in mechanical design, CAD, manufacture, basic research, electrical and electromechanical design project management, and software applications development. These groups operate the Institutions dynamic simulation laboratory (SimLab) as well as the clinical 3D printing laboratory adding a new dimension to exploiting technology and engineering development. The SimLab provides a unique dynamic design and development testbed enabling clinical device and software upgrade testing, and the evaluation of new devices and interfaces, cybersecurity vulnerabilities, new technologies, the creation of new workflows, and staff training in an isolated environment minimizing patient safety and risk. The 3D Printing laboratory originally implemented as a rapid prototyping and production tool, was quickly focused and enabled patient-specific treatment solutions, such as anatomically accurate models, custom surgical guides, and tooling.

Responding to a Crisis with 3D Printing, Design, Engineering, and Production

With the onset of COVID-19 pandemic the value of this type of in-house capability and functionality was quickly realized and demonstrated. Innovations both of our own initiation as well as those defined by groups within Memorial Sloan Kettering Cancer Center (MSKCC) and outside organizations where quickly designed, prototyped, evaluated and developed for production. Dealing with uncertainty and supply chain failures, these teams designed and implemented medical devices, PPE, and novel solutions to meet the needs of the hospital staff and patients. COVID-19 demonstrated the need for immediate parts, mechanical devices, and medical devices.

As the COVID-19 pandemic exploded within the hospital these biomedical investigation and development groups were targeted to support the most critical needs of our hospital. This capability quickly focused on the development of COVID-19-related innovations which included the design of medical devices, PPE, and novel solutions to meet the escalating needs of the hospital staff and patients. The following projects were successfully implemented and deployed to aid in the battle against COVID:

■ Modification of Snorkel Masks for Use as PPE
■ Filter Adapters for 3M Face Masks
■ 3D Printed Face Shields
■ 3D Printed Testing Swabs
■ HEPA Filter Conversion to Spot Ventilation
■ MSK Octopus: Multi-Patient Ventilator Splitting
■ Crisis Vent: Emergency-Use Ventilator
■ Intubation/Extubation Aerosol Boxes

These programs are detailed in subsequent chapters along with several developments and diverse solutions outlined below.

Ventilation Support Systems

As previously discussed in the early stages of the pandemic, hospital systems were overwhelmed with patients needing mechanical ventilation and consequent shortage of ventilation systems [27]. A number of solutions were proposed to meet the demand: emergency production of new ventilators (both by existing manufacturers and non-medical/automotive manufacturers), home-made ventilators created by medical providers or universities, alternative ventilation solutions, and splitting/sharing of existing ventilators. An immediate solution enabled rapid turn-around focused in on the splitting of ventilator systems between patients. In March of 2020, when the New York State approved the emergency use of ventilator splitting for COVID-19 patients [28], a collaborative MSKCC team with members from Biomedical Engineering, Anesthesiology and Surgery came together to work on this challenge and established the requirements. The proposed solution, shown in Figure 2.7, incorporated the use of an adjustable, fixed-pressure regulator on each parallel ventilation circuit and allowed completely independent adjustment of inspiratory pressure for every patient [29](Figure 2.9).

Crisis Ventilator

In a parallel effort a team consisting of Surgeons, Biomedical Engineers, Respiratory Therapists, Anesthesiologists, and Device Development Engineers came together to design, and build a prototype of what we

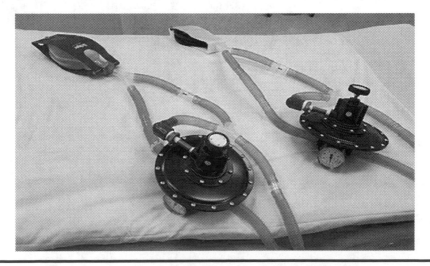

Figure 2.9   Ventilation splitter—enabling multiple patients/ventilator.

characterize as an emergency-use crisis ventilator or "Crisis Vent." The intent of this device was to provide a compromise between functionality, simplicity, and ease of building to facilitate the broadest possible distribution of lifesaving care in the event of a traditional equipment shortage. This was not a traditional ventilator, but rather a method to provide a bare minimum of functionality to maintain a sick patient when no other option exists.

3D Printing and PPE Development

Intubation/Extubation Boxes

Various types of PPE were promptly adopted or developed to protect patients and healthcare providers (HCP) from airborne viral exposure to COVID-19. Clinicians working with a patient's airway were objectively determined to be in the highest risk category. One area of particularly high potential exposure risk for HCPs is during intubation/extubation of patients with COVID-19. The insertion and, even more so, removal of endotracheal tubes can generate aerosols exiting the patient's mouth and are thought to potentially contain high viral loads which might put those nearby at risk of infection. A solution known as "the aerosol box" was created by Dr. Hsein Yung Lai at Mennonite Christian Hospital in 2020 to help contain these aerosols during intubation/extubation of patients [30]. The box consists of a plexiglass enclosure that fits over the patient's head/neck and contains arm holes in the superior (head) side for the HCP to work as well as a flap on the inferior (chest) side to allow ventilation tubing access. His idea garnered a lot of attention and multiple adaptations and iterations on the design were quickly created and deployed at MSK and by teams across the world.

MSK was able to leverage our in-house fabrication capabilities in order to manufacture several items which were not readily available for purchase. In particular, 3D printing technology was critical in enabling us to deliver many of the items which were needed early in the pandemic and others where we were able to proactively plan for the heightened risk of a potential shortage in the future. Our Biomedical Engineering group used 3D printing in the production of face shields, mask adapters, respirator adapters, ventilation tubing adapters, and nasopharyngeal test swabs amongst others. More than 700 face shields were internally produced over the course of a month, 300 more were printed and donated to us by non-medical business partner companies and this kept many of our healthcare workers protected until we were again able to purchase them from commercial suppliers.

Case Study: 3D Printed Nasopharyngeal Test Swabs

Another critical supply which was difficult to source in early 2020 were nasopharyngeal test swabs used for COVID-19 testing. A collaborative effort between a printer manufacturer (Formlabs) and two hospital groups (Northwell Health and USF Health) yielded a design which could easily be printed and sterilized for clinical use [31]. We were able to quickly set up a system to print and process up to 2,000 swabs daily. Within a few days, we made test prints, ran through sterilization, and had our internal teams validate efficacy and approve for use (Figure 2.10).

Emergency Preparedness Lessons Learned

The events of the Coronavirus pandemic have clearly identified the need for expanded emergency preparedness and preparation for the unexpected. These events can be natural events such as hurricanes, floods, or earthquakes, or deliberate events such as terrorist attacks. As we read through the chapters and reflect on the steps that were taken by the many institutions across the United States and the world, it becomes clear that the successful implementation of solutions is largely dependent on having specific

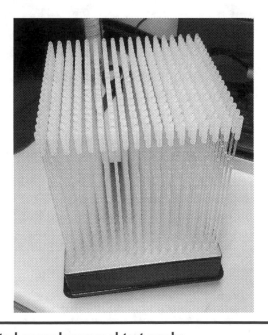

Figure 2.10   3D printed nasopharyngeal test swabs.

technologies, capabilities, workflows, and plans in place prior to any event occurring. Though the world has moved to supply on demand business model, COVID has demonstrated that there is a realistic need to maintain at least a minimum level of supplies, or maintain in-house capability to design and produce alternative PPE, and hygiene products, etc. to support unplanned events. Fortunately, the pandemic did not affect power and utility disruptions, however, it is easy to envision how these could have significantly further impacted our COVID response and further introduced risk to patient outcomes and safety. Any emergency preparation planning needs to address a broad set of unplanned events enabling healthcare systems to continue to deliver quality and continuous patient care.

References

1. The Editorial Board (29 January 2020). "Is the World Ready for the Coronavirus?—Distrust in Science and Institutions Could Be a Major Problem if the Outbreak Worsens". *The New York Times*. Retrieved 30 January 2020. https://www.nytimes.com/2020/01/29/opinion/coronavirus-outbreak.html
2. Page J, Hinshaw D, McKay B (26 February 2021). "In Hunt for Covid-19 Origin, Patient Zero Points to Second Wuhan Market—The Man with the First Confirmed Infection of the New Coronavirus Told the WHO Team that His Parents Had Shopped there". *The Wall Street Journal*. Retrieved 27 February 2021. https://www.wsj.com/articles/in-hunt-for-covid-19-origin-patient-zero-points-to-second-wuhan-market-11614335404
3. https://www.worldometers.info/coronavirus/.
4. McNeil Jr DG (2 February 2020). "Wuhan Coronavirus Looks Increasingly Like a Pandemic, Experts Say". *The New York Times*. ISSN 0362-4331. Retrieved 4 April 2020 (1st Case Coronavirus). https://www.nytimes.com/2020/02/02/health/coronavirus-pandemic-china.html
5. *Medical News Today Newsletter*, ZawnVilinette May 5, 2020.
6. https://www.seattlechildrens.org/conditions/a-z/covid-19-exposure-but-no-symptoms/Transmission without symptoms.
7. https://www.cdc.gov/coronavirus/2019-ncov/symptoms-testing/symptoms.html.
8. U.S. Centers for Disease Control and Prevention (CDC) (22 February 2021). "Symptoms of Coronavirus". Archived from the original on 4 March 2021. Retrieved 4 March 2021. https://www.cdc.gov/coronavirus/2019-ncov/symptoms-testing/symptoms.html
9. Grant MC, Geoghegan L, Arbyn M, Mohammed Z, McGuinness L, Clarke EL, Wade RG (23 June 2020). "The Prevalence of Symptoms in 24,410 Adults Infected by the Novel Coronavirus (SARS-CoV-2; COVID-19): A Systematic

Review and Meta-Analysis of 148 Studies from 9 Countries". *PLoS One*. 15 (6): e0234765. Bibcode:2020PLoSO.1534765G. doi:10.1371/journal.pone.0234765. PMC 7310678. PMID 32574165. S2CID 220046286.

10. Oran DP, Topol EJ (January 2021). "The Proportion of SARS-CoV-2 Infections That Are Asymptomatic: A Systematic Review". *Annals of Internal Medicine*. 174 (5): M20–6976. doi:10.7326/M20-6976. PMC 7839426. PMID 33481642.

11. U.S. Centers for Disease Control and Prevention (CDC) (6 April 2020). "Interim Clinical Guidance for Management of Patients with Confirmed Coronavirus Disease (COVID-19)". Archived from the original on 2 March 2020. Retrieved 19 April 2020. https://www.cdc.gov/coronavirus/2019-ncov/hcp/clinical-care/clinical-considerations-index.html?CDC_AA_refVal=https%3A%2F%2Fwww.cdc.gov%2Fcoronavirus%2F2019-ncov%2Fhcp%2Fclinical-guidance-management-patients.html

12. Jump up to: CDC (11 February 2020). "Post-COVID Conditions". U.S. Centers for Disease Control and Prevention (CDC). Retrieved 12 July 2021. https://www.cdc.gov/coronavirus/2019-ncov/long-term-effects/index.html?CDC_AA_refVal=https%3A%2F%2Fwww.cdc.gov%2Fcoronavirus%2F2019-ncov%2Flong-term-effects.html

13. https://www.nytimes.com/interactive/2021/us/new-york-covid-cases.html.

14. http:/worldometer.info/coronavirus.

15. https://covid.cdc.gov/covid-data-tracker/#datatracker-home.

16. Chiam T, Subedi K, Chen D, Best E, Bianco FB, Dobler G, Papas M (26 June 2021). "Hospital Length of Stay among COVID-19-Positive Patients". *Journal of Clinical and Translational Research*. 7 (3): 377–385. Published online June 5 2021.

17. *Lancet* Journal May 19, 2020.

18. https://coronavirus.health.ny.gov/hospital-bed-capacity.

19. https://www.beckershospitalreview.com/patient-flow/2-healthcare-leaders-talk-icu-capacity-5-sound-bites.html, Lancer Journal.

20. https://fox11online.com/newsletter-daily/what-you-need-to-know-about-icu-capacity-in-the-united-statesFox News.

21. Wunsch H, Wagner, J, Herlim M, Chong DH, Kramer AA, Halpern SD (December 2013). "ICU Occupancy and Mechanical Ventilator Use in the United States". *Journal of Critical Care Medicine*. 41 (12): 2712–2719. doi: 10.1097/CCM.0b013e318298a139.

22. https://www.google.com/search?q=NYC+Hopsital+lenght+of+stay&rlz=1C1GCEA_enUS976US976&oq=NYC+Hopsital+lenght+of+stay&aqs=chrome..69i57j33i10i160j33i10i299.5912j1j7&sourceid=chrome&ie=UTF-8.

23. Hunter A, Johnson L, Coustasse A (April to June 2014). "Reduction of Intensive Care Unit Length of Stay: The Case of Early Mobilization". *Health Care Manager (Frederick)*. 33 (2): 128–135. doi: 10.1097/HCM.0000000000000006. PMID: 24776831 Review.

24. Vekaria B, Overton C, Wiśniowski A, Ahmad S, Aparicio-Castro A, Curran-Sebastian J, Eddleston J, Hanley NA, House T, Kim J, Olsen W, Pampaka M, Pellis L, Ruiz DP, Schofield J, Shryane N, Elliot MJ (2021). "Hospital Length of Stay for COVID-19 Patients: Data-Driven Methods for Forward Planning". *BMC Infectious Diseases*. 21: 700.
25. https://www.barclaydamon.com/alerts/covid-19-nys-hospital-capacity-to-increase-amidst-unprecedented-regulatory-pragmatism.
26. https://covidtracking.com/data.
27. Rosenbaum L (2020). "Facing Covid-19 in Italy—Ethics, Logistics, and Therapeutics on the Epidemic's Front Line". *New England Journal of Medicine*. 382: 1873–1875.
28. Cuomo A (2020). *New York State Governor's Daily Coronavirus Press Briefing*. New York City.
29. Chen GH, Hellman S, Irie T, Downey RJ, Fischer, G (2020). "Regulating Inspiratory Pressure to Individualise Tidal Volumes in a Simulated Two-Patient, One-Ventilator System". *British Journal of Anaesthesia*. 125 (4): 366–368.
30. Everington K (23 March 2020). "Taiwanese Doctor Invents Device to Protect US Doctors against Coronavirus". *Taiwan News*.
31. Formlabs, Inc., "3D Printed Test Swabs for COVID-19 Testing" [Online]. https://formlabs.com/covid-19-response/covid-test-swabs/.

Chapter 3

Hospital at Home: Transformation of an Old Model with Digital Technology

Alisa L. Niksch

Contents

The COVID-19 pandemic has highlighted the limitations and vulnerabilities of the US healthcare system. While over the years innovators had tried to reimagine healthcare models and practices, the practical drivers had not been there to push these solutions forward. This included the rapidly evolving home care

DOI: 10.4324/b23264-3

space, which found itself in the forefront in the management of millions of hundreds of thousands of patients affected by the pandemic.

The practice of medical care at home is not new. Whether this was a house call for scarlet fever or a centuries-old practice of midwifery, medical care was largely done in the home until the last century. However, the reach of that practice was limited by what a physician or nurse midwife could physically carry in a satchel. For this reason, among other social, technological, and economic advancements, there was a rapid move toward centralization of health care. Over a series of decades, however, there were distinct risks which came to be identified within hospital care. Home care began to emerge again, this time for specific clinical purposes, including post-hospital discharge care, palliative care, and rehabilitation services. The span of services has continued to grow, and, with the co-development of telemedicine and mobile technologies able to collect and transmit patient data, has expanded into the care of sicker and more complex patients. Unifying a vetted care model with cutting-edge digital technology and advanced logistics has led to the current state of Hospital at Home, unifying intelligent patient insights with established cost and outcome benefits to scale this model of care.

Drivers for Change

With the sudden endorsement and expansion of acute care at home during the COVID-19 pandemic, it seemed from afar that a new model of care had appeared out of nowhere—this was far from the real story. In fact, hospital at home was a mature logistical operation which made a nimble adjustment to meet the moment. For decades, the medical industry relied on an increasingly complex epicenter of acute care. However, cost of care for inpatient hospitalizations continue to rise year over year in the United States, rising to $1.1 trillion in 2017 and comprising a third of all healthcare costs.[1] This continued despite the growth of value-based care models and attempts at cost mitigation via service bundling. Meanwhile, clinicians and researchers were working on perfecting a home care model which would provide the same quality of care with the additional benefit of decreasing costs for health systems. Many of these efforts were taking place internationally, in countries like Australia, Canada, Sweden, and Brazil. However, initially, each country may have had different incentives for developing a Hospital at Home model; while Australia appears to have had motivation to offer acute care services in the home to improve system efficiency, certain provinces in Canada may have resorted to acute care at home due to regional bed closures.[2]

In the United States, the right technology, care model, and financial incentives needed to converge to incentivize adoption and expansion of acute care at home by institutions, payers, and patients. The model of care at home in the United States was truly reborn in in the early 1970s through efforts of Veterans Administration Medical Centers, with recognition that an aging population of veterans might outpace hospital capacities. The expansion to acute care was achieved with further research in academic medical centers, providing data and an opportunity to present this as a feasible option for private payers, and ultimately Medicare. And when COVID-19 hit hospital systems hard, it was a viable option to expand hospital capacity while reducing risk of infectious exposures for non-infected patients.

The Role of the Veterans Administration

In the United States, the hospital at home model has been developed the longest within the Veterans Affairs network, which was able to tie its services to an effective single-payer system for its patient population. The Veterans Administration (VA) system has sustained a robust blend of traditional home nursing care, palliative care, and then developed an acute care at home program prior to its adoption to a broader array of medical centers. In the 1970s, the VA expressed concern that the proportion of aging World War II veterans would expand out of proportion to the general population by the year 2000. These projections led to the development of the VA Hospital-Based Home Care (HBHC) program.

Early evaluations of this program were not complete; they were limited in scope and did not include any cost analysis. Finally, the Edward Hines, Jr. VA Hospital in Illinois, which instituted their HBHC program in 1971, conducted a randomized controlled study on the impact of their physician led, interdisciplinary home care program on severely disabled or palliative care patients.[3] This study selected patients from those admitted to the 1,100 bed hospital, ultimately enrolling 491 to be randomized to usual care versus home care. The two groups did not have any difference in hospitalization days, though the HBHC group had lower inpatient acuity. The usual care group, however, had much greater utilization of outpatient services. Through mostly lower institutional costs, savings in the HBHC group was 13% lower than the usual care group, with no statistically significant differences in patient outcomes. As would be echoed in future research, patients and caregivers expressed higher levels of satisfaction with the level of care provided in the home, and there was no perceived deterioration in functional status in the patients which received care in a home setting.

This study was one of the hallmark evaluations of a comprehensive care program which involved a multi-disciplinary team led by a physician. This was a new model of care which demonstrated longitudinal success, and resulted in cost savings to the system. Smaller studies, such as one published in 2018 evaluating a hospital at home program at the VA Hospital in Cincinnati, OH, continued to show benefits in terms of cost and resource utilization, including a lower rate of admissions to nursing homes.[4] This accelerated the adoption of this HBHC model throughout the VA healthcare system, and inspired future iterations of the care model and definition of quality metrics. In addition, the early adoption of telemedicine within the VA system in 2003 enabled even more access to care from home and augmented home monitoring for veterans, and by 2014, had reduced inpatient bed days by 59%.[5] This encouraging data, again, served as an incentive to develop future iterations of Hospital at Home utilizing virtual encounters to enable patient monitoring.

Finding Traction in Academia

Many large academic hospital systems were the first to join the initial group of centers approved through the CMS Acute Hospital Care at Home program in November 2020, prompted by the needs of the COVID-19 pandemic. However, their capabilities were honed over years of research and practice. The safety and functional impact of hospitalization on the elderly became a focus of Drs. Bruce Leff and John Burton, members of a team of geriatricians at Johns Hopkins Medical Center, in the early 1990s. The team's efforts gained support from the John A. Hartford Foundation, a non-profit organization which has historically partnered with innovators re-examining care for older adults.[6] Care for older adults in hospital settings has always carried risk of iatrogenic complications, including infection, cognitive difficulties, and functional decline. The goal of hospital at home was to prevent these complications, and even enhance speed of recovery by maintaining mobility and orientation.

Leff's team ultimately developed a program which yielded an early pilot study of hospital at home outside the VA medical system. Published in 1999 in the *Journal of the American Geriatric Society*, the study enrolled 17 patients from the emergency department or outpatient clinic setting. A physician visit was performed daily, and nursing supervision was performed in the home for the first 24 hours, after which a Lifeline Medical Alert system (Philips, Inc., Framingham, MA). While comparable percentages of patients had services like oxygen therapy, blood cultures, and intravenous antibiotics, "difficult services" at home were noted to be echocardiography, cardiac telemetry and arterial blood gases. Patient outcomes compared to traditional inpatient hospital care were equivalent for similar diagnoses, and the cost of the acute care at home was 60% of inpatient care.[7] Leff's work led to a keen interest in hospital at home within academic medical centers, even though at the time there was no Medicare coverage available.

Since this time, there have been over 60 publications documenting the clinical benefit and the potential cost savings of acute care performed in the home. A meta-analysis of Hospital at Home data from 61 randomized controlled trials was first published in 2012 in *Medical Journal of Australia*. This looked at metrics regarding mortality, readmission rates, and cost savings among the multiple studies which qualified. The analysis demonstrated a consistent and statistically significant reduction in mortality and readmission rates. Among the 11 studies which evaluated cost of care, the mean reduction in cost involving 1,215 patients was $1567.11 per admission.[8]

In November 2020, the Centers for Medicare & Medicaid Services launched the Acute Hospital Care At Home program to provide hospitals a payment structure, and therefore, expanded flexibility to care for patients in their homes. The provisions for the model involved the following requirements:

- Having a physician or advanced practice provider evaluate each patient daily either in-person or through a virtual care platform
- Having a registered nurse (RN) evaluate each patient once daily either in-person or remotely
- Having two in-person home visits daily: by either an RN or mobile integrated health paramedics
- Having capacity for immediate, on-demand remote audio connection with a care team member who can immediately connect either an RN or MD to the patient
- Having the ability to respond to a decompensating patient within 30 minutes (e.g., ambulance transfer to an emergency department)
- Tracking defined patient safety metrics with weekly or monthly reporting
- Establishing a local safety committee to review patient safety data
- Ability to provide or contract for other services required during an inpatient hospitalization (e.g., mobile phlebotomy, radiology, or food services)

The COVID-19 pandemic certainly accelerated this decision given the massive demand for inpatient care. However, the acceleration of virtual care and adoption of FDA approved digital medical devices which could substitute for conventional human tasks were the most practical drivers to enable the movement of patients outside a congested medical infrastructure. Meanwhile, the compelling cost and outcomes data had gradually gained traction with private payers. Programs and service providers continue to watch how CMS will view these models as the United States moves beyond the COVID-19 pandemic.

Technology Entering the Home

The COVID-19 pandemic created pressures to maximize access to medical care in an atmosphere encouraging isolation. Virtual care and remote patient monitoring systems had always been an industry of interest to those who were looking for the potential of technology to disrupt healthcare. Telemedicine services had been in existence for years before COVID-19 hit the United States. These services were finally deregulated for Medicare beneficiaries in March of 2020 in response to the pandemic, and expanded access to outpatient care to millions of patients.

However, many early attempts at building remote monitoring platforms failed to gain traction because of the arduous, expensive, and time-consuming regulatory pathways in the face of unclear consumer adoption prospects. Patients with ongoing health concerns were often left out of the design process, and persuading a medical care team to endorse a non-FDA-approved technology was nearly impossible. Potentially the most impactful piece was the lack of reimbursement structure, either directly or indirectly, which could incentivize the broader incorporation of wearable technology and other data tracking devices into patient care. It became clear that "disruption" of a highly regulated industry needed a different perspective to succeed.

Since 2017, however, the environment for developing medical-grade remote patient monitoring platforms began to shift. The year 2017 was the year when the FDA provided official guidance on the handling of medical software and functions of that software which required regulatory oversight.[9] In 2019, the FDA published a subsequent document which gave specific categories of software functions where the agency would not enforce oversight.[10] This maturity of the FDA's understanding of digital medicine helped accelerate the clearance of a large number of newer patient-facing devices, many of them designed for a range of functionalities, from vital sign acquisition or population health applications.

Many of the burgeoning hospital at home programs, as well as contracted service providers, rapidly incorporated these technologies to solve some of their biggest challenges, among them augmentation of care coordination, and reducing the higher cost of human capital to perform lower complexity tasks. Between the devices and the connected platforms which supported them, the technology applied to hospital at home has been key in several ways. For instance, connected devices have become increasingly skillful at informing clinicians of accurate patient data. Telemedicine has increased the number, quality and efficiency of patient "touches" over the period of acute care performed in the home. Finally, newer health IT infrastructure streamlines clinical workflow, emphasizes technology integration, and creates an intelligent network of coordination of care.

Ian Chiang, an investor at Flare Capital Partners and founding member of CareAllies, which ran home-based care business within Cigna, spoke about the key features of technology in the home that were particularly valuable in the context of Hospital at Home:

> "From a technology perspective, there are several ways that we
> need to see continuous improvement. One is a technology platform
> that can continuously curate diagnostics for the home, especially
> point of care diagnostics. Second, it's essential to have a well-built
> API with the layers available to add additional services, and can
> be deployed to the field in days or weeks. Third, predictive ana-
> lytics and data science—as the data grows in complexity this will
> become even more important. Lastly, the user experience for both
> patient and provider is so important, a technology needs to be
> functional out of the box to drive engagement.[11]

From a product design strategy, the flexibility of the software and API infrastructure is equally, if not more important than the device it supports. This allows the multi-functionality and versatility of a platform to support monitoring for a range of patient diagnoses and acuity.

Digital Solutions Solving Management Gaps

There is a vast array of continuous vital sign monitors available to support clinical decision making within a hospital at home care model. These tools, enabling longitudinal monitoring, were able to be used for clinical insights into the conditions of COVID-19 and non-COVID patients cared for at home. The VitalPatch (VitalConnect, San Jose, CA), which received its 501K clearance in 2018, is a wireless monitor able to detect eight different parameters, including patient position and fall detection. It also provides a continuous single lead ECG function, which overcomes some of the prior difficulties with continuous cardiac telemetry. Incorporating an access point within the home, and a multi-patient continuous monitoring dashboard on the clinician end, VitalConnect clearly markets itself to hospital at home providers.

The all-in-one vital sign wearable from Current Health (Boston, MA, and Edinburgh, UK), extensively used during the pandemic for at-home monitoring, offers an array of vital sign monitoring devices, a tablet for video connection, and a wireless access point. The platform gained FDA approval in 2019 for its platform, as well as its Bluetooth integration with other devices. The company also states that their API has the capability to integrate over 200 additional devices into their platform. They ultimately entered into a partnership with the Mayo Clinic to provide at-home data on convalescing patients with COVID-19 patients who were at risk for deterioration.[12] The company most recently announced in June 2021 that it will become the backbone of the hospital at home program at UMass Memorial Hospital (Worcester, MA). These newer companies are competing with more established companies like Royal Philips, which acquired out-of-hospital cardiac monitoring company BioTelemetry in December 2020. Philips had previously contracted with Partners Healthcare to supply their "Hospital to Home" telemedicine and monitoring technology to patients enrolled in various home care programs within the network.

The more complex patient populations are benefiting from rapid development of truly mobile technologies for acute care needs. One of the "difficult" home care tasks noted in early trials was echocardiography, which had no option for portability in the 1990s. However, as the model of healthcare increasingly focused on community outreach, portable equipment became very attractive as an investment. The technology has evolved over the last 20 years from a briefcase sized device weighing about 6 kg (Vivid IQ, GE Healthcare), to smaller hand-held units weighing about 2–3 kg (VScan, GE Healthcare; Acuson P10, Siemens), to now 0.5 kg probes which can plug into a smart phone (Lumify, Philips; Clarius C3, Clarius Mobile Health).[13] The Butterfly IQ device is marketed as a hand-held ultrasound device, of which cardiac echocardiography is one of 20 presets. The smaller devices tend to have more limited capabilities of color and Doppler imaging, but these new devices have become widely used for point of care imaging by specialists outside of cardiology. With the number of options available to clinicians, echocardiography at home is no longer an obstacle to care. With the very real risk of myocardial injury related to COVID-19 infection, the routine accessibility of echocardiography in evaluating convalescing patients at home has increased in importance.

Dialysis has been studied in home care due to a rapidly expanding population of individuals with chronic renal failure. However, most feasibility studies focused on chronic, relatively stable renal failure; a home care nurse would still be required for supervision. One of the more interesting mobile devices in the dialysis space, which was approved in 2019 as a breakthrough device by the FDA, is the AWAK Peritoneal Dialysis Device, which allows the user to self-administer 6–8 hours of treatment through a portable 3 kg device. The device is able to extract peritoneal fluid, filter out toxins through a cartridge integrated into the device, and then infuse the filtered fluid as new dianeal. Traditionally, this process had to be done manually using a new supply of dianeal with each treatment. Other competitors such as Nanodialysis and Triomed are building similar devices which may on the market in the next couple of years.[14]

Overcoming Systemic Challenges

Hospital at home is fundamentally a value-based service, offering acute care of comparable to a subset of admitted patients with reduced cost. These types of programs were able to scale in countries with single-payer healthcare systems—Canada and Israel, for example. In the Australian state of Victoria, every urban and regional medical center has a hospital at home program, which serves 6% of all admitted patient bed-days in the state.[15] In the United States, while this service did have early success under the auspices of the Veterans Administration, it wasn't until the Affordable Care Act incentivized value-based care payment structures that a greater number of private hospital systems grew interested in building programs.

Having a reimbursement structure in place appears to be an essential foundation for the scalability of these services. Hospitals or hospital systems which wanted to enter into the Acute Hospital Care At Home program had to apply for a waiver on the CMS website. A cohort of six programs were automatically given a waiver after CMS reimbursement was put in place (https://www.cms.gov/files/document/what-are-they-saying-hospital-capacity.

pdf); these included Mount Sinai Health System (NY), Massachusetts General Hospital (MA), Brigham Health Home Hospital (MA), Huntsman Cancer Institute (UT), Presbyterian Healthcare Services (NM), and UnityPoint Health (IA). These centers had demonstrated extensive experience with Hospital at Home services, including publishing results of patient outcomes and cost effectiveness in peer-reviewed journals. However, as of April, 2021, there were at least 200 programs which had enrolled in the program.[16]

Many hospitals and hospital systems are still evaluating their capabilities and strategy for taking on increasingly ill patients for home care. Systems like Intermountain Healthcare, based in Utah, have had a foundational home care program since 1984. With experience spanning palliative care to primary care taking place in the home, resources are now in place to take on higher acuity patients. Nickolas Mark, who is a Managing Director and Partner at Intermountain Ventures, sees that

> payer reimbursement, provider buy-in, and high-quality coordina-
> tion of care continue to be the headwinds which may curtail the
> scalability of hospital-level care at home. However, a demographic
> of patients over 65, and patient preferences for care after the
> COVID-19 pandemic are now driving demand for increase home-
> based medical services, especially in rural catchment areas.[17]

Care Model Execution

Brigham Health officially launched their Hospital at Home program in 2018. Screening patients presenting to their network emergency departments, patients were triaged to acute care at home. The majority of these patients had manageable conditions such as pneumonia, COPD, cellulitis, or urinary tract infections.[18] With an annual volume of about 300 patients, the system was able to demonstrate a significant drop in need for lab draws and radiologic studies, increased patient mobility and sleep, and an overall drop in cost of 38% compared to traditional inpatient care. Among the 91 patients studied, there was also a significantly lower rate of readmissions (7% vs. 23%).[19]

The history of hospital at home, with years of experience and data showing good outcomes, comparable safety, and cost savings compared to traditional inpatient acute care, justified the investment of larger medical systems in these programs. The programs evolved to partner hospital physicians with contracted services to provide nursing care and monitoring capability, which allowed the care model to scale. Mount Sinai Health System in New

York City formed their Visiting Doctor's Program in 1995. This evolved into a Mobile Acute Care Team in 2015, which was funded by a $9.6M Health Care Innovation Award sponsored by CMS.[20] While waiting for a payment plan proposal to be considered by CMS, Mount Sinai ultimately partnered with a third-party service provider, Contessa Health (acquired by Amedisys in 2021), to provide home services and care coordination which were reimbursed by private insurers. Negotiated contracts with several private insurers, including with their Medicare Advantage plans had been put in place. However, until CMS approved a payment and quality structure for hospital at home in November of 2020, the largest market for these services, those over 65 years old, were often deemed ineligible for this option.

Like Contessa Health, Medically Home is another company providing third-party care coordination which leveraged incipient research supporting a scalable Hospital at Home model using telemedicine and robust logistical operations in 2010. It took five years until the data was published in the American Journal of Managed Care in 2015.[21] Their data persuaded their first customer, Atrius Health, which was spending hundreds of millions of dollars on hospital care, but did not own a hospital themselves. Medically Home stepped in to provide needed services and a revenue stream for Atrius Health. However, it became clear that there were limitations within certain health systems for providing full service medical care to patients designated appropriate for acute care at home. As the CEO of Medically Home, Rami Karjian, stated:

> While discussing the model with health systems, we quickly realized it wasn't going to develop into thousands of beds across the country by us providing the care. So, we moved to an enablement model. We weren't going to change the country's healthcare if we were going to be the providers.[22]

Karjian also weighed in on the approach to the type of patient that would be an attractive candidate for Hospital at Home. He eschewed the idea that home care infrastructure should only be designed for the least acutely ill patients:

> Even though the care is happening in the home, this is hospital-level care in the home, not low acuity home health. You have to build it for high acuity, otherwise you are not going to keep the patient safe, and also you are not going to get the volume…so we said, let's build this for the high acuity patient, and then you can scale all the way down.[22]

There was recognition by the company that in order to gain adoption, the model had to gain trust and assimilate seamlessly into a hospital system. This included utilization of the system's own clinician services and integrating patient-generated data into existing electronic health record software, primarily Epic and Cerner. Adding to the challenge, it was evident that many hospital systems did not have the skills or bandwidth to organize the logistics and supply chain for appropriate care coordination and patient monitoring. Therefore, hospitals could keep their existing payor contracts, maintain a command center with a team of their physicians, but allow Medically Home to deploy technology and personnel to operate an acute care bed at home at a fraction of the cost of care within the walls of a hospital.

A Crisis of Traditional Workflows: Funding and Adoption

The conceptual design of hospital at home models had demonstrated important advantages over traditional inpatient care for many of the common diagnoses now targeted by population health initiatives. However, effective virtual care technologies, which mostly came into the market in the mid-2010s, were essential for the scalability of the model and ability for clinical staff to access and respond to patient needs at home. This became particularly vital for patient management during the COVID-19 pandemic, where physical human contact had potentially higher risks than benefits.

The COVID-19 pandemic rapidly expanded the patient population which were candidates for hospital at home. However, the pressures brought by waves of infection were not all positive. Some smaller institutions actually contracted or shuttered their home care programs to mobilize clinician resources to intensive care units and other COVID-19 inpatient wards. However, other systems found home care was able to decompress their overloaded inpatient census, conserve personal protective equipment (PPE) and kept infected individuals from mixing with the non-infected on hospital wards.[23] These incentives were also seen internationally, where more or less organized home care efforts were taking place in hard-hit countries like Spain[24] and Italy.[25]

Michigan's Metro Health, a health system serving 250,000 patients per year, saw a massive surge in patients infected by the COVID-19 virus in 2020 which threatened to overflow their patient census and safe nursing ratios. When the surge hit their region of the state, Metro Health partnered with Health Recovery Solutions to provide a telehealth and remote patient monitoring infrastructure which was customized for COVID-19 patients. About 20%–25% of all COVID-19 patients presenting within Metro Health's system were enrolled in the home care program, and they achieved a 90% adherence to prescribed vital sign measurements.[26] According to the case report published through Health Recovery Solutions, Metro Health prevented an average of 9.5 hospital days for a series of 80 patients.

The COVID-19 pandemic created stress on traditional clinical workflows. In March of 2020, CMS made a determination as part of the 1,135 waiver that telemedicine visits using audio and video technology would be reimbursed at the same rate as in-person visits. A key change also liberalized the location where patients could receive care, including their own home, and there were no restrictions to rural geographies. No enforcement against virtual visits for initial encounters would take place during the public health emergency, which had not been allowable for reimbursement before 2020.[27]

While telemedicine encounters made up 1.1% of primary care claims for private insurers in Q2 of 2018 and 2019, this skyrocketed to 35.2% of primary care encounters by Q2 of 2020.[28] A Rock Health consumer survey of 7,980 patients in 2020 also documented a 11% increase in patient utilization of live video telemedicine (43% vs. 32%), as well as a 10% increase in the use of wearables (43% vs. 33%) over the prior year. However, the report also revealed that populations least likely to utilize technology to augment or replace conventional models of medical care were in lower socioeconomic groups, residents of rural areas, and those over 55 years of age. More encouraging data was the higher adoption rate within populations with chronic disease states, which are known to drive a significant percentage of healthcare costs in the United States.[29]

Another measure that the US government established was a provision in the 2020 CARES Act for a $200M funding program administered by the Federal Communications Commission (FCC). This appropriation, which went into effect on June 25, 2020, was put in place to support and expand telehealth and remote patient monitoring services to improve access to patients during the COVID-19 pandemic. Several centers received funding through this program's first round, including the Mayo Clinic, Ochsner Clinic Foundation, Grady Memorial Hospital, Mt. Sinai Health System (NYC), Hudson River Healthcare, UPMC Children's Hospital, and Neighborhood Health Care (OH). Funding for services, which were invoiced and submitted to the FCC for reimbursement, included expansion of telehealth and remote patient monitoring services to high-risk homebound patients, focusing on geriatric, palliative, and underinsured patients.[30] A second round of funding to the FCC for support of telemedicine programs was approved within the Consolidated Appropriations Act of 2021; applications for this second round of funds closed on May 6, 2021.

While outpatient usage of technology to augment access to medical care increased during the COVID-19 pandemic, inpatient care was significantly impacted by the volume of patients inundating regional hospital systems with acute illness. As previously stated, hospital census limitations became a crisis, with many non-COVID infected patients avoiding or delaying care, or alternatively, competing with COVID-infected patients for hospital beds. This phenomenon likely contributed to excess deaths tabulated in 2020.[31] Hospital at Home use grew within certain hospitals and hospital systems, but relied on payment systems which fell outside the Medicare reimbursement system. Despite these reimbursement barriers, systems utilizing Hospital at Home like Mount Sinai and Atrium Health tripled their acute home care patient census during the pandemic as a result of excess inpatient numbers.[32]

Future Challenges

Hospital at home received a terrific boost from last year's Medicare coverage determination. Evaluation of several of the existing acute care at home programs before and after the onset of the COVID-19 pandemic contributed to the development of the waiver. A massive market opened up for patients over 65 years old primarily receiving benefits from Medicare. It appears that the waiver for participation in the Acute Hospital At Home program will be extended until 2022 until further Congressional oversight can take place. The hope is that with more programs entering the program, there will be enough momentum to keep the reimbursement structure in place. Many participants in the program are systems which already had significant home care services in place and were more easily able to pivot toward a more acutely ill population before and during the peak of the COVID-19 pandemic. Adam Wolfberg, Chief Medical Officer of Current Health, states that even though numbers of institutions participating in the waiver program continue to increase, "larger hospital systems will continue to have an advantage of standing up a Hospital at Home program—they already have the ancillary services set up, or they have existing relationships with contract service providers."[33]

As with telemedicine adoption seen at the beginning of the COVID-19 pandemic, larger medical facilities had a greater proportion of telehealth adoption than smaller practices as a percentage of their pre-pandemic visit volume, reflecting infrastructure and resources which could be shifted to new technology and workflows.[34]

Hospital systems that are rapidly moving toward acute care for their home-based care services may also be faced with the challenge of managing remote patient monitoring data. Integrating this data with a workflow that makes sense for the types of patients admitted to Hospital at Home programs will require time, education, and a strategic focus. This has been an historical dilemma in the commercialization of digital health technologies. The problem of "data dumping" without intelligent curation of actionable information has consistently been an obstacle for timely and accurate clinical evaluation. Again, this speaks to a clinical infrastructure needed to manage data and understand appropriate times to acquire data from patients undergoing home care of acute conditions.[35] The aggregation of even more data from increasingly complex patients will need higher sophistication in data analytics and predictive capabilities to assist clinicians in recognizing potential deterioration in patient status.

In addition, there still exists an educational barrier for patients who may be eligible for this model of care. A level of hesitancy exists regarding the safety and privacy of home care and building of confidence around this model will be a heavy burden for clinicians recruiting patients for their program. Compounding this hesitancy is an intimidation factor of having to master new technology in the home. While telehealth and remote patient monitoring companies have recognized this barrier and have designed out of the box telehealth kits, some with their own wireless access points, the initial sale to a candidate patient may still be a challenge.

Other temporal factors could also contribute to low patient enrollment into hospital at home programs. A low enrollment rate of 29% was noted at a study site in a 2005 study published in *Annals of Internal Medicine*—this was attributed to a nursing shortage which would have precluded requisite visits at the frequency needed to carry out the protocol.[36] Appropriate personnel with requisite training will take time to develop, even in mature home health programs. The cultivation of a workforce including specially trained paramedics has alleviated the concerns over nursing shortages, and the natural mobility of paramedic duties has proven to adapt to this model of care splendidly. Case managers are also vital to perform intake screening, and they carry a crucial role of identifying candidate patients in outpatient settings, promoting awareness of home care options, and managing rapid deployment of technology and clinical personnel.

Conclusions

Despite the challenges in implementation, the demonstration and reproducibility of cost savings and outcomes metrics to health systems which utilize hospital at home is undeniable. This, in addition to the reduction in hospital acquired infections and functional decline in elderly patients, make hospital at home an attractive investment, although challenging for smaller institutions with larger infrastructural gaps. Third-party services have started to step in to provide logistical support and coordination of care services, while allowing medical facilities to manage patient care using their own clinical staff. Remote patient monitoring technology supporting the hospital at home care model continues to advance in its sophistication. The growing potential of predictive analytics to have an active role in anticipating deterioration in patient status is another driver that can increase the scale of home care for acute conditions. The role of the COVID-19 pandemic has not only shaped patient preferences but also highlighted the value of hospital at home for clinicians who otherwise would have been hesitant to engage with a new operational workflow. While reimbursement structure from CMS continues to have an uncertain future, successful implementation of hospital at home services continues to rapidly expand and will create undeniable pressure on federal agencies to allow these programs to mature.

References

1. Liang L, Moore B, Soni A. "National Inpatient Hospital Costs: The Most Expensive Conditions by Payer, 2017". *AHRQ Statistical Brief #261*, July 2020.
2. Chevreul K, Com-Ruelle L, Midy F, Paris V. "Issues in Health Economics Newsletter". Institute for Research and Information in Health Economics, Paris, France. December 2004.
3. Cummings JE, Hughes SL, Weaver FM, et al. "Cost-Effectiveness of Veterans Administration Hospital-Based Home Care: A Randomized Clinical Trial". *Arch Intern Med.* 1990;150(6):1274–1280.
4. Cai S, Grubbs A, Makineni R, Kinosian B, Phibbs CS, Intrator O. "Evaluation of the Cincinnati Veterans Affairs Medical Center Hospital-in-Home Program". *J Am Geriatr Soc.* 2018;66(7):1392–1398.
5. "7 Key Findings on VA Telehealth Outcomes". Becker's Hospital Review. June 24, 2014. https://www.beckershospitalreview.com/healthcare-information-technology/7-key-findings-on-va-telehealth-services-outcomes.html.
6. Anthony M. "Hospital-At-Home". *Home Healthcare Now.* 2021;39(3):127.

7. Leff B, Burton L, Guido S, Greenough WB, Steinwachs D, Burton JR. "Home Hospital Program: A Pilot Study". *J Am Geriatr Soc.* 1999;47(6):697–702.
8. Caplan GA, Sulaiman NS, Mangin DA, Aimonino Ricauda N, Wilson AD, Barclay L. "A Meta-Analysis of 'Hospital in the Home'". *Med J Aust.* 2012;197(9):512–519.
9. "Software as a Medical Device (SAMD): Clinical Evaluation – Guidance for Industry and Food and Drug Administration Staff". Software as a Medical Device Working Group, Food and Drug Administration. September 2017. https://www.fda.gov/regulatory-information/search-fda-guidance-documents/software-medical-device-samd-clinical-evaluation.
10. "Policy for Device Software Functions-Guidance for Industry and Food and Drug Administration Staff". Food and Drug Administration. September 27, 2019. https://www.fda.gov/regulatory-information/search-fda-guidance-documents/policy-device-software-functions-and-mobile-medical-applications.
11. Ian Chiang, Flare Capital Partners. Personal Interview, May 24, 2021.
12. Wholley S. "Current Health, Mayo Clinic Launch AI-based COVID-19 Detection Collaboration". MassDevice. April 29, 2020. https://www.massdevice.com/current-health-mayo-clinic-launch-ai-based-covid-19-detection-collaboration/.
13. Chamsi-Pasha M, Sengupta PP, Zoghbi WA. "Handheld Echocardiography: Current State and Future Perspectives". *Circulation.* 2017;136:2178–2188.
14. Hu M. "Singapore Startup's "Portable Kidney" Can Give Patients their Freedom Back". TechInAsia. January 21, 2020. https://www.techinasia.com/singapore-startup-portable-kidney-give-patients-freedom.
15. Montalto M. "The 500-Bed Hospital That Isn't There: The Victorian Department of Health Review of the Hospital in the Home Program". *The Medical Journal of Australia.* 2010;193(10):598–601.
16. Donlan A. "CMS Hospital-at-Home Program Closing in on 200 Participants". *Home Healthcare News.* April 19, 2021.
17. Nickolas Mark, Managing Director Intermountain Ventures, Personal Interview, June 18, 2021.
18. Levine DM, Ouchi K, Blanchfield, B, et al. "Hospital-Level Care at Home for Acutely Ill Adults: A Pilot Randomized Controlled Trial". *J Gen Intern Med.* 2018;33:729–736.
19. Levine DM, Ouchi K, Blanchfield B, et al. "Hospital-Level Care at Home for Acutely Ill Adults: A Randomized Controlled Trial". *Ann Intern Med.* 2020;172(2):77–85.
20. Siu A, DeCherrie L. "Inside Mount Sinai's Hospital at Home Program". *Harvard Business Review.* May 10, 2019. https://hbr.org/2019/05/inside-mount-sinais-hospital-at-home-program.
21. Summerfelt WT, Sulo S, Robinson A, Chess D, Catanzano K. "Scalable Hospital at Home with Virtual Physician Visits: Pilot Study". *Am J Manag Care.* 2015;21(10):675–684.
22. Rami Karjian, CEO, Medically Home. Personal Interview, June 2021.

23. Weiner S. "Interest in Hospital at Home Explodes During COVID-19". *AAMC News*. September 19, 2020. https://www.aamc.org/news-insights/ interest-hospital-home-programs-explodes-during-covid-19.
24. Pericàs JM, Cucchiari D, Torrallardona-Murphy O, et al. "Hospital at Home for the Management of COVID-19: Preliminary Experience with 63 Patients". *Infection*. 2021;49(2):327–332.
25. Berardi F. "The Italian Doctor Flattening the Curve by Treating COVID-19 Patients in Their Homes". *Time*. April 9, 2020.
26. Siwicki B. "Metro Health's Telehealth and RPM Program Is Helping Patients Avoid Hospital Stays". *Healthcare IT News*. June 29, 2021. https://www.health-careitnews.com/news/metro-healths-telehealth-and-rpm-program-helping-patients-avoid-hospital-stays.
27. "Medicare Telemedicine Health Care Provider Fact Sheet". Centers for Medicare and Medicaid Services Newsroom. May 17, 2020. https://www.cms.gov/ newsroom/fact-sheets/medicare-telemedicine-health-care-provider-fact-sheet.
28. Eberly JA, Kallan MJ, Julien HM, et al. "Patient Characteristics Associated with Telemedicine Access for Primary and Specialty Ambulatory Care during the COVID-19 Pandemic". *JAMA Netw Open*. 2020;3(12):e2031640.
29. DeSilva J, Zweig D. "Digital Health Consumer Adoption Report 2020". Rock Health. April 2021. https://rockhealth.com/reports/ digital-health-consumer-adoption-report-2020/.
30. Wicklund E. "6 Health Systems Receive Funding from FCC's COVID-19 Telehealth Program". mHealth Intelligence. April 17, 2020. https://mhealthintelligence.com/ news/6-health-systems-receive-funding-from-fccs-covid-19-telehealth-program.
31. Czeisler MÉ, Marynak K, Clarke KEN, et al. "Delay or Avoidance of Medical Care Because of COVID-19-Related Concerns – United States". *MMWR Morb Mortal Wkly Rep*. 2020;69(36):1250–1257.
32. Weiner S. "Interest in Hospital-at-Home Programs Explode during COVID-19". Association of American Medical Colleges. September 29, 2020. https://www.aamc.org/news-insights/ interest-hospital-home-programs-explodes-during-covid-19.
33. Adam Wolfberg, Chief Medical Officer, Current Health, Personal Interview, June 23, 2021.
34. Mehrotra A, Wang B, Snyder G. "Telemedicine: What Should the Post-Pandemic Regulatory and Payment Landscape Look Like?" Commonwealth Fund. August 5, 2020. https://www.commonwealthfund.org/publications/ issue-briefs/2020/aug/telemedicine-post-pandemic-regulation.
35. "AMA Digital Health Implementation Playbook". American Medical Association Publications. 2018. https://www.ama-assn.org/system/files/2018-12/digital-health-implementation-playbook.pdf.
36. Leff B, Burton L, Mader SL, et al. "Hospital at Home: Feasibility and Outcomes of a Program to Provide Hospital-Level Care at Home for Acutely Ill Older Patients". *Ann Intern Med*. 2005;143(11):798–808.

Chapter 4

Biomedical Engineering's Response to Drive COVID-19 Patient Care Solutions: Lessons Learned from the Front Lines

Ashley Jackson and Jennifer Larbi

Contents

DOI: 10.4324/b23264-4

Introduction

The novel coronavirus, COVID-19, surprised the world. COVID-19 was the first pandemic to occur in over a century. Due to technological advances and societal connectivity, COVID-19 was able to spread across the world faster than any other pandemic in history. Since the first reported case in Wuhan, China on December 31, 2019, the COVID-19 virus has infected over 181 million people causing over 597,727 deaths in the United States and 3,899,172 deaths worldwide. Furthermore, as new variants surface, these numbers will continue to rise.

On March 1, 2020, the first case of COVID-19 was confirmed in New York City. New York City, being a densely populated city, loomed with anxiety about the ramifications of the COVID-19 virus and the best way to combat it. Hospitals suddenly found themselves on the front line sharing one chilling reality, "We are not prepared."

COVID-19 is a virus like no other. It was not something seen in this generation and hospitals were not prepared to take this on; however, there was no choice in the matter. Hospitals had to quickly spring into action, addressing anything and everything from personal protective equipment (PPE) shortages to operationalizing surges that would stretch hospitals to two–three times their capacity. At the onset of COVID-19, little was known about how the virus was spread or how it would affect people both in the short term and the long term. Regardless of the countless unknowns, Biomed had a job to do: to help clinicians prepare for the worst-case scenario with limited supplies.

This section will provide a detailed description of the Biomedical Engineering response to the increased medical equipment needs within the clinical space at Memorial Sloan Kettering Cancer Center (MSK) during the onset of the COVID-19 pandemic. Topics will be covered such as medical equipment surge planning, streamlining onboarding, expanding critical care and acute care, increasing monitoring capabilities, and minimizing staff exposure.

Preparing for Surge

The most significant challenge that MSK had to overcome related to the impending surge was the lack of, or more appropriately the absence of, time to create comprehensive plans prior to implementation. Typically, the "planning phase" comes before the "operational phase," but in this case there was simply not enough time. These phases were forced to happen in parallel, forcing hospitals to operate within this duality. Burnout amongst leadership and staff was a significant concern. An overwhelming amount of information needed to be presented, understood, and ultimately acted upon, essentially at the same time. One strategy that proved to be success-ful was an early adoption of subcommittees that essentially acted as a task force. These subcommittees were tasked with presenting solutions to specific challenges. Establishing this structure helped to reduce burden on leadership while empowering collaboration between diverse multi-disciplinary groups. Capitalizing on the collective expertise of multi-faceted teams to push the boundaries and drive creative solutions proved to be an effective way to expand the capabilities of the institution. At the same time, the creation of these various groups established a much-needed structure and predictability that enabled teams to maintain focus. Ultimately, the MSK Hospital Incident Command System (HICS) leadership somewhat naturally separated into two functional groups: a planning group that analyzed the predictive analytics to make high-level decisions, and an operational group that focused on estab-lishing solutions to implement these plans.

Medical Equipment Planning

The first questions that come to mind when beginning any medical planning exercise are clearly; "what do we have?," "what do we need?," "is what we need available?" These questions, though seemingly simple, can be daunt-ing especially when supply is scarce and the timeline for decision-making is seemingly non-existent.

As the clinical operations expanded for hospitals across the greater met-ropolitan area, the challenge of acquiring medical equipment to accommo-date new surge areas became increasingly difficult. The global pandemic severely impacted all supply chains making it more difficult to source equip-ment. This was exacerbated by the fact that all hospitals across the country were fighting over the same limited stock of equipment due to the wide reach of the virus and the rate at which it spread. Available medical supply stock was decreasing at such a rapid rate that there was significant concern that delaying a purchase decision even one day could result in the inability to acquire the medical equipment necessary to accommodate the surge of critically ill patients. Hospitals had no time to go through the typical channels of formalized proposals and layers of approval chains. Still, with limited stock across the country, it was equally important to mitigate compulsive decision-making to reduce surplus at the individual hospital level that would exacerbate the shortage for others. Belaboring the issue further, the uncertainty around the virus made it nearly impossible for hospitals to predict how long they should expect to maintain surge capacity and at what level. Generally, surge equipment is not expected to remain in-service for a significant period. Thus, the ideal approach to outfit a surge care area is to either reallocate underutilized medical equipment from other areas within the institution or rent the necessary equipment. Every piece of equipment that the hospital acquires has a "cost of ownership," largely comprised of the cost to store or maintain the device for the duration of the asset lifecycle. Performing a risk-benefit analysis prior to acquiring new equipment allows decision-makers to limit unnecessary capital spending and avoid inventory surplus. Affective analysis ultimately increases equipment utilization and decreases the overall cost of ownership. However, in this case, the lack of equipment availability combined with the ambiguity around the duration of the surge forced many hospitals to react quickly leaving institutions with a surplus of equipment after the immediate need had passed.

It became clear early on that the only reliable way to manage the overwhelming number of requests and facilitate rapid decision-making is to rely heavily on data. Establishing a proactive approach to medical equipment planning given a condensed timeline is virtually impossible without metrics. That said, data cannot be the only factor that drives equipment decisions in the hospital environment. Clinical expertise is crucial. Data can provide insight, but clinical expertise drives relevance.

MSK navigated these challenges by establishing a multi-collaborative task force, referred to as the Medical Equipment HICS team, to manage the medical equipment purchase decisions for the hospital. The group was led by Nursing and comprised of representatives from Critical Care, Biomedical Engineering and Supply Chain. The success of this collaboration was rooted in the combination of a reliable predictive model, clear surge plan, accurate inventory, and support of hospital leadership. The group reported directly to the HICS leadership team, and all other pathways for acquiring medical equipment were suspended temporarily. Centralizing all medical equipment requests provided the institution a singular pathway eliminated competing priorities which allowed the team to fast-track the process for vetting, sourcing, and onboarding medical equipment.

Critical Care Needs versus Acute Care Needs—Creating a Template

Challenges can only be addressed if they are identified. Predictive modeling can be a vital tool in preparing for potential needs especially when multiple scenarios need to be considered.

To anticipate equipment needs, biomed and nursing leadership collaborated to create a template to identify the essential medical equipment items needed to accommodate a baseline standard of care. The template focused on two general patient acuity levels, Acute Care (or MedSurg) and Critical Care, while considering any COVID-19-specific equipment needs.

Table 4.1 shows an example of the main equipment identified as part of the template. The leftmost column indicates the type of equipment needed while the middle columns indicate the ratios of equipment needed either per patient or per care unit to support a typical acute care or critical care setting. The ratios were based on an oncology patient population and approximated using clinical expertise. With more time, this equipment list and associated ratios could be further vetted to provide a holistic picture of all equipment needs for the institution as a function of bed or unit count. However, this exercise provided a simple baseline that could be used to predict basic medical equipment requirements as operations start to expand.

In parallel, the HICS leadership team was working to finalize the list of surge areas. The initial surge plan outlined an incremental plan that was separated into four capacity levels: Conventional, Contingency (standard surge), Contingency (non-standard surge), Crisis. If the surge plan were to be fully implemented, critical care capacity would increase by 570% and acute care capacity would increase by 159%. Fortunately, MSK did not reach that heightened level of surge largely because it is a specialized cancer hospital, but we planned for it, nonetheless.

After the surge areas were decided and released by the HICS leadership, Biomed started working to determine the medical equipment needs that would accompany the implementation of the surge. Table 4.2 shows the anticipated bed and unit counts associated with the four main surge capacity levels.

Table 4.1 Medical Equipment Requirements Template—Acute Care versus Critical Care

Equipment Type	Ratio of Devices Needed		Per
	Acute Care	Critical Care	
Bed/Stretcher	1	1	Patient
Physiological Monitor or Vital Signs Monitor	1	1	Patient
Bispectral Index (BIS) Monitor	0	3/20	Patient
Ventilator	0	1	Patient
Suction Unit	0	2	Patient
Portable Suction	1/10	4/10	Patient
Infusion Pumps (Brain)	1	2	Patient
Infusion Pumps (Channel)	4	8	Patient
Thermometer	1	1	Patient
Sequential Compression Device (SCD)	1	1	Patient
Feeding Pump	1/10	1	Patient
Defibrillator	1	1	Unit
Scale	1	1	Unit
12L EKG Machine	1	1	Unit

Table 4.2 Surge Capacity Levels with Associated Bed and Unit Counts (Acute and Critical)

Surge Capacity Levels	Acute Care		Critical Care	
	Bed Count	Unit Count	Bed Count	Unit Count
Conventional	484	14	20	2
Contingency Standard Surge	580	22	20	2
Contingency Non-Standard Surge	752	36	73	7
Crisis	1252	58	134	11

Creating a detailed surge plan including the identified surge areas and associated bed counts proved vital. With the list of all surge areas, it was easy to identify areas that would bring forth challenges as well as areas that were well equipped and did not require as much focus. Cross-matching the Surge Plan with the Medical Equipment Requirements Template provided a basic understanding of the medical equipment needs. Table 4.3 and Figure 4.1 show the maximum equipment requirements for each surge capacity level.

While this information provided a sufficient overview of what the equipment requirements were or could have been, it did not provide the context necessary to determine if/when the inventory will be at a deficit. To provide context, this data needed to be cross-matched with the

Table 4.3   Equipment Requirements for Each Surge Capacity Level

Equipment Type	Conventional	Contingency Standard Surge	Contingency Non-Standard Surge	Crisis
Bed/Stretcher	504	600	825	1,386
Physiological Monitor or Vital Signs Monitor	504	600	825	1,386
Bispectral Index (BIS) Monitor	3	3	11	21
Ventilator	20	20	73	134
Suction Unit	40	40	146	268
Portable Suction	57	66	105	179
Infusion Pumps (Brain)	524	620	898	1,520
Infusion Pumps (Channel)	2,096	2,480	3,592	6,080
Thermometer	504	600	825	1,386
Sequential Compression Device (SCD)	504	600	825	1,386
Feeding Pump	127	146	260	452
Defibrillator	16	24	43	69
Scale	16	24	43	69
12L EKG Machine	16	24	43	69

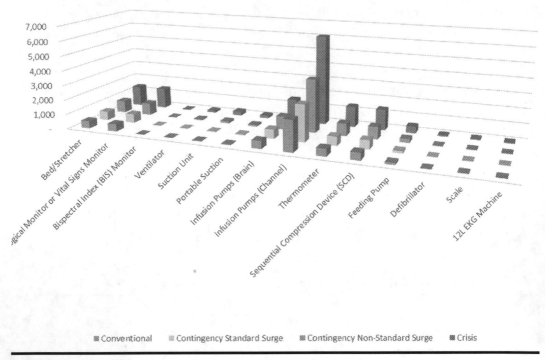

Figure 4.1   Equipment requirements for each surge capacity level.

equipment inventory providing a high-level view at the equipment most at risk of a shortage.

Comparing the equipment needs to the available inventory made clear the equipment groups listed below had sufficient inventory to accommodate a max surge:

- *Infusion Pumps (Brain)*
- *Thermometers*
- *Physiologic Monitors/Vital Signs Monitors*
- *12L EKG Machines*
- *Defibrillators*
- *Bispectral Index (BIS) Monitors*
- *Suction Units*
- *Scales*

This allowed for a shift in focus to only the equipment groups that had an insufficient amount of inventory to accommodate a max surge. In Figure 4.2, these select equipment groups are graphed as a function of bed count (or patient count).

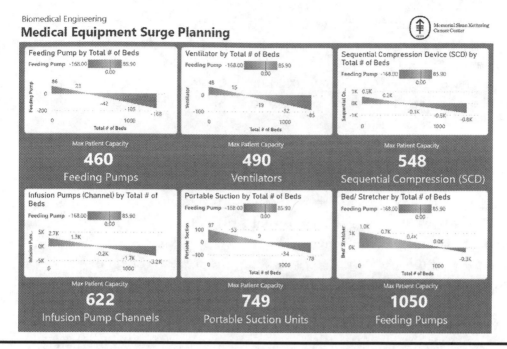

Figure 4.2   Equipment groups with expected shortage as a function of bed count.

This visual makes it clear not only which equipment groups will experience a shortage, but also how soon to expect that shortage with respect to increased surge capacity. For example, feeding pumps experience a shortage when patient capacity exceeds 460. This proved to be an incredibly helpful tool to quickly determine which devices would need to be reallocated/sourced, and most importantly, "when."

Implementation of the Surge Plans

The care units were divided into two: non-COVID patients and COVID patients with a further separation of critical care COVID and acute care COVID patients.

The requirements for any COVID patient were to have the following PPE: N95 mask, gown, face shield/goggles, gloves, and surgical cap. Due to shortages nationwide, creativity was needed to help ensure that the expansion plans were met. The first hurdle was PPE. In preparation of going into any COVID patient rooms to install any new technology, the Biomed staff needed proper PPE to ensure their safety. Thankfully, the hospital provided an N95 mask to each staff member to use per week, a reusable face shield, and a daily gown, while there was limited allocation. This precaution ensured that Biomed as well as the clinical staff were protected when entering a COVID room. To further reduce exposure amongst the Biomed staff and facilitate social distancing, Biomed shifted to a 12-hour shift model. This allowed the group to limit the number of team members on-site at one time and expand to 24-hour coverage.

Managing Specialty Emergency Equipment with Real-Time Location Tracking

Equipment rarely used in the hospital tends to get placed in areas that are out of the way, and naturally, hospital staff is not as familiar with how to use or locate the equipment. This was highlighted during the pandemic when the use of emergency equipment like HEPA Filters, PAPRs, and Demistifiers was at an all-time high, and in many cases there was a limited supply of equipment that had to be utilized across the institution. It was quickly realized that there needed to be a centralized resource assigned to manage the distribution and optimization of emergency equipment use. To accomplish optimization of emergency equipment use, there needed to be a way to track whether equipment was being used at any given time, and initiate a team to clean and redistribute the equipment if it was not being used.

Thus, the Emergency Management Resource Center (EMRC) was created as well as a EMRC "SWAT" team. The EMRC desk acted as a dispatch coordinator for emergency equipment like HEPA Filters, PAPRs, and Demistifiers. They received requests for the emergency equipment and would dispatch the "SWAT" team any time equipment needed to be disinfected and redistributed to another area. This workflow was implemented by the use of existing RTLS, Active button tags, and custom-made RTLS-Enabled Dashboards. Figures 4.3 and 4.4 show the workflow utilized and associated dashboard view.

Expanding Critical Care

Critical care was set to potentially surge by114 additional beds or to 570% normal capacity at MSK. To accommodate that level of surge, multiple spaces had to be brought up to the same Critical Care standard of care, each space with their own unique challenges. The fundamental approach to all strategies during the pandemic, especially during the early months when PPE was scarce and very little about the virus was known, was to

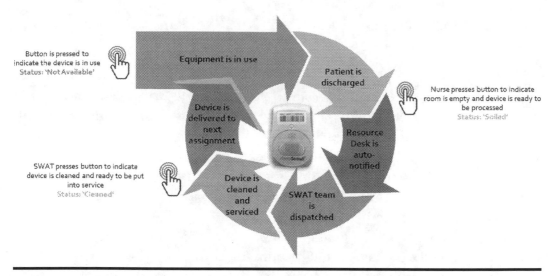

Figure 4.3   RFID workflow for emergency management equipment.

Emergency Management Equipment (All)

Equipment Type	Manufacturer	Model	Building	Floor Desk	RT Room	Alias	Asset Status/Last Checked	...	Business Status
Grand Total									Not Available
									Clean
Air Cleaners, Particulate, High-Efficiency Filter	Baikal Mechanical	BKL-PHF-ZS...	Bobst	Floor 9		HEPA Filter	Not Set Jun 24 2021 3:24AM		Not Set
					C-950 Multi Purpose Room	HEPA Filter	Not Set Jun 24 2021 3:21AM		Soiled
					C-984	HEPA Filter	Not Set Jun 24 2021 3:21AM		
				Floor 10		HEPA Filter	Not Set Jun 24 2021 3:20AM		
							Not Set Jun 24 2021 3:21AM		

Figure 4.4   Emergency management resource desk dashboard.

"increase caregiver interaction with the patient for closer monitoring while limiting staff exposure." Seemingly, these are two opposing requirements, but during the PPE shortage, both objectives held equal importance. It was imperative to not only ensure the health of the patients, but also the staff entrusted to care for them. To accomplish a reduction of staff exposure while maintaining, not only the same standard of care, but also (in many cases) an increased standard of care, various creative and innovative approaches were explored most of which made possible by utilizing technology.

Converting the Surgical Acute Care Unit (SACU) to a COVID ICU

Prior to the pandemic, the SACU unit at MSK was a step-down unit primarily targeted for patients recovering from thoracic surgery. As the need for critical care spaces continued to grow, the SACU was identified as the most optimal unit to accommodate the surge. However, prior to the pandemic this area was very ill-equipped to act as a critical care space. The SACU ultimately became MSK's main critical care unit for COVID-positive patients, but it was not a simple transition. There were multiple roadblocks identified along the way that required near immediate solutions.

To monitor patients in critical condition, at a bare minimum clinical staff need to be able to: (1) have a line-of-sight to the patient; (2) visibly monitor the patient's physiological monitor; (3) hear alarms from the patient's physiological monitor; (4) be stationed within close proximity of the patient to be able to quickly respond to any alarms.

First and foremost, the doors installed in the SACU did not have a window, so there was no line-of-sight to the patient. This was addressed in two ways. The doors themselves were modified by the facilities team to incorporate a window. This allowed for a direct line-of-sight into the room. However, that was still not sufficient in every room so a webcam was added as well to allow for better visibility of the patient.

Additionally, the care unit was initially setup and configured to have a centralized monitoring of patient's vitals and subsequent alarms at the central nurse's station with the assumption that nurses would be seated and able to respond to alarms from the nurse's station. Essentially, this workflow pulls the nurses to the nurse's station to remotely monitor vitals and subsequent alarms taking them away from the bedside.

In a typical "SACU" setting, this workflow and setup would be typical, however, converting this area to care for critically ill patients, specifically critically ill COVID-positive patients, it was necessary to provide the care team the ability to monitor their patient right outside the room. To enable the workflow necessary to bring the care team to the patient, a few things needed to be implemented in parallel. First, a temporary "pop-up nurses station" was created outside each room. Subsequently, remote monitoring was increased to accommodate the new workflow. Though the window was added, the existing monitor had a very small screen that was hard to view from outside the room. Multiple approaches were discussed to create better visibility of the monitor (Figures 4.5–4.7).

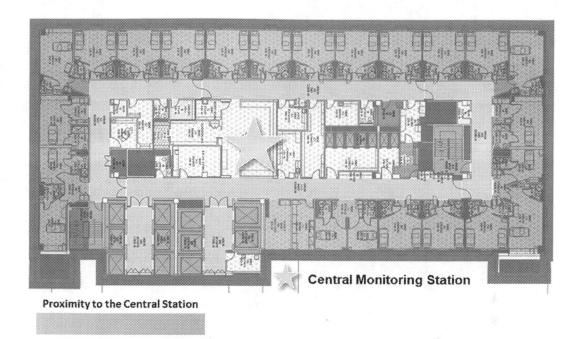

Figure 4.5   SACU heat map of room proximity to central station.

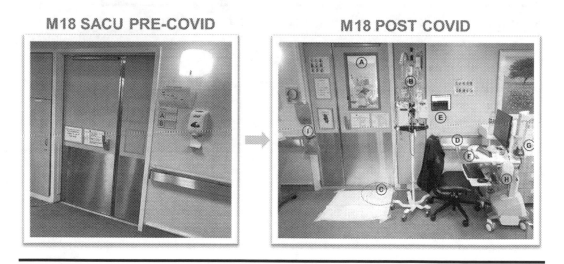

Figure 4.6   Pop-up nursing stations on M18 SACU.

■ Relocation of the monitor in closer proximity to the door
   This solution required a roll-stand for the monitor as well as
extended cables and/or an extended patient data acquisition module
docking station to accommodate the additional distance. The roll-stand,
the extended cables, and the extended patient data acquisition module

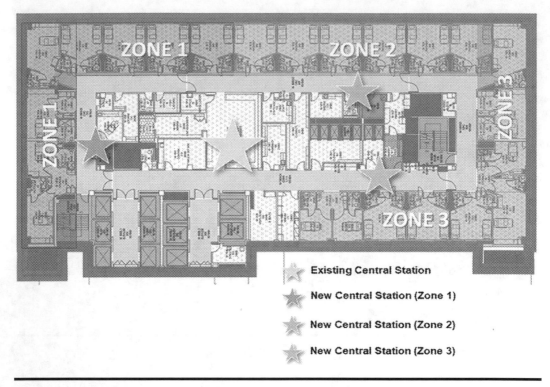

Figure 4.7 SACU zones and additional central station placement.

docking stations were extremely difficult to source due to the supply chain shortages at the time. In addition, it could not have been a consistent approach. In some rooms, the monitor could be placed in a visible area that was out of the way of incoming clinical staff, but in most rooms the monitor ended up in the direct pathway of the clinical staff, impeding their ability to swiftly engage with the patient.

■ Purchasing additional physiological monitor displays to mount outside the room

The issue of the added roll-stand and associated blockage of entry to the room did not exist with this solution. Though, it required the purchase of an additional display, wiring installation to connect the remote display to the monitor, and a mounting solution for the secondary display outside the room. This solution would allow for the clinician to respond to alarms directly outside the room, a feature highly desired. However, this solution was also subject to massive supply chain delays for the mounting hardware as well as the additional display. In addition, this was a costly solution. It was ultimately not pursued further due to the costliness as well as the potential delays in supply chain.

■ Custom Remote Application installed on iPADs outside each room

Because the iPads were existing hardware for MSK and the remote application was already available (though not used in this manner), this solution required the least amount of upfront capital investment. The only drawback to this solution initially was that the web application was only able to view one patient at a time. Because the nursing staff was typically monitoring two patients at a time, the ability to view only select patients was a feature that was required to make this solution ideal. Luckily, the remote application vendor was able to make the appropriate development adjustments to enable a patient "Multiview." This addressed the ability to view patient vitals outside the room but did not address the ability to respond to alarms outside the room nor did it address the need for audible alarms.

■ Purchasing/Installing extended remotes

This solution did not address the visibility issue at all. However, it did allow the clinician to respond to alarms outside the room.

■ Purchase and install additional Central Stations

Purchasing additional Central Stations provides the clinician with an audible and visible alarm and allows for the view of multiple patients (up to 16) at one time. Purchasing and installing central stations outside every other room would allow for multi-patient monitoring as well as the ability for clinicians to address alarms from outside the room. Nevertheless, this was quickly ruled out due to the overwhelming cost (most costly of all solutions) and the requirement of an extensive amount of added network infrastructure (additional two cable runs to each Central).

Exhausting all options, ultimately a combination of solutions was determined to best fit our needs. An iPad was installed outside each room with the custom "multi-view" application. Remotes were purchased and installed as needed throughout the unit. In conjunction, the unit was divided into three sections, and central stations were installed in each respective section.

The three solutions in combination made way for a relatively low-cost solution to bring monitoring outside the room in a way that the caregiver could see, hear, address, and ultimately respond to alarms rapidly while primarily stationed outside the patient room.

Operating Room Conversion

Though the expansion of Critical Care throughout SACU, would increase the Critical Care capacity by 180%, adding 36 extra beds at full capacity (total of 56 critical care beds), it was still not enough to accommodate the original projections. Thus, it was necessary to find space for additional Critical Care beds.

The operating rooms (ORs) were quickly identified as a possible surge area. Converting the OR space to a critical care space had several advantages during the pandemic, especially regarding equipment and staffing. As mentioned previously, ventilators are essential for the treatment of critically ill COVID-positive patients and, thus, were in extremely high demand as the infection rates around the nation (and the world) continued to climb. Ultimately, this resulted in a nationwide shortage of ventilators. The OR was specifically chosen due to the abundance of anesthesia units that could be repurposed as ventilators for patients. Additionally, the OR space was already staffed with trained anesthesiologists, doctors, and nursing staff capable of caring for critically ill patients. Generally, the OR is not an optimal surge area because surgical operations must be halted to accommodate the use of the rooms. However, in this case, all non-essential surgical operations were already halted due to infection risks, making it an ideal space to house additional critically ill patients.

The original plan at MSK was that each of the 20 OR rooms would be filled as private rooms. Then, if the number of Critical Care patients surpassed the increased capacity, each OR room would be split to accommodate a double patient room utilizing the same footprint. Subsequently, the OR would be doubled from 20 beds to 40 beds resulting in an additional 71% increase in critical care capacity (total of 96 critical care beds).

On the surface, reconfiguring OR space to inpatient beds appears to be relatively straightforward. However, any major conversion of hospital function within a particular space requires several considerations that are not always visible to the user.

■ Obtain/acquire necessary equipment to support the needs of the inpatient space

Though the OR had the anesthesia units necessary to supplement ventilators, there are a few types of equipment that are not typically used in the OR that needed to be obtained: portable suction units, infusion pumps, sequential compression devices (SCDs), and feeding pumps (Table 4.4).

Table 4.4 Essential Equipment Requirements: OR versus Critical Care

Equipment Type	OR # of Devices Existing	Critical Care # of Devices Needed	Per
Portable Suction	0	0.4	Patient
Infusion Pumps (Brain)	0*	2	Patient
Infusion Pumps (Channel)	0*	8	Patient
Sequential Compression Device (SCD)	0	1	Patient
Feeding Pump	0	1.5	Patient

*Pumps in the OR are a different model than inpatient (IP) and outpatient (OP). They are used for anesthesia, not general drug delivery. Drug library would need to be modified on existing units to accommodate.

To setup any surge area within the hospital, it is important to first pull from existing inventory that is not being utilized. The best way to accomplish this is to identify a singular medical equipment management (planning and logistics) group that is responsible for assessing existing inventory, escalating equipment needs to sourcing, and relocating equipment when necessary. Decentralization of equipment management and associated logistics can drastically slow down the process of relocating equipment and can lead to confusion amongst disjoint hospital groups.

Apart from feeding pumps, there was enough of the essential equipment throughout the institution that could be relocated to the OR to accommodate all 40 beds. Additional feeding pumps were rented to have on standby.

■ Build/configure beds within the hospital information management system and reconfigure physiological monitoring

Because the physiological monitors were originally configured as OR beds within the medical record, the informatics team had to build out all the additional rooms within the hospital's Clinical Information System (CIS). Then, the monitor itself needed to be reconfigured to connect to the newly built "OR inpatient rooms." Luckily, there were enough data jacks available to accommodate the added monitoring equipment, so no additional cabling was required to properly connect the physiological monitors to the network.

■ Add Central Station

The Central Station has a 16-patient limitation. The OR typically has 2 Central Stations to view all 20 patients. However, doubling the capacity throughout the OR also doubled the number of licenses required to monitor all 40 patients. Thus, another central station was required and added view licenses were acquired.

In the end, MSK did not reach the projected capacity of Critical Care patients and did not have to care for any patients on the M6 OR platform. Nevertheless, the exercise of converting the space was enlightening and the workflows built to operationalize the conversion will be referenced and further refined in future disaster planning.

Treating COVID-19 Patients: Addressing Medical Equipment Needs

Increased Monitoring Needs—Staying Agile

Caring for COVID-19-positive patients during the months of March through May (2020) came with quite a bit of uncertainty. Little was known about the virus and treatment plans were only beginning to be developed. Naturally, with that uncertainty, there was an overwhelming desire and need to understand and learn everything possible about the COVID-19 patient population at each stage of their treatment and recovery.

Modifying physiological monitoring to best fit the present need was crucial and required adopting multiple approaches. In some cases, configuration needed to be modified to accommodate the capture (and/or emphasis) of different parameter(s) that were of interest. Other situations called for monitoring expansion to enable the monitoring of more patients. In other cases, the frequency of monitoring needed to be increased. Every varied clinical need required a thoughtful approach and many times the approaches were very different based on the existing infrastructure and the scope of the clinical need. Unyielding collaboration and coordination between the clinical and technical teams was paramount to create physiological monitoring that was both agile and accessible to fit the needs of the institution.

Introducing Episodic Pulse Oximetry (SpO₂) Monitoring

Because MSK is a cancer-care facility that specializes in the treatment of an already immune-compromised patient population, infection control is at the forefront of equipment planning. In many cases, this results in dedicated equipment for each room, that would be shared by the entire floor in a typical institution. Having equipment dedicated to each room, made it possible to significantly reduce the amount of necessary disinfections required when equipment is moved from room to room. In the case of vital signs monitoring, it enabled the implementation of near-continuous vital signs monitoring across all MSK acute care units.

Due to the significant nature of the impact the COVID-19 virus has on the respiratory system, pulse oximetry or continuous SpO_2 monitoring can be the earliest indicator of patient decline. Pulse oximetry is the percent of oxygen within the blood (typical versus typical for COVID-19).

The first immediate challenge was a lack of equipment that was setup to monitor continuous pulse oximetry to cover the projected capacity. Shifting practice to utilize the existing vital signs monitors that were dedicated to each room already to accommodate this monitoring easily remedied the issue of insufficient equipment quantities. However, utilizing the existing vital signs monitor in the room at the increased frequency introduced a new issue. A nurse typically takes vitals every four hours. The COVID-19 patient population requires near-continuous vitals monitoring, in some case as much as every 20 minutes. Requiring a nurse to increase the number of vitals taken on each patient from every four hours to as much as every 20 minutes would increase the number of times that a nurse is required to enter the room, and subsequently his/her exposure to a patient with COVID-19, by 92%. Increasing nursing exposure, especially by such a significant amount, was not an option for MSK, so a new approach needed to be developed to obtain these frequent vitals that did not require the nurse to increase the number of times that they needed to enter the patient room.

Ultimately, to increase pulse oximetry monitoring while minimizing nursing exposure, the monitors needed to be able to extract vitals automatically at a set interval. Though, automatic vitals collection implies that the patient remains wearing the SpO_2 finger probe and blood pressure cuff, requiring the patient to wear the sensors for an increased duration potentially causing discomfort. To increase the comfort level as much as possible, disposable SpO_2 finger probes, with a significantly more comfortable design, were stocked on the floor to replace the hard plastic reusable SpO_2 finger probes.

Now, reconfiguring the existing vital signs monitors allowed for vitals to be taken as frequently as required without requiring the nurse to enter the room. However, in many cases the layout of the room was such that the vitals could not be viewed from outside the room. To address this, remote viewing options were explored (i.e., connecting to the network, installing cameras). Luckily, the vital signs monitors at MSK are connected (via wired or wireless connection) to the vendor network. Because the network infrastructure for the vital signs monitors was already in place, remote viewing at a central viewing station became an option.

In the end, Biomed worked closely with Nursing Informatics, IT (DigITs), and the vendor to quickly test and stand-up a solution by which vitals were automatically captured at a set interval and displayed at a central viewing station. This solution was implemented across five acute care floors at MSK requiring the reconfiguration of a total of 117 monitors and the installation of five central viewing stations.

Expanding Telemetry Monitoring

To monitor COVID-19-positive patients more methodically, the need for telemetry monitoring increased rapidly. The telemetry monitoring system at MSK requires a proprietary wireless antenna system and associated proprietary network infrastructure. Thus, scalability can be a challenge. For this type of system design, rapid expansion is limited to the footprint of the existing antenna placement due to the cost and time that would be required to install new cabling for additional antennas. Nevertheless, MSK was able to maximize telemetry monitoring as much as possible within the existing footprint, increasing the telemetry monitoring capacity by 37% from 108 patients to 148 patients.

Increased Ventilator Needs—Management of Multi-Vendor, Multi Model Ventilators

Patients suffering from COVID-19 often require assisted breathing by way of a mechanical ventilation until their immune system can clear the infection to the point where proper lung function can be restored. As COVID-19 spread through the United States and an accelerated pace, so did the demand for ventilators to treat COVID-19-positive patients. However, hospitals across the nation were not equipped with enough ventilators to accommodate the rapid surge resulting in a nationwide shortage. Hospitals were then given no other choice but to source any ventilators available, regardless of hospital equipment standards, as well as establish creative solutions to utilize existing ventilators. The government was able to aid in creating stockpile.

To manage an increased (and varied) fleet of ventilators, MSK's approach to secondary alarm routing for ventilator alarms had to quickly adapt to the increased demand. Prior to COVID-19, primary local alarms were addressed by nursing while a secondary alarm was sent to Respiratory Therapy and in rare cases the charge nurse of the unit, through middleware and pagers. As patients requiring ventilators started to rise, it became clear that there would soon be a lack of bridge hardware to accommodate the typical MSK middleware alarm routing strategy. In addition, it was evident that the uptake of alarms would soon be unmanageable for Respiratory Therapists alone. Thus, an overwhelming need to extend the notification to nursing as well as Respiratory Therapy was required.

Knowing the current alarming setup was not going to be a sufficient option, it was apparent that a new strategy needed to be implemented that could accommodate the use of ventilators in all Expanded Critical Care areas. In all the Critical Care spaces, at this time, the physiological monitoring system was connected to the hospital network infrastructure and configured to route alarms to central station monitors, and in some cases, nursing handheld phones. Because this technology already spanned the areas of interest, it was clear that this was the clearest pathway to be able to achieve the desired workflow of routing alarms from the ventilator to the necessary clinical staff. However, the challenge of capturing alarms from a varied fleet of ventilators remained. Ultimately, every model of ventilator used at MSK, whether MSK-owned, rented, or donated required extensive testing in a condensed time frame.

The Role of Biomedical Engineering

Through innovative solutions and close collaboration with many groups within the institution, Memorial Sloan Kettering (MSK) was able to increase the bed capacity to 150% meeting the state requirement. COVID-19 changed the way things were done in the hospital. As we braced for the surge, Biomed roles expanded to meets the needs the hospital. Biomed staff had to find the balance with using technology to limit the exposure from the clinical staff while keep their exposure at minimum.

As the Medical Equipment HICS team determined the medical equipment needs for the institution, several items were purchased to help the hospital uphold its usual standard of care. While supply chain teams were diligently monitoring the PPE supply, Biomed took on the ask to onboard countless items purchased for the surge. This was the biggest intake of inventory that the team had to turnover in a brief period. Most of the challenges arose from having to do the physically labor of unboxing and prepping the inventory with reduced staffing. To combat the shortage, Biomed resources from other non-inpatient sites were temporarily reassigned to support the inpatient operation while we prepared for this time of uncertainty. With the additional workforce, there were task forces created that tackled specific needs of the hospital: general inventory, maintenance/repair, acute care, critical care. With this division, the Biomed team was able to success onboard more than 500 new devices and eventually install/customize it to fit the COVID patients.

General Inventory and Repair Task Force

The onboarding/staging and repair team consisted of four techs and one engineer. The responsibility of this team was to ensure that all the devices that were transferred from other sites, moved out of storage, or recently purchased/rented was accurately captured in the database and certified for patient use through testing. The large uptake in the number of rental devices in circulation introduced a significant concern with respect to the ability effectively locate and return the rented items in a timely manner. Failure to do so could result in additional charges and fees. Thus, extreme diligence is required to effectively manage the location of rental devices of this magnitude. Utilizing the existing Real-Time Locating Systems (RTLS) significantly helped in this endeavor. The Biomed Inventory Team tagged all rental devices as they were onboarded significantly reducing the amount of time spent searching for the equipment at the time of return. Ultimately, all rented equipment was able to be collected and returned without facing any fees.

The onboarding/repair team was the biggest task force in Biomed due to the volume of incoming equipment. Each day the group onboarded around 60 devices on average. Naturally, the major hurdle that was faced early-on to accommodate a large team with a large volume of incoming equipment was space, or more appropriately a lack of staging space. Staging space is notoriously rare within hospital settings. Yet, it is crucial to have a dedicated staging space when looking to stage large batches of equipment, especially when that equipment has a large footprint (i.e., Hepa Filters). Biomed does not have a dedicated staging area, so one of the unused conference rooms had to be converted into a staging area where the team was able to inventory, test, tag, and store all incoming devices. Centralizing the medical equipment delivery provided a controlled, consistent, environment for the team to significantly increase efficiency. Since this team was not directly exposed to COVID patients, it was safe for older workers and those with any comorbidities. Without the diligence of this team, the other two teams would not have been able to be effective.

Acute Care Task Force

The acute care team had a rotation of two engineers and two techs. The acute care team was bigger since they would cover majority of the inpatient hospital. The goal of the team was to ensure that the vital sign devices can be used as an indicator of when a COVID patient would begin to desaturate so that medical intervention can take place. They worked on creating a solution where the continuous vitals will be visible at a central station and the nurses will get alerts to their phones when levels reached a critical value. This solution required a firmware update that took 20 minutes to load via laptop. To minimize staff exposure in the rooms, the firmware updates were performed on purchased devices that have not been installed yet and swapped out in the rooms which allowed the Biomed staff to be in the patient rooms for a shorter period.

Critical Care Task Force

The critical care team consisted of one engineer and a manager who was responsible for setting up the COVID ICU. This team was small but had an assortment of skills with healthy and willing employees. Their task consisted of turning the SACU care unit into the COVID ICU, expanding the current ICU capabilities, turning the ORs into a critical care space, minimizing the amount of time clinical staff had to enter a room. When entering a COVID room, safety was the main objective for both the Biomed and clinical staff, and countless measures were taken to ensure that the safety of the worker such as wearing the proper PPE. The manager was responsible for communicating with leadership about the progress of the ICU expansion, securing the resources that was needed for each ICU bed and working with various departments to ensure that the task was completed. The engineer went into each room and updated the clinical profiles, made equipment accessible outside of the patient room and installed new devices.

Finding the "Right" Solution

During a crisis, it is important to take stock of what is available, especially when facing seemingly insurmountable challenges. Each hospital is unique with varied access to space, technology, and available capital equipment at their disposal. Truly understanding all available options requires the consideration of many factors and how those factors impact each other such as staffing, inventory, technology, infrastructure, and hospital design. The best medical equipment planning occurs at the intersection of clinical necessity, facility design, and technology (ECRI). Thus, it is imperative to establish strong multi-disciplinary teams with varied expertise to ensure that all options are fully explored when determining the "right" solution to address difficult challenges. For MSK, oftentimes the solution that was not purchasing more capital but rather investing in the expansion of existing technology. Giving the Medical Equipment HICS team the space and backing to be proactive and thoughtful about equipment surge planning created the space for innovative solutions. As a result, MSK was able to mitigate reactionary spending and invest in technology-driven solutions that will outlive the pandemic.

Lessons Learned and Impacts on Future Operations

The success of any project or implementation, large or small, is directly related to the ability to plan effectively. Prepping for a surge, is no different. Thus, advanced disaster planning preparations can be crucial to ensure that hospitals are nimble enough to react to any crisis.

Chain of command to manage clinical equipment decision-making and logistics can and should be defined prior to the crisis. The hospital should establish a clear surge plan that identifies areas that will be allocated as Critical and Acute Care surge spaces as well as areas with the potential to be utilized as isolation areas. These areas should be reviewed periodically with clinical and emergency management teams to keep them up to date. In addition, standards of care for surge spaces should be established and reviewed periodically.

With surge areas identified and standards of care established, operational teams (Biomedical Engineering, Informatics, Facilities, etc.) should review and work alongside clinical teams to ensure that each area is setup to be easily converted to accommodate the hospital surge plan. For Biomedical Engineering, this means investing and implementing medical devices and systems that are easily scalable. Scalability is crucial in major medical systems (e.g., physiological monitoring, nurse call, infusion systems) to effectively expand care spaces rapidly. Systems that rely on the existing hospital wireless network are ideal. However, if the hospital has any of the aforementioned medical systems that are not scalable and therefore cannot accommodate the surge plan, the surge space plan should be either be modified or approved equipment substitutes should be sourced in advance. Furthermore, a small stock of critical medical devices necessary to support a low-level surge should be maintained and stored centrally.

Chapter 5

Data Management and Analytics to Drive COVID Response

Jim Beinlich

Contents

The COVID-19 pandemic heightened the importance and use of healthcare data and analytics in a way that has not been seen before. Accurate, reliable data and information have played a critical role in providing healthcare executives and caregivers with tools needed to make decisions that in some cases literally could mean life and death. Unlike the normal operations of a health system and the associated information flow which is very predictable (seasonality, service volume norms), COVID-19 has proven to be anything but predictable. Healthcare systems have relied on experience, intuition, and "predictable" data for years to run their operations. COVID-19 made it nearly

DOI: 10.4324/b23264-5

impossible to rely on those three elements, leaving many to turn to real-time data for information from which to make key decisions. This chapter will explore the issues, responses, and lessons learned from the experiences during my time at a large academic multi-hospital system and the use of data and analytics during the pandemic.

Early Days

During the early days of the pandemic, hospitals and health systems reacted by cancelling elective appointments and procedures. While this might not seem like a very challenging thing to accomplish, indeed it is, especially from a data perspective. It is not uncommon to have to cancel procedures or appointments for a particular day due to unexpected provider unavailability, unexpected equipment failure, or weather-related events. But to cancel ALL your elective appointments and procedures is quite out of the ordinary. First, there had to be agreement on what exactly constituted an elective appointment or procedure from a clinical risk perspective. As you might imagine, data was needed to provide an electronic listing of all candidates that might constitute "elective." Criteria for data inclusion needed to be decided and a starter list could be generated. Then the list was culled to separate the easy decisions from those that might need additional clinical review. This all could not happen immediately so manual work looking at schedules and calling patients provided interim support until a more automated method could be implemented that was able to send electronic notices to patient to ease the manual effort. This very first reaction to COVID-19 would not have been possible without data.

Another immediate effort focused on standing up testing centers, many of them located outside of hospitals and clinics. One of the first data challenges was how to handle citizens that showed up for COVID-19 testing but were not already patients of the health system. The first reaction was to just enter them into the health system EMR. This would provide for robust data tracking and reporting capabilities for COVID-19 testing. It would also leverage the existing workflows that clinicians familiar to clinical staff. That approach was soon seen to have several important implications:

- EMRs are sized and licensed based on a health system's normal patient population and visit volume, what would be the implications on performance?
- Would the system crash if it was overwhelmed with unexpected volume?

- Would we pay a penalty for a surge in software licensing?
- Would some existing reporting systems become unusable if we now co-mingled non-patient and regular patient data?
- How would all our regular processes be impacted (billing, etc.) if we were to co-mingle non-billable testing activities (COVID-19 testing was never going to be billed to individual patients or insurers) with regular patient activity?

While some of these issues may appear to be strictly administrative in nature, unfortunately, they are critical to the normal operation of any health system. Causing unnecessary disruption to any of those processes would have caused incredible confusion and distraction at a time when health system leadership needed to be able to focus completely on all the COVID-19 challenges that were thrust upon them, including how to shift a large part of the workforce to remote operations in response to stay-at-home orders. Those of you in healthcare already know what a complex and interconnected system it is. You need all the pieces to function to deliver care.

Once a decision was made to track and manage the drive-up testing volume in a separate database from the EMR, we could avoid all the distractions of answering the questions posed above and focus on the next challenge which was the daily reporting cycle for all COVID-19-related activity. This is what helped to guide organizations through what turned out to be over a year of daily reporting.

COVID-19 Reporting

Data and reporting in the early days of the Pandemic (March and April 2020) focused in many ways on basic information about capacity and volumes such as:

- Impact on scheduled appointment and procedure volumes due to cancellation of electives
- Estimation of volumes and patient lists needed to support remote patient screening (tele-screening)
- Emergency Department volumes
- Admissions, discharges, and length of stay (COVID-19 and non-COVID-19)
- Intensive care unit (ICU) volume and capacity (COVID-19 and non-COVID-19)

- Ventilator usage and capacity
- COVID-19 patient inflows and outflows
- Positive Potential Patients (tested patients not confirmed but likely COVID-19 positive)
- COVID-19 positive patients recovering at home
- COVID-19 admissions by geo-location (to identify hotspots)

This may not seem like much of a challenge to gather and report this data but there were two initial ones that made this harder that it might seem. How to define a hospitalized COVID-19 patient (remember, many patients already have chronic disease and other issues and may not have entered the hospital specifically because of COVID-19) and how to report the data to tell a meaningful story that could be understood and used for executive decision-making. One might think the easiest thing to do would be to take any patient tested for COVID-19 and simply take their test results and count any patient tested positive as a COVID-19 patient. There are a few problems with that approach that we identified:

- In the early days and weeks of the crisis, rapid changes were occurring regarding how lab testing was managed. New orderables, result components, testing agencies, and workflows were added daily. The number of changes to data tracking and EMR configuration would have caused a lot of confusion.
- Some early results came back on fax and were scanned into the EHR; a few early positive results came back electronically, but without the expected abnormal flags.
- Additionally, some patients had both positive and negative lab results.

It's easy to forget that early in the pandemic laboratory testing was a moving target and there was much confusion about exactly how to test for COVID-19 (remember the invasive nasal swabs). Questions about testing equipment, reagents needed for the tests, etc. The situation on the ground was changing rapidly and that's not a good thing when you are trying to capture data from which to make decisions. Not just any decisions, potential life, and death COVID-19 decisions.

What we decided is for patients that have tested positive for non-severe COVID-19 and could recover at home, a positive lab test was an appropriate data point (and probably the most reasonable one). For patients who tested positive for COVID-19 with severe symptoms and admitted to the hospital, infection control staff reviewed the patient's medical chart and used an infection status flag in the EMR to denote a patient with active COVID-19 infection. It was critical at that time to closely monitor capacity within the hospital for ICU beds, ventilators, etc. Closely monitoring patients that were confirmed by not just a lab test but also based on the clinical judgment of infection control specialist was critical. This provided for high-quality data on the COVID-19 inpatient population in real-time and avoided the issues associated with simply relying on a lab test result that could have been mis-read, false positive or negative, and the timing associated with test turnaround. As inpatients were recovering from active COVID-19 infection, we were also able to leverage the same process of managing the infection status flag that would be removed by the infection control team. This provided for additional trust and confidence in the data on our inpatient COVID-19 population. Any question about the data was easy to isolate to individual patients whose medical records could be audited by one of the infection control team to ensure data was accurate and up to date.

The infection status flag also allowed us to easily identify patients confirmed to be COVID-19 positive and provide a source of truth not just for reporting but also for workflow to support the clinical teams, Environmental Services (EVS), and others who could look to the red "COVID-19 Confirmed" banner in the EMR. Since everyone was using the same source of truth, we were able to quickly develop reports that aligned with workflow.

Projections and Predictions

Hospitals and health systems wrestled with understanding what might happen with COVID-19 hospitalizations as the daily numbers of reported infections grew at an alarming rate. Inpatient census in the United States for COVID-19 patients exploded by 666% in just 26 days from March 26 to April 21, according to statistics from the COVID Tracking Project (https://covidtracking.com/data). This left healthcare administrators scrambling to plan for unknown surges in hospitalizations, ICU admissions, and ventilator needs. Under "normal" circumstances that might be experienced during a bad flu season, there are historical data that can be used to model projections for hospital capacity in the ER and on inpatient units. No historical data existed for a COVID-19 pandemic which meant that there were no historical data from which to project future data. Another complication was the projected effect of mitigation strategies (masking, distancing, etc.) that could be factored into projection. These factors introduced a new and significant set of variables into projection models.

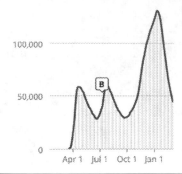

Figure 5.1   Pattern of virus spread.

What was available was current data that was flowing in from counties and states. This data was the only reliable historical data that could be used to start projecting future cases, hospitalization, etc. Looking back on it now, it's easy to see that one of the faults in that data is that it was a result of the initial surge of cases. That virus was spreading at an alarmingly fast rate. A rate that did not sustain as cases eventually leveled out, declined, rose again during the second surge, and so forth as shown in Figure 5.1.

These surges distorted the rate of infection and severity, not only at any given point in time, but also by point in time by locality. These factors led to individual models that looked more like hurricane path prediction spaghetti charts with a wide range of possible outcomes. Many also projected an alarming number of deaths, much of which did not materialize as the initial surge subsided. This very scientific approach to projections might have been technically the "right" thing to do but the unknowns in the model assumptions made them confusing and too wide-ranging in possible outcomes to be understandable by many hospital administrators and thus not very useful. For many organizations, it was back to basics.

Since normal hospital statistical projecting using seasonality and historical data was not available, we built new projection based on existing COVID-19 census data. This was a very new data set with no apparent linear pattern (except for the steep initial increase in March and April) so we started with simple moving averages (MA). Originally, we started with a seven-day MA thinking that would smooth out any weekly variation (Sunday admissions versus Monday, etc.). As it turned out, that did smooth things out but a little too much. Leadership was sensitive to daily changes in census and projections for the following week and the smoothing effect of a seven-day MA was not helpful, so we switched to a three-day MA. This gave us the sensitivity we needed for admissions, but we had to do something a little different for discharges.

Most healthcare executives know that a typical healthcare week has a defined rhythm to it from busy surgical days to heavy admission days and varying degrees of discharge activity. For example, it is common to see more discharges at the end of a week versus a weekend. As full-time staffing levels are lower on the weekends and physician availability is lower, many more discharges are processed on a Friday versus a Sunday. We found the same dynamic with COVID-19 patients as they recovered and prepared for discharge. This created a cyclic fluctuation in discharges dependent of the day of the week. This created a challenge with our three-day MA that we wanted to use to project next week's admissions, discharges, and census. During the three-day window on days with higher discharge volume, the three-day MA was higher due to the cycle of the week. Conversely, the weekend window for three-day MA was lower due to the same dynamic. A simple fix was to use a three-day MA but use the last three Sundays, the last three Mondays, etc. None of this is complex but the point is to demonstrate the subtleties that we had to tune to do a little better job of predicting the next day's admissions and discharges. We also had to keep it simple. When we fielded questions about how we were determining projections, these points were very helpful:

- Projections were only for the next seven days, anything further out was too unpredictable.
- Using simple MAs made explanations understandable to a wide audience.
- Re-baselining census on days we had days that were outliers for activity helped us better project tomorrow's census.

Projecting future census also meant that we had to project length of stay. This was challenging in many of the same ways admissions and discharges were to project. It took a few months to get a sense for the true average length of stay for COVID-19 patients and this certainly changed as new treatment protocols were identified and implemented. During the first few weeks of the pandemic, we took the small data set of existing patients and determined an assumed length of stay based on that data and constantly monitored and tuned it based on newer patients which helped us establish a reasonable baseline for projecting future census as the weeks progressed. It highlighted once again, the challenge that COVID-19 presented with respect to the lack of prior historical data from which to make assumptions.

We were constantly trying to identify leading indicators for hospital admissions but like everyone else, really struggled to find dependable correlations. While increased Emergency Department visit volume and positivity rates in the community certainly correlated in general with hospitalizations, those were widely known variables and while helpful to indicate potential for increased hospitalizations, were not specific beyond general expectations for increases in admissions. We did not complicate our projections with these outside factors and instead relied on the general MA's to project volumes. We did, however, rely on that information as anecdotal indication that hospitalizations may increase. One thing that did help was identifying cases in certain localities, especially ones where we knew there were nursing homes and senior living centers. Increased COVID-19 activity in those areas helped identify homes and centers that would benefit from intervention at their site to keep hospitalizations from occurring in the first place as these locations were becoming high-risk due to the concentration of elderly populations.

Government Reporting

While all hospitals and health systems were trying to project COVID-19 census data, we also had responsibility for reporting statistics to city, county, and state agencies. What we found to be most effective was to create a central repository of COVID-19 statistics and provide access to our local hospital staff who, in turn, were responsible for reporting this data. This allowed for the required individual reporting requirements set forth by the agencies while allowing central management of data to ensure accuracy and quality. This hybrid approach of central collection and management along with local submission was another lesson for us; hybrid approaches satisfy multiple needs in a coordinated manner.

Data-Driven Decisions

I cannot stress enough how import the COVID-19 census data was to the continued health system and hospital operations. There were multiple critical operational and strategic decisions that needed to be made, some daily, that were highly dependent on this data. Remember, historical management experience and "gut instinct" were challenging because of the many unknowns with COVID-19. Some of these critical decisions were:

- Surge units (should we open them?)
- What is going to happen to Emergency Department volume, impact on staffing?

- Can our lab process test fast enough? Do we have enough supplies?
- Do we have enough ventilators? Do we need more?
- How are telemedicine visit volume changing, can we keep up?
- How many of our employees have been exposed to COVID-19? How many are quarantined? How many are COVID-19 positive? What is the impact on staffing and how do we adjust?

As you can see, there were a lot of considerations to be made on a regular basis. With all the unknowns surrounding COVID-19, the early days of the pandemic were riddled with questions that had to be answered to continue operation. The need for data on a regular, digestible, and understandable basis became our focus and was another lesson—the keep it simple approach served us well. Ultimately, we never did open our COVID-19 surge unit, which would have required transport of some very sick patients, placing them at risk. While I was not personally involved in that decision, I believe that the data we were generating daily informed that decision to a great extent.

Besides the challenges specific to data, we also had to wrestle with reporting of the data:

- How often are reports needed?
- What time horizon do we report on? As of now? As of midnight, last night?
- How do we best combine data from multiple EMRs?
- What is the most critical data needed for executive decision? What is just enough versus what is too much?
- What visualizations best convey the story behind the data?
- Do we trend only some data points? All of them?

COVID-19 Reporting

As with everything else surrounding COVID-19, we learned as we went and continued to refine our reporting based on feedback from the executive teams and key stakeholders. In the early days of the reporting, we leveraged manual processes for synthesizing and visualizing data using Microsoft Excel. This was labor intensive but allowed us to make rapid changes to the way we reported data and the way we visualized it.

Initially we were reporting volume activity three times per day:

■ Morning report—data as of the prior midnight census as a basis for daily executive meetings.
■ Noon report—data from midnight to mid-day to capture activity for the current day.
■ 4 pm report—appended any addition volume that occurred since noon and support an end of day executive meeting.

The three times per day reporting cycle gave us the opportunity to make requested changes to visualizations and then get feedback in a quick time-frame. This helped us respond quickly to enhancements requested by our executive team. We could also "demo" new visualizations or additional data points quickly and get feedback the same day. The three times per day reporting also provided a predictable reporting cycle for the organization, another seemingly small but important outcome.

We had considered several delivery methods for the daily COVID-19 executive reports including an online dashboard, a centralized intranet site, and a PowerPoint slide deck. Ultimately, we decided on the lower-tech PowerPoint deck for a few reasons:

■ Online access with the EMR or our analytics platforms would have required a login to an environment that not all our users were familiar.
■ Some platforms would have required users to be logged onto the net-work which would have required multi-step login activities.
■ Email was a preferred method as it was a channel that our target audi-ence could access easily and was already using throughout the day, in the evenings, at home, or when away and was dependable enough to be "always on".

We decided on an email "push" of a PowerPoint deck that was easy to prepare, review, and view on a mobile device, computer, or a tablet. This was another one of those "keep it simple" decisions that served us very well.

One of the other things that we planned for very early on in the pan-demic was an onslaught of requests that might come our way for COVID-19 reports. Every corner of our health system was impacted by what was going on and everyone certainly needed "information" to help them plan whatever aspect of their operations was being impacted. We made the decision to form a small group of very knowledgeable analytics and clinical reporting staff from Information Services, Quality Management, and Administration. The group acted as a funnel to handle requests (in meetings, via our I/T ticketing system, etc.) from a triage perspective to ensure we were not (i) overwhelming our reporting staff, (ii) duplicating efforts, and (iii) creating confusion by generating conflicting data. We also had to factor in changes that were being made on a very regular basis to our EMR to account for changes in unit configurations, lab tests, etc. These changes had a ripple effect on data and reporting and we needed to ensure tight change control. Without it, our data and reporting systems could have been littered with incorrect data. That tight coordination with this small group was critical to keeping us organized and working in a unified fashion as we navigated some rough seas at time. We met daily to make sure we were aligned and later as things became more under control, we were able to move to twice week touch-point meetings.

After a few months as the initial surge was beginning to wane and we had settled in on the data collection and presentation format, we did start to automate as much of the manual data aggregation and visualization using our analytics platform. This relieved what was becoming a tiresome, laborious, manual process of spreadsheets and validation. Over time, manual processes can lead to human error due to the rote-ness and impracticality of continuous error-free focus. The good thing is that manual work really solidified what was needed to be automated and ensured that we had a very firm grasp of the data and visualization requirements. Once we automated into online dashboards, it became a simple process of validating those dashboards and capturing screenshots for the executive reporting package. Another good lesson learned was not jumping too quickly into automation. Ultimately, we saved time and were much nimbler using simple tools until we understood exactly what we needed.

Recovery

As we settled into the automation and a more relaxed reporting cycle as the initial COVID-19 surge waned into the summer of 2020, healthcare organizations were shifting from pandemic mode to resumption of normal operations. Elective surgeries were opening back up and patients were coming back to clinics and primary care offices. Staff were pivoting to resume their normal job duties, and all were looking forward to getting back to financial health as normal business was resuming. The big question was, how long was it going to take to get back to "normal" volumes and how could we ensure that if another COVID-19 surge hit in the fall, we weren't rushing too quickly back to volumes that would have left no capacity to deal with new COVID-19 patients. We continued to track and report our daily COVID-19 data points but used lessons we learned for those and adopted what we called "resurgence metrics" to track our recovery. It meant that the team that was so heavily focused on gathering, curating, and reporting COVID-19 metrics had to completely change focus on a new set of metrics. Leveraging what we had already learned, it was much easier to build on that experience and quickly provide the data needed to track our recovery.

Summary of Lessons Learned

There were certainly valuable lessons learned from the COVID-19 experience and hopefully ones that will shape and propel healthcare data and analytics into the future on a better trajectory that what might have otherwise been achieved. A recent study by the Virtusa Corporation indicates that healthcare firms typically lag about a decade behind other industries in adopting business technologies that would help with customer engagement. The relaxation of legislative barriers to adoption of digital technologies such as telemedicine are hopefully a signal that healthcare can start to make up precious ground compared to other industries. While data privacy and security are very important, healthcare must find ways to leverage the rich data that can help address future pandemics and other promising initiatives such as precision and genomic medicine. A harsh lesson that we should also take from the COVID-19 experience is that while AI, machine learning, and predictive analytics are technologies with great promise to advance diagnostic and therapeutic healthcare, they are only as good as the data used to develop and train them. Algorithms and predictive models were no match for the unpredictable nature of COVID-19. We should all learn that lesson and tread carefully into the integration of those technologies into patient care.

Healthcare struggled with some very simple aspects of data management and reporting during COVID-19. The gaps in these areas were highlighted for every organization to see where they need to focus and invest. Luckily, my organization had already been investing and implementing technologies and processes that allowed us to better collect, curate, and synthesize data in a common technical platform. We had implemented governance processes and data standards and had a centralized data analytics center. Even with those advantages, we found gaps and struggled with some aspects of data management and reporting. Others who were not as far along, really had a tough time doing simple things like getting data in a common format into a common repository. There has been much criticism about the state of reporting at the county, state, and federal level during COVID-19. This criticism is justified as the current system proved to be difficult to trust at times, but hospitals and health systems contribute to problem. The lack of local sound data management capabilities flows upstream and creates issues that ripple through every level.

Here is a summary of our lessons learned from the data and reporting aspect if managing COVID-19:

- Established a "tiger team" of data managers from I/T, Quality, and Administration in the first weeks of the pandemic to oversee and manage COVID-19 data.
- Made an early decision as to how to consistently identify COVID-19 patients that saved us from great confusion and miscommunication that could have resulted.
- Initially evaluated existing population Health registries to help manage COVID-19 population, but most are built to manage "alive" populations and proved to be problematic.
- Built a single repository of COVID-19 positive patients which became source of truth for all COVID-19 reporting.
- Local hospital entities handled state reporting but used data from a curated central source of truth.
- Leveraged a single team to evaluate all reports and dashboards to ensure consistency and avoid duplication of effort.
- Inventoried and managed all COVID-19 reports and dashboards on a single portal to improve visibility and consistency to the organization.
- Kept it simple.
- Leveraged easy-to-use tools like PowerPoint and email distribution to ensure we consistently communicated in a user-friendly way.
- Decided early on to leverage simple tools like Microsoft Excel to model data and create visualizations; this was the right decision.
- Established consistent reporting cycles and published reporting horizons to be clear about data freshness.

Bibliography

Landie, Heather. (March 30, 2018). Study: Healthcare Lags Other Industries in Digital Transformation, Customer Engagement Tech. *Healthcare Innovation*. https://www.hcinnovationgroup.com/population-health-management/ news/13030021/study-healthcare-lags-other-industries-in-digital-transformation-customer-engagement-tech.

The COVID Tracking Project at The Atlantic. (March 7, 2021). The COVID Tracking Project. https://covidtracking.com, Copyright © 2021 by The Atlantic Monthly Group. (CC BY 4.0)

Chapter 6

The Role of Real-Time Location Systems in Ambulatory Care in the Post-Pandemic Era

Mary Jagim and Joanna Wyganowska

Contents

DOI: 10.4324/b23264-6

As communities begin to re-open after COVID pandemic, a "new-normal" began for ambulatory care practices. Ambulatory care practices undertake the difficult task of restoring patient volumes through the practice while limiting exposure risks for patients and staff. This chapter explains the role of real-time location systems (RTLS) in implementing new processes necessary to optimize patient flow while creating safer environment.

Background and Challenges

Around the globe, the COVID-19 pandemic has caused the illness of millions and a death toll in the hundreds of thousands.[1] The event has altered daily life and impacted businesses. Ambulatory care medical practices are no exception. The operational and financial impact on medical practices has been significant. Many of these practices are smaller and privately owned by providers or groups of providers with fewer financial resources to sustain the practice.

Impact on Patient Volumes and Revenues

In an effort to reduce potential exposures, many medical practices temporarily closed or had to limit their number of daily appointments, or they transitioned their model of care primarily to telehealth as advised by the CDC.[2] In some cases, these services have incorporated in-home diagnostic testing such as lab draws or electrocardiograms.[3] These changes significantly reduced their daily patient volumes, compared to pre-COVID-19 volumes. This was highlighted in a survey done by the Medical Group Management Association, in which it was found that medical practices have experienced a 60% average decrease in patient volume and a 55% average decrease in revenue since the beginning of the coronavirus pandemic.[4]

Impact on Workforce

In addition, ambulatory care practices reported that 48% of them have temporarily furloughed staff, and 22% have permanently laid off staff due to decreased patient volumes and revenues.[5]

In those organizations where staff have been furloughed, the staff may choose other opportunities, leaving vacant positions that result in staff shortages once active patient scheduling resumes.

Impact on Workflow and Operations

Ambulatory practices that have remained open and were actively seeing patients have had to alter their existing patient workflows and staff processes in order to maintain social distancing to prevent the potential spread of the virus. All staff had to wear appropriate PPE, including a surgical face mask, at all times. Patients were also required to wear a face mask. Screening protocols were put in place to identify potentially infectious patients or staff. Cleaning practices within the facility were hypervigilant and all non-disposable equipment used in patient care had to be thoroughly cleaned after every use.[6] Check-in areas had to allow for ample distancing of 6 feet between patients, and the time patients spent in waiting areas had to be limited or even eliminated.[7] Of further concern was that patients with underlying health conditions, which tend to make up the frequent patient visits to ambulatory care sites, are at increased risk for community-acquired infections. Patients with cancer and autoimmune diseases were also at higher risk due to their immunocompromised state.[8] These concerns forced practices to implement processes to limit the congregation of patients in areas and the number of patient-staff contact points to reduce exposure risk.[9]

As communities began to re-open, a "new-normal" started to begin for ambulatory care practices. There were new challenges as they were restoring patient appointment volumes, including the backlog of appointments, while simultaneously implementing new processes necessary to maintain patient and staff safety.[10]

Practices are now faced with new priorities as they start to operate in the post-pandemic era. These priorities include:

- Screening processes to identify patients and staff who may be infectious
- Securing PPE resources for staff and patients
- Maintaining social distancing of 6 feet apart
- Eliminating waiting lines for check-in
- Reducing or eliminating patient time spent in waiting rooms
- Minimizing person-to-person contact while providing the patient with an optimal experience
- Efficiently performing thorough contact tracing to identify patients and staff in the practice at risk in the event of any exposures

Solution

Ambulatory medical practices must develop plans and processes to fully re-open to patients while providing a safe space for patients and staff. Many practices turned to technology for solutions. However, with the economic impact on healthcare, funds for solutions are still limited, so the need for affordable technology solutions has never been greater.

Real-Time Tools

RTLS offer solutions to support ambulatory care practices in overcoming many of these new challenges. Specifically, RTLS tools can provide insight into processes aimed at improving staff workflow and patient throughput and reducing the risk of infections. Traditionally, RTLS solutions tend to be very cost-prohibitive and time-consuming to implement. That is no longer the case with the incorporation of new technology that is more affordable and easier to install. The following are examples of ways in which RTLS can support ambulatory care practices in meeting their goals regarding access and safety.

The Need to Eliminate a Physical Waiting Room and Create Virtual Waiting Rooms

Historically, the reduction or possible elimination of time spent in clinic waiting rooms has always been about patient satisfaction.[11] This includes any waiting in lines to register in addition to the general waiting to be called back to the exam room. However, in the post-COVID-19 era, reducing or eliminating waiting is also about patient safety, by reducing infection risk.[10] As part of reducing the risk of exposure, it is critical to prevent patients from congregating in registration and waiting spaces. Making the transition from a physical waiting environment to a virtual waiting room with contactless check-in is now a top priority for healthcare organizations.

Streamlined Door to Exam Patient Flow

An example for improving the door to exam room patient flow is to leverage RTLS badges upon a patient's arrival to the clinic. The patient can be automatically placed into a queue to register, allowing the patient to be seated and avoid standing in line, or even to wait in their car; HIPAA-compliant notification tools can alert the patient when it's time for them to register, and with two-way texting, patients can notify the clinic of their arrival or if they're running late. Clinical staff are immediately made aware of the patient's readiness for care to efficiently get the patient into the exam room. RTLS tools have supported ambulatory care centers in eliminating check-in lines and reducing patient wait times by up to 50%,[12] creating a safer and more satisfying patient experience. In Figure 6.1, as an example, the staff can readily see the critical information related to the patients' locations and wait times through the Workflow[RT] solution. In addition, optional tools can be added and utilized for patients to self-room, further improving both patient throughput and safety.

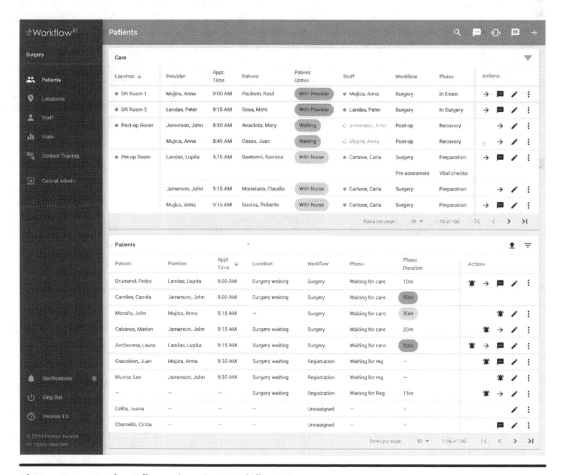

Figure 6.1 Patient flow view in Workflow[RT].

Use of RTLS Data to Improve Staff Workflow and Improve Patient Throughput

As ambulatory care practices begin recovering from the impacts of COVID-19, they need to accommodate as many patients as possible into their schedule, while simultaneously minimizing overall patient time in the ambulatory center. When patients have RTLS badges, staff can quickly know where a patient is, what phase of care they are in, and how long they have been in a specific patient phase (i.e., vital signs, waiting for care, or waiting for registration). Furthermore, with staff wearing RTLS badges, it is also known when a provider/clinician is with a particular patient and for how long. As an example, in Figure 6.2, an onsite patient list from Workflow[RT] allows clinicians to see an at-a-glance list of patients waiting to be seen, the order in which they should be seen, and their status. They know which rooms are occupied and which are available. Clinicians are also able to clearly identify how long the patient has been alone, potentially waiting on a provider or service. Finally, it is also easy to identify which staff the patient is with, and other status indicators. By using RTLS tools, real-time views can highlight the key pieces of information clinicians need to efficiently see patients while minimizing delays. By using these RTLS tools and data effectively to drive staff workflow and patient flow changes, ambulatory clinics have been able to decrease total patient visit time by 8%–15%, resulting in a decreased risk for exposures while enabling the opportunity to drive more patient throughput.[12]

RTLS can automatically capture data related to location, time, and duration, without requiring manual entry by staff. By leveraging key metrics, ambulatory practices can identify delays in care and modify processes to gain improvements. As a result of workflow efficiencies, ambulatory care practices have been able to increase their patient visit capacity by 5%–10% without increasing staff or number of rooms, while at the same time decreasing patient risk of exposure.[12] Figure 6.2 from Workflow[RT] provides an example of trend data that could be used to improve clinic capacity.

Contact Tracing to Aid in Mitigating Post-COVID-19 Concerns

Part of the "new-normal" during the pandemic recovery period, along with future cold and flu seasons, is the ongoing monitoring for COVID-19 cases. Infection prevention practices continue to be put into place to minimize

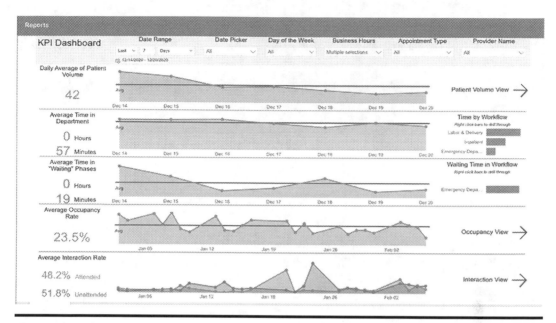

Figure 6.2   Workflow^RT KPIs dashboard.

exposure risk to patients and staff. However, there is also a critical need to be able to conduct efficient, thorough contact tracing for appropriate follow-up when needed. When staff and patients wear RTLS badges, all patient and staff contacts that occurred in the same location, along with the duration of contact time, are monitored. This data enables the ambulatory care practice to promptly take any necessary follow-up action for patients and staff, such as isolation, monitoring for symptoms, and/or prophylactic treatments if appropriate. In Figure 6.3, a sample contact tracing report is shown from Workflow^RT, which quickly summarizes and shows the contacts and contact duration that occurred between patients and staff, along with the location(s). This provides the necessary information for staff to decide on optimal next steps for patient and staff follow-up.

Staying Connected to Families and Visitors

Visitor restrictions have been put in place at many healthcare facilities, meaning patients are either allowed one person to accompany them or they are required to come alone. Keeping track of visitors, identifying the one visitor per patient, and family communication in general can be difficult and time-consuming for staff. The same workflow tools that support patient flow can assist with visitor management and family communication. As an

Figure 6.3 Contact tracing report in Workflow^{RT}.

example, the Workflow^{RT} solution allows staff to easily text family members. Each patient can have an unlimited number of recipients, and staff can then send custom messages or select from a list of common messages. This messaging tool keeps families informed while easing the level of effort needed by staff. The same solution can also be used to identify a patient's designated visitor and communicate with them. In addition, with two-way texting, the patient can let the clinic know they've arrived at the hospital, or that they're running late.

Summary

Ambulatory care practices during the pandemic recovery period are experiencing a unique set of challenges. There is a focus on restoring their normal patient volumes while at the same time providing a safe environment for patients and staff that is focused on social distancing and limiting exposure opportunities. Workflow efficiency and heightened awareness of delays are critical when operating in the post-pandemic era.

RTLS-enabled solutions such as Workflow^{RT} provide ambulatory care sites an opportunity to leverage technology to improve their patient experience and decrease wait times while increasing capacity. The workflow solution also helps to reduce exposure points for patients, such as those in check-in lines or waiting areas.

The real-time location solution enables ambulatory care sites to:

■ Eliminate wait lines for check-in
■ Decrease patient wait time
■ Allow patients to bypass the waiting room and self-room
■ Increase throughput
■ Enhance care coordination
■ Improve resource utilization
■ Provide contact tracing reports for any potential exposures
■ Enable family communication
■ Provide visitor management

These benefits provide a critical role in ambulatory care in the post-pandemic era, and prepare us to face the challenges that lay ahead.

References

1. World Health Organization (WHO) (2020). Coronavirus Disease (COVID-19) Outbreak Situation. Retrieved from https://www.who.int/emergencies/diseases/novel-coronavirus-2019.
2. Castellucci M, Meyer H (2020). Physician Practices Modify Operations to Cope with COVID-19. Modern Healthcare, March 17, 2020. Retrieved from Physician practices modify operations to cope with COVID-19. https://www.modernhealthcare.com/physicians/physician-practices-modify-operations-cope-covid-19.
3. Centers for Disease Control (CDC) (2020). Outpatient and Ambulatory Care Settings: Responding to Community Transmission of COVID-19 in the United States. Retrieved from https://www.totalmedicalcompliance.com/wp-content/uploads/Handouts416.pdf.
4. Medical Group Management Association (MGMA) (2020). COVID-19 Financial Impact on Medical Practices. Retrieved from https://www.mgma.com/getattachment/9b8be0c2-0744-41bf-864f-04007d6adbd2/2004-G09621D-COVID-Financial-Impact-One-Pager-8-5x11-MW-2.pdf.aspx?lang=en-US&ext=.pdf.
5. Wu Z, McGoogan JM. Characteristics of and Important Lessons from the Coronavirus Disease 2019 (COVID-19) Outbreak in China: Summary of a Report of 72 314 Cases from the Chinese Center for Disease Control and Prevention. *JAMA*. 2020;323(13):1239–1242. doi:10.1001/jama.2020.2648.
6. Centers for Disease Control (CDC) (2020). Interim Infection Prevention and Control Recommendations for Patients with Suspected or Confirmed Coronavirus Disease 2019 (COVID-19) in Healthcare Settings. Retrieved from https://www.cdc.gov/coronavirus/2019-ncov/hcp/infection-control-recommendations.html.

7. Centers for Disease Control (CDC) (2020). Characteristics of Health Care Personnel with COVID-19—United States, February 12–April 9, 2020. *MMWR Morb Mortal Wkly Rep.* 2020;69:477–481. http://doi.org/10.15585/mmwr.mm6915e6.

8. Cavallo J (2020). Mitigating the Spread of COVID-19 and Its Impact on Cancer. The ASCO Post. April 10, 2020. Retrieved from https://www.ascopost.com/issues/april-10-2020/mitigating-the-spread-of-covid-19-and-its-impact-on-cancer/.

9. Rivera A, Ohri N, Thomas E, Miller R, Knoll MA (2020). The Impact of COVID-19 on Radiation Oncology Clinics and Cancer Patients in the U.S. *Adv Rad Oncol.* Advance online publication. http://doi.org/10.1016/j.adro.2020.03.006.

10. Centers for Medicare & Medicaid Services (2020). Recommendations for Re-Opening Facilities to Provide Non-emergency Non-COVID-19 Healthcare: Phase I. Retrieved from https://www.cms.gov/files/document/covid-flexibility-reopen-essential-non-covid-services.pdf.

11. Bleustein C, Rothschild DB, Valen A, Valatis E, Schweitzer L, Jones R (2014). Wait Times, Patient Satisfaction Scores, and the Perception of Care. *Am J Manag Care.* 2014;20(5):393–400.

12. Infinite Leap (2020). Ambulatory Care Data Analytics. Retrieved from http://infiniteleap.net.

Chapter 7

Medical Devices: Responding to a Crisis with 3D Printing, Design, Engineering, and Production

Samuel Hellman, Paul H. Frisch, and Paul Booth

Contents

DOI: 10.4324/b23264-7

Introduction

In the early phases of the COVID-19 pandemic, the healthcare community was faced with uncertainty around how we would respond to the critical nature of the threat. There were many unknown areas surrounding both the nature of the disease and—more importantly from the perspective of a technical team seeking to support the response—how best to maximize the use of our skills and resources to address challenges. How could we most effectively restructure our operations to provide solutions utilizing our core competencies? We had a responsibility not only to perform and maintain our normal operational goals, but to also identify needs that we could quickly and realistically address for the local as well as the broad COVID-19 response initiative. It was important for us to avoid duplicating the work of others and channel our resources; we wanted to address unmet needs that would add to global efforts and find ways to complement, implement, or incorporate others' existing work whenever possible. While our primary focus was on addressing our hospital's internal needs and requirements, we emphasized the goal of contributing to the broader medical community. We factored this goal into our approach toward solving problems and disseminating results and information. This multitiered approach was central to our adapted mission, and we routinely addressed the potential impacts to our institution, our regional, national, and international response, and where our work might impact the broadest possible community.

In traditional hospital systems, Biomedical Engineering's role is primarily focused on facilitating the technical function of clinical hospital operations; having medical equipment maintained and certified, implementing commercial medical technology, overseeing technical projects etc. In addition to the traditional role, at MSKCC, the Biomedical Engineering department (Biomed) also carries out R&D activities including design, testing, and fabrication services. Working in conjunction with other providers in the hospital, the clinical and research needs of the institution are supported by technical developments which can be fully executed in-house from concept to device. Biomed also provides extensive expertise, both broad and specialized depending upon the need, covering all facets of the medical equipment spectrum. These operational specialties are broken down into clearly defined sections, with each falling under one of two general areas of responsibility: Operations or Development. While each of the sections falls predominantly into one of these two categories, there is a degree of overlap and flexibility where practitioners in each group are routinely involved in collaborative projects. For instance, we have design engineers who work on the development of new systems, process engineers who are involved in deployment, and technicians who troubleshoot and repair the equipment, yet all at different times can be seen working together on collective projects. The range of capabilities and specialties allow us to run day-to-day operations and continuously improve and expand the hospital's advanced practice.

When the COVID-19 pandemic began, we needed to decide how to employ our staffing and resources in order to support the critical needs of our hospital while best serving our patients, staff, and the global medical community. We were able to effectively organize our resources to best match our capabilities with where they were needed. In this chapter, we focus on the developmental aspects of Biomedical Engineering and on the critical and pivotal role that it represented in our overall institutional response to the COVID-19 pandemic. The value of these technical services and infrastructure—specifically in times of crisis—is highlighted along with the organizational systems which can enable successful implementation.

How Projects Were Chosen and Organized

A key element to our departmental response was in deciding which projects to work on and how best to implement them. In the early stages of the pandemic, there was little room for extra capacity, and we found ourselves in a supply-limited environment from which we would have to respond, adapt, and pivot as new requirements unfolded. We needed to be nimble regardless of the direction of any outcome and it was as important for us to exit unfruitful projects early as it was for us to keep moving forward on projects with a high impact score and high probability of success. We could not afford to be in a situation where the law of diminishing returns dominated and we allocated limited resources for less and less impact. Constant evaluation and objective analysis were critical in determining our direction. With this concept in mind, we needed to take a critical look at the resources and capabilities available to us and decide how best to focus them. We were always aware that any effort that did not contribute to established goals was taking critical resources from another area that might have a significant impact to our COVID-19 response. As a result, we took an honest and direct approach to identify key areas where we felt we could make a material contribution while eliminating work that was out of scope or expertise for what we could offer. In this critical examination of our capabilities, we didn't simply look to restrict ourselves by identifying what we couldn't do, rather, we pushed our teams to find areas we felt confident we could make a material contribution.

We had to make relatively quick decisions about which projects receive our resources— money, materials, time, and staff. In addition to standard resource allocation, we focused on individual core competencies and allowed people uniquely poised to solve a particular problem the ability to focus on that task exclusively without the overhead normally associated with traditional business operations.

This internal assessment formed the backbone of our project-based triage where we picked the projects that were solidly within our existing mission. Once started, we evaluated the projects on an ongoing basis and were proactive in avoiding sunk-cost-driven decision making; that is, if project no longer made sense based on progress, results, or changing requirements, we were quick to stop working on it.

Case Studies

In this section, we outline some of the medical devices and projects which resulted from our efforts and discuss their implementation. We outline the process and challenges for each project and stress the way engineering projects were prioritized and selected in order to focus on available resources. Additionally, we discuss the global and communal aspects of our approach; how we worked to contribute to global problems and focus on quickly sharing and disseminating all information.

Case Study: Multi-Patient Ventilator Splitting

In the early stages of the pandemic, there was a great deal of attention placed on the potential shortage of ventilators for COVID-19 patients. Experience in Italy, for instance, was that hospital systems were overwhelmed with patients needing mechanical ventilation and the existing supply could not keep up with demand [1]. In some cases, doctors were forced to select which patients could receive care and which could not or attempt to share a ventilator with multiple patients [2]. A number of solutions were proposed to meet the demand: emergency production of new ventilators (both by existing manufacturers and non-medical/automotive manufacturers), home-made ventilators created by medical providers or universities, alternative ventilation solutions, and splitting/sharing of existing ventilators.

The idea of splitting ventilators had been previously proposed, and a proof-of-concept was demonstrated by Neyman et al. [3] in 2006 when they successfully set up a four-limbed parallel circuit system with lung simulators using a standard emergency room ventilator. The intention was to show that a typical ER could use readily available equipment and supplies to ventilate multiple patients in an emergency case. This four-limbed setup was validated in 2008 by Paladino et al. [4] when they successfully intubated, paralyzed, and maintained four sheep using a single ventilator successfully for 12 hours. Ventilator splitting was put to a real-world test in 2017 with the mass shooting at the Mandalay Bay Hotel in Las Vegas, Nevada, when nearly 200 gunshot victims were brought to the nearby Sunrise Hospital ER. In addition to implementing an emergency triage and logistics system, Dr. Kevin Menes and his team successfully ventilated several pairs of patients using y-tubing to create parallel circuits and matching patients of roughly the same body mass while doubling the tidal volume settings required for a single patient [5].

One challenge with these existing approaches was in addressing the varying ventilation parameters required by different patients. Not everyone on a ventilator can be supported using the same settings and a functional solution which allowed for independent adjustment for patients was critical for this to work. The machines also needed to be able to operate a split venting system without sensing an alert (or abnormal) condition and shutting down. However, given the previous experience with ventilator splitting, it seemed like a viable option for use with COVID-19 patients when ventilator shortages were expected.

There were many teams proposing this idea along with various solutions to address concerns around implementation. Multiple experts and professional societies warned against the use of ventilator splitting due to concerns over the ability to properly maintain a patient's health due to lack of independent control for pressure, volume, O_2 saturation, and viral containment [6]. Additionally, unlike in the scenario of supporting gunshot victims, COVID-19 patients often require extended duration of ventilation—lasting days or weeks [7]—and disease progression often requires continuous adjustment of ventilation parameters. Despite these concerns, late in March of 2020, New York State approved emergency use of ventilator splitting for COVID-19 patients [8]. Some solutions were publicly proposed which included the ability to regulate inspiratory/expiratory pressures (per patient) and some included the ability to adjust tidal volume.

We analyzed the work being performed in this space and opted to work on the issues facing implementation of ventilator splitting systems, however, we did not want to tackle all of the challenges or spend our time working in areas where other competent teams were already making progress. We had to objectively determine where our expertise and available resources should be focused for maximum immediate benefit of our patients while positively impacting the global medical community. Although we could have chosen many areas of this problem to explore, we knew that there was limited time available to work and test any solutions due to the impending demand of COVID-19 patients. We discussed multiple strategies and ultimately felt that the best use of our resources was to focus on the independent regulation of inspiratory pressure because (a) we believed this to be the single most important variable to control, (b) the existing proposed solutions did not adequately address the problem, and (c) we had the clinical and engineering expertise to make a positive impact. The publicly disclosed pressure-regulation solutions to that point allowed independent adjustment of inspiratory pressure, however, the settings were not fixed with respect to other variables in the system; for instance, changes in one patient (pressure, tidal volume, lung elasticity, etc.) could change the resulting pressure in other patients in parallel circuits of the split ventilation system resulting in suboptimal treatment and/or danger to the patient.

A collaborative MSKCC team with members from Biomedical Engineering, Anesthesiology, and Surgery came together to work on this challenge. Established goals were selected to (a) focus solely on inspiratory pressure regulation, (b) create something simple to implement, (c) provide hardware needed to accomplish the goals, (d) perform proof-of-concept testing, and (e) make results public immediately. The proposed solution, shown in Figure 7.1, incorporated the use of an adjustable, fixed-pressure regulator on each parallel ventilation circuit and allowed completely independent adjustment of inspiratory pressure for every patient [9]. A working system with lung simulators was tested to demonstrate the regulators' ability to handle multiple changes in parallel circuits while maintaining a fixed inspiratory pressure setting. It was found that changes in one circuit (even extreme changes such as complete tubing removal or coughing/lung spasms), had no effect on the other circuit in the system. Additionally, the regulators provide adjustment relative to atmospheric pressure and, thus, fixed-pressure settings are independent of ventilator pressure settings (assuming the ventilator pressure

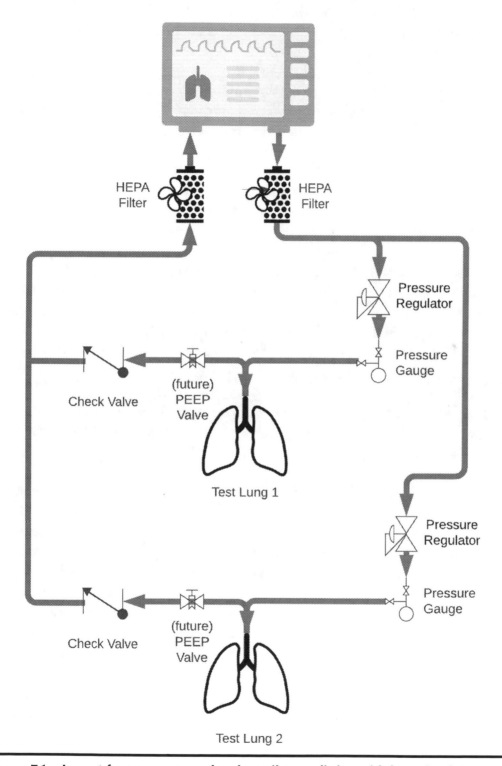

Figure 7.1   Layout for pressure-regulated ventilator splitting with lung simulators. Two manually adjusted, fixed-pressure regulators with analog pressure gauges independently control each circuit's pressure. PEEP valves are proposed for future tests.

setting is equal to or greater than the regulator setting). Combined, this solution allows for the adjustment of each patient's inspiratory pressure and avoids safety concerns of over-pressurization which can cause lung damage. In order to meet the goal set for simple implementation and thus a more broad and available solution, the system employs manual (mechanical) adjustment and analog pressure gauges in order to keep setup and operation simple while avoiding the expense and potential failure of electronic systems.

In-line with the commitment to making all work publicly available as quickly as possible, results were pre-published on the MSKCC website immediately and submitted to a rapid publication, peer-reviewed journal. The goal of tackling a finite, achievable problem allowed the team to quickly implement an engineering solution, test system function, and rapidly share results with the global community. This approach, taken by multiple teams in parallel at various institutions can allow rapid progress on complex problems, where no individual team would be able to implement all steps and testing in the same timeframe.

Case Study: Intubation/Extubation Boxes

Various types of personal protective equipment (PPE) were promptly adopted or developed to protect patients and healthcare providers (HCP) from airborne viral exposure to SARS-CoV-2. Alongside our clinicians, we had to identify what were the areas with the highest potential for exposure to COVID. We were faced with the scenario that some of our most valuable clinicians who would be on the front line of treating patients were also the most vulnerable. Clinicians working with a patient's airway were objectively determined to be in the highest risk category for patient to clinician exposure and we worked to mitigate the risk that these clinicians faced on a daily basis. One area of particularly high potential exposure risk for HCPs is during intubation/extubation of patients with COVID-19. The insertion and, even more so, removal of endotracheal tubes can generate aerosols exiting the patient's mouth and are thought to potentially contain high viral loads which might put those nearby at risk of infection. As we have now seen, airborne exposure in indoor spaces is believed to be the most common way the disease is transmitted [10, 11] and any solution to this risk factor would add an extra layer of protection for staff involved. A solution known as "the aerosol box" was created by Dr. Hsein Yung Lai at Mennonite Christian Hospital in … of 2020 to help contain these aerosols during intubation/extubation of patients [12]. The box consists of a plexiglass enclosure that fits over the patient's head/neck and contains arm holes in the superior (head) side for the HCP to work as well as a flap on the inferior (chest) side to allow ventilation tubing access. His idea garnered a lot of attention and multiple adaptations and iterations on the design were quickly created by teams across the world. Some of these designs incorporated negative pressure ventilation into the enclosure to aid in containment of aerosols/virus. There were several safety concerns regarding the use of these enclosures including (a) limited arm mobility for the HCP, (b) limited access to patient in case of emergency or assistance needed with, for example, difficult airways, and (c) unknown efficacy of aerosol containment.

A team from Biomedical Engineering and Anesthesiology decided to work on a revised design to address these concerns. The established goals were to come up with a design which (a) allowed increased HCP arm mobility, (b) provided emergency access to the patient and to (c) evaluate efficacy of aerosol containment, (d) make the device with readily available materials and processes, and (e) make results available immediately. In this case, the team's expertise and resources were sufficient to address each of these issues. Several designs with varying shapes/features were quickly assembled and given to a team of anesthesiologists to evaluate. Several iterations of this process lead to the final configuration. The resulting design [13] shown in Figure 7.2 incorporated a single large aperture for the HCP's arms which was sealed using a disposable surgical gown/sleeves clipped onto the opening. This allowed for a fuller range of flexible arm mobility while keeping the

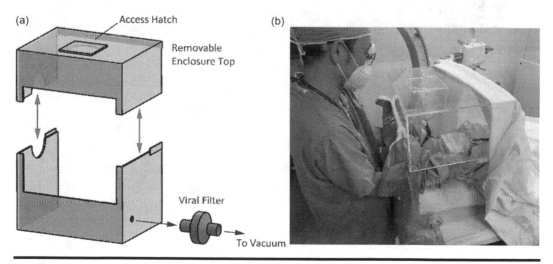

Figure 7.2 **(a) Intubation enclosure diagram showing removable top, access hatch, and exhaust port via viral filter. (b) Simulated use of enclosure with surgical gown clipped in place.**

enclosure sealed. Additionally, the box was made in two pieces with a top portion that could be quickly lifted off (with the intubator's arms remaining in position) during an emergency which would provide full access to the patient. A smaller access port was also included which allowed a second HCP to reach into the box if needed for assistance without completely opening the enclosure. Lastly, an exhaust port was included with negative pressure ventilation of the enclosure through a viral filter.

An experiment was carried out to assess the efficacy of aerosol containment and establish the proper ventilation requirements for negative pressure. A particle generator was placed inside the enclosure and airborne particle level measurements were taken inside and outside of the enclosure. Multiple tests were run at varying ventilation flow rates to establish the requirements and efficacy of negative ventilation. The team showed that negative ventilation dramatically increased the containment efficacy and reduced the amount of time needed to clear aerosols after a procedure. It also showed that a relatively inexpensive vacuum pump could be used in conjunction with a common viral filter to allow quick and simple implementation in most settings.

Again, the team pre-published results on MSKCC's website and made full design documents available with an open license for anyone to use. A rapid publication, peer-reviewed journal was used in order to make results quickly available. Emergency authorization was approved for the immediate clinical use of this device and it has been used on countless patients in treating airway issues and for providing an increased layer of safety for our staff while effectively adding no risk to the patient. This was a great example of our team using some of the excellent publicly shared external work and contributing to improve upon the design.

Case Study: Crisis Vent

A team consisting of Surgeons, Biomedical Engineers, Respiratory Therapists, Anesthesiologists, and Device Development Engineers came together to design, and build a prototype of what we characterize as an emergency-use crisis ventilator or "Crisis Vent." The intent of this device was to provide a compromise between functionality, simplicity, and ease of building to facilitate the broadest possible distribution of life-saving care in the event of a traditional equipment shortage. As a result, we did not seek to recreate a traditional ventilator, but rather to provide a bare minimum of functionality to maintain a sick patient when no other option exists. As with other projects we worked on, there were many proposed solutions in the public domain to address the problem. There were non-medical companies (e.g., auto manu-facturers) working on building conventional, fully controlled ventilators as well as research teams at universities and institutions coming up with make-shift solutions with excellent functionality. We felt that the latter category had many competent teams working on them and we did not need to con-tribute to this effort. In particular, we felt that many of these projects tried to include too many features and functions to be reliable without an extensive testing and development process. From our perspective, computer controls, extensive mechanical systems, complex plumbing, etc. all were possible sources of failure and made operation, assembly, and repairs too compli-cated for an emergency-use scenario. We decided to work on an option that was as simple and reliable as possible while meeting the bare-minimum requirement of keeping a patient sustained during an equipment shortage.

Our resulting solution employs a relatively simple mechanism which operates a standard self-inflating manual resuscitator or "bag resuscitator." The design incorporates a bag resuscitator since these are (a) in ready sup-ply and (b) perform the needed clinical requirements with proven reliability and safety. While we developed the idea for this independently, a quick internet search identified many other groups working on similar concepts with varying degrees of complexity. Again, we felt that our approach offered a solution that was not already existing and was something that we could realistically implement and share with others.

Since our goal was to make something as simple as possible, we had to determine the minimum requirements needed for clinical use. While it is desir-able to have control over all aspects of ventilation, we had to narrow it down to the most critical. We decided, along with our critical care and respiratory therapy colleagues, that adjusting tidal volume, respiratory rate, and positive end expiratory pressure (PEEP) would be the required parameters which must be controlled. In terms of physical requirements, we agreed that there should be no computer programming or complex adjustments required. Additionally, we wanted all adjustments to be possible while actively ventilating a patient. We also wanted the resulting design to be relatively simple to build and main-tain from readily available parts by people with a reasonable level of technical skills. Finally, in order to ensure patient safety, the bag resuscitator needed to be quickly accessible for manual operation in the event of a mechanism failure.

The resulting design (Figure 7.3) consists of an aluminum frame which holds the bag in place with a motor-driven crank arm which compresses the bag resuscitator. The motor has a simple speed controller which controls the rate of the crank arm and thus the respiratory rate. The crank arm pivot

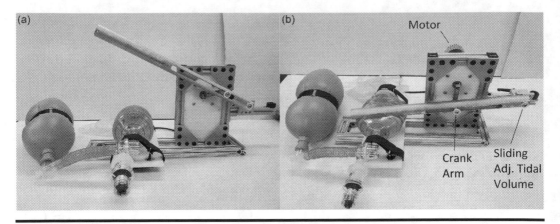

Figure 7.3 **(a) Crisis vent with compression arm in up position, bag fully inflated (exhale). (b) Compression arm in down position, bag fully compressed (end inhale).**

point can be adjusted dynamically such that the stroke length of the arm changes and varies the tidal volume by varying the amount of bag compression. The geometry was designed such that a fixed I:E (inspiratory to expiratory) ratio of 1:2 is maintained when the tidal volume is changed. While the geometry could be altered to provide different I:E ratios, this would be the most commonly used setting and thus was chosen as our fixed value. This geometry could be altered; however, we did not incorporate a dynamic adjustment for I:E ratio since it would alter the tidal volume at the same time and require back-and-forth adjustment of the two parameters ... again, we chose simplicity over versatility. A PEEP valve on the expiratory line controls for back pressure. While not required for basic operation, supplemental oxygen can easily be incorporated if available.

While simple, the device has proven to be very reliable and has run in tests for over ten days without interruption. Additionally, it has performed as designed on a test lung in a simulated environment. The simplicity of the design enables it to be easily and quickly constructed to facilitate the potential for speedy and extensive distribution, while not compromising basic functionality. The frame was designed using extruded aluminum t-slot framing which is commonly available throughout the world and simple speed-controlled DC motor is also a part that be easily sourced, and many models/substitutes are available to suit the application. In-line with our sharing of information, we made full design drawings with parts list and instructions and published them on our website for free use [14]. It is a design which can be easily built from locally available materials and parts and maintained by anyone with relatively common technical skills.

While we designed this device such that it could be used in Tier 1 medical facilities in the event of equipment shortage, we also see the potential for this device in low-resource facilities and health systems worldwide. We envisage its application in the global health system in areas with persistent shortages of such life-saving equipment. We were particularly intrigued with the potential for using a device like this in power limited environments around the world where electric grids are unreliable but would have access to power resources like car batteries or even the cars themselves.

3D Printing

One of the main challenges presented by the pandemic was the limited capability of the supply chain to meet the enormous demand for medical equipment—some basic and some complex. The sudden increase in demand for medical supplies—PPE, testing supplies, cleaning supplies, treatment devices, drugs, etc.—overwhelmed existing stockpiles, distribution chains, national distribution strategies, and manufacturing capability. Additionally, the production side was stressed by a reduction in labor due to COVID-19 shutdowns and an overall breakdown of supply chains upstream for raw materials. All of these factors contributed to a shortage in available supplies and left many healthcare workers and patients without much-needed equipment.

We were able to leverage our in-house fabrication capabilities in order to manufacture a number of items which were not readily available for purchase. In particular, 3D printing technology was critical in enabling us to deliver many of the items which were needed early in the pandemic and others where we were able to proactively plan for the heightened risk of a potential shortage in the future. Our Biomedical Engineering group used 3D printing in the production of face shields, mask adapters, respirator adapters, ventilation tubing adapters, and nasopharyngeal test swabs amongst others.

3D printing (more broadly called additive manufacturing) has historically been emphasized for its application in rapid prototyping, however, there has been a steady increase in adoption for creating end-use products. While it is generally limited in its mass-production throughput, 3D printing can be a viable option for low-production numbers and is vastly more flexible than many traditional fabrication technologies. Particularly in the hospital environment, it allows for the creation of a wide range of products and devices without the overhead and lead time required for other methods. The flexibility of 3D printing is extremely valuable for the creation of patient-specific treatment devices, custom surgical tools, and on-demand parts in the medical setting … during the pandemic, this flexibility became indispensable.

Because 3D printing technology was already in regular use for a number of clinical modalities, particularly in printing 3D dental guides, we had clinically tested printing materials that could be reallocated to different use modes while taking advantage of their inherent medical characteristics—notably, biocompatible materials with the ability to be sterilized.

With much of the global supply chain optimized for efficiency and specialization, this leaves it vulnerable to breakdown if there are disruptions anywhere along the way and, during early 2020, we saw these disruptions occur across much of the globe. This is an excellent demonstration of why it is critical for hospitals to adopt 3D printing technologies as a part of their infrastructure to enable a robust and resilient facility.

Case Study: 3D-Printed Face Shields

One of the items we produced in-house to meet supply shortages were protective face shields using 3D-printed structures. There were several designs made publicly available early in the pandemic and this was an excellent example of both the usefulness of the technology and the spirit of public collaboration across the globe. Many non-medical companies and hobbyists printed these face shields on their printers and sent to healthcare professionals or frontline workers in their local communities.

We started with a design by Prusa Research [15] which they made freely available for anyone to use. We made several modifications to the design to enable faster production and increase the comfort for wearers. The original design was intended for use with either a perforated rubber strap or rubber bands for the headband section. We did not have the perforated strapping on-hand and could not easily source it. Additionally, our initial tests with elastic bands were that they were not very comfortable—these had to be worn for extended periods of time by healthcare workers.

We came up with a design modification that used round rubber cord that could be adjusted to fit the wearer's head and was held in place by a friction loop. This rubber cord was low cost, readily available, and provided increased comfort by eliminating the constant tension of elastic headbands. We also changed the design of the frame to yield faster printing time and allow us to stack them on our printer beds to produce 10–20 at a time (depending on which printer model was used). The final design modification was to change the size and layout of the pegs which hold the clear plastic

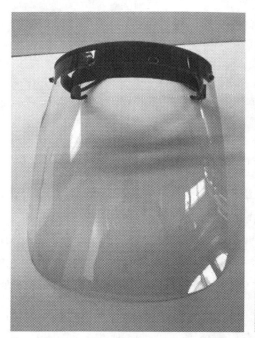

Figure 7.4 Modified face shield design with 3D printed frame, rubber cord with adjustable length.

shield to match hole punches which we had in the hospital. This ability to easily alter a design based on available materials and needs is one of the many advantages of 3D printing technology (Figure 7.4).

These were produced using various models of fused deposition modeling (FDM) printers and several different materials that we had available including ABS, PP, Nylon, and PLA. For this application, the relatively low cost of FDM printing and insensitivity to material selection allowed us to use whichever materials were available. More than 700 face shields were internally produced over the course of a month (300 more were printed and donated to us by non-medical companies) and this kept many of our healthcare workers protected until we were again able to purchase them from commercial suppliers.

Case Study: 3D Printed Viral Filter Adapters for Respirators and Snorkeling Masks

Another PPE item which was in short supply were face masks and respirators. There was a national/international shortage of both disposable cloth face masks (N95, surgical, etc.) and respirators and supplies. We did some initial testing and felt that we would not be able to directly 3D print cloth face mask replacements;

there were some designs for face masks which were widely distributed, but they were not able to sufficiently adapt to a wearer's face unless designed specifically for each user and form fitted. This was not a practical solution to produce in a significant quantity. Similarly, we did not find that printing respirators (half- or full-face masks with replicable filter cartridges) would work for the same reasons. We did still have some half- and full-face respirators in the hospital but were having a hard time sourcing the filter cartridges for them.

We did, however, have a large supply of viral filters which are typically used in ventilator circuits both during surgery and for extended respiratory support. These are used in-line with standard 1″ ventilator tubing and typically come with stated/certified viral filtering efficiencies. We designed and printed adapters, shown in Figure 7.5, which allowed us to fit the viral filters to existing respirators. For this application we used a biocompatible material, Stratasys MED610 [16], with our Stratasys Objet 260 Connex 3 printer. There were other biocompatible materials available, but we were not aware of others which had been specifically tested for respiratory application safety. This type of material and printer technology is significantly more costly than FDM printers and is more commonly found in larger and/or more specialized hospitals and dental practices.

The efficacy of the setup was verified using the equipment we already have in the hospital for fit testing of N95 masks and respirators. It was found

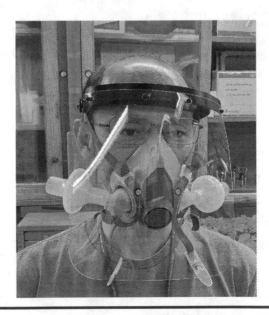

Figure 7.5 3D printed adapters allow viral filters to be used with a 3M half-face respirator.

that the respirators with viral filters fit using 3D printed adapters met the required particle filtering levels for occupational use [OSHA/NHSA?].

While the adapters for existing respirators were successful, we also wanted to have a backup solution ready in case we needed a larger supply of aerosol PPE. We made similar 3D-printed adapters to enable the use of recreational snorkeling masks as a full-face respirator alternative. Full-face snorkeling masks are recreational swimming devices which incorporate a snorkel and full mask which seals the entire face (eyes, nose, and mouth). They are designed with a one-way breathing circuit that pulls in fresh air to the face mask via an air pipe (snorkel) above the water surface; exhaled air is then directed out either above the water through a second channel in the snorkel pipe or underwater through a check valve in the mask. We used a model of snorkel mask which had the dual air tube setup and made an adapter, shown in Figure 7.6, which connected to the mask using the same mechanism as the snorkel. The adapter thus had an air intake and air exhaust pathway. We fit a viral filter to the inlet and a check valve to the exhaust so that air could only flow one direction.

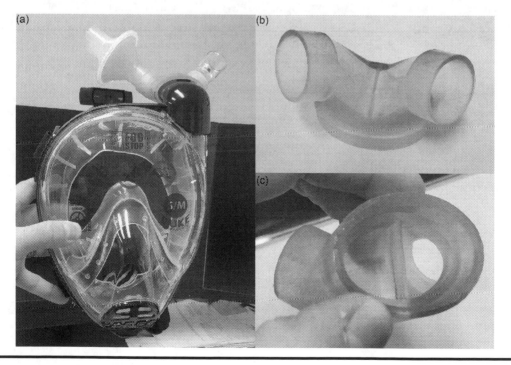

Figure 7.6   (a) Snorkel mask with 3D printed adapter, viral filter for air intake and check valve for one-way air exhaust. (b) 3D printed adapter view from top. (c) 3D printed adapter view from bottom.

Again, the snorkel mask system was tested and found to satisfy the particle filtering requirements for a full-face respirator. It was noted, however, that this configuration did require more effort to breath (slow steady breaths were needed) than a standard respirator and would only have been used as a last resort. While we had snorkel masks on-hand and ready to deploy, it did not become necessary. Though it was not used in clinical practice, it is a good example of the application of 3D printing to quickly implement an operational solution in emergency situations.

Case Study: 3D Printed Nasopharyngeal Test Swabs

Another critical supply which was difficult to source in early 2020 were nasopharyngeal test swabs used for COVID-19 testing. This is a critical part of pandemic management and the swabs were quickly becoming a potential bottleneck for widespread testing. The swabs typically consist of a long, thin polymer/aluminum shaft with flocked tips for collecting mucosal samples. Multiple groups came up with 3D printed versions and made their designs publicly available. A collaborative effort between a printer manufacturer (Formlabs) and two hospital groups (Northwell Health and USF Health) yielded a design which could easily be printed and sterilized for clinical use [17]. We had the same printer and biocompatible resin on hand in our 3D print lab and were able to quickly set up a system to print and process up to 2,000 swabs daily. Within a few days, we made test prints, ran through sterilization, and had our internal teams validate efficacy and approve for use (Figure 7.7).

We were ultimately able to purchase sufficient test swabs commercially just before we ran out of our existing supply and the 3D printed versions were not needed. However, if the hospital had been unable to secure swabs, we were prepared to fill the need without disrupting critical testing operations. Though we did not use these clinically (beyond initial testing), and our team did not design the swabs, we felt this was an excellent example of many of the advantages of 3D printing infrastructure, collaborative work, and open sharing of information. Having 3D printing capability in a hospital (along with supporting engineering, technical, and medical services) provides the ability to respond to myriad challenges which cannot always be anticipated. MSKCC has a 3D Printing Laboratory with a large range of technology and material choices. This serves us during normal operations to meet the demands of an advanced oncology center and provides us the flexibility to respond to many unforeseen needs.

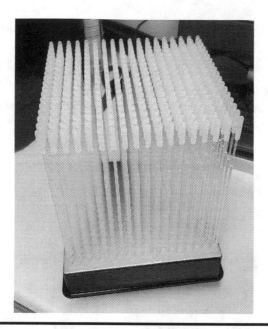

Figure 7.7   Tray of 3D printed nasopharyngeal test swabs. 324 swabs could be printed on each tray.

Operational Changes during COVID-19 and Lasting Impact

In this section, we discuss the operational changes that occurred within the Biomedical Engineering Department as a result of the pandemic and in response to the needs of our institution. While some of the changes were temporary and limited in application to the COVID crisis, many of these changes have been beneficial for our daily operations going forward and lessons learned have been implemented into our revised workflows. Within our institution, there was a general increase in awareness of the developmental operations of Biomedical Engineering during COVID-19. Specifically, the **Mechanical Engineering** section—centered largely around device design, CAD, manufacturing, and basic research—and **Biomedical Systems**—centered on system design, project management, and team dynamics—were deeply involved with implementing COVID-19 solutions. We had daily, in-depth development meetings with our internal teams and, equally as important, had direct access and routine interactions with the key clinicians, leaders, and decision-makers in the hospital that allowed these solutions to be quickly evaluated for clinical practice. While operations were streamlined, it is important to note that safety was never sacrificed, and a high level of quality and patient focus were always first and foremost.

An internal operational impact for Biomed has been the increased involvement and collaboration between Mechanical Engineering, Biomedical Systems, and other hospital teams outside of Biomed. While these groups have a history of close collaboration, this environment has strengthened the link and allowed us to specialize on our internal competencies while supporting one another to more efficiently advance technical projects. In addition to a drastic change in the focus and operational pace of our work, the COVID-19 crisis necessitated a number of operational changes.

Enhanced and Streamlined Administrative Support

There was a notable change in the ways with which we engaged administrative decision-makers in supporting projects. We were more easily able to meet directly with the administrators and leaders who generally have the authority to approve projects and funding. This led to a level of efficiency that has very positively impacted the progress of projects and allowed for optimal decisions as to whether to move forward or cancel a project. As a result, we were nimbler in reallocating limited resources to the most significant challenges and were enabled to align our goals more directly with higher-level directives and needs. The administrative decision-makers, in turn, have been extremely supportive and accessible on an as-needed basis.

Reduced Development Timetables

While we have always strived to be efficient in our operations, the crisis streamlined the process from concept to deliverable. In responding to the COVID-19 crisis, we were able to move the development of simple devices from the more-typical weeks or months to days. More complex device development changed from months to days or weeks. While some of this reduction in time stemmed from a shifting of internal priorities, much of the efficiency was due to a fundamental shift in the developmental environment as outlined in this section.

Shifting Technical Innovations—3D Manufacturing

The COVID-19 crisis has stepped up the transition to 3D fabrication for not just prototyping but, more significantly, for making operational parts. While this transition was well underway, the need for immediate parts as well as an increased reliance on internal resources to supply needed solutions highlighted the value of this technology and has helped define a roadmap for the future.

In addition to the general shift toward 3D printing, there is a corresponding internal shift in how these devices have been allocated and managed. The addition of new printers—directly purchased to support needs during the crisis—and new materials has increased the need for well-trained individuals to be able to design devices, operate the machines, keep them maintained, and schedule them efficiently.

A Shift from Research Support to Immediate Clinical Support

While Biomed has always maintained developmental support for clinical operations, there has traditionally been a balance between clinical applications and fundamental research. While we have transitioned to a return of normal operations for research, we have found that the clinical focus of development has continued at the enhanced level created in response to COVID. Developing enhancements to PPE equipment and novel airway management systems have been some of the new areas where we have been asked to participate in and help develop solutions.

A New Evaluation of Required Skillsets

Development for the COVID environment highlighted the need for highly skilled individuals with an ability to work both in specialized fields and in broad-based, multi-disciplinary teams. One of the lessons learned during our COVID-19 operations was in the realization that there is a need for individuals with a range of high-level skills to be able to focus on specialized areas. This necessitated good leadership to coordinate operations but has also identified areas where future staffing requests should be prioritized. Having a team with diverse backgrounds and skillsets provides the most flexible toolbox to respond to unforeseen needs during a crisis and also to the continuously advancing technology required of a modern hospital.

Defining More Focused Scope of Clinical Deliverables

In normal developmental projects involving the high-caliber researchers and clinicians at MSKCC, there is often a wide array of requirements that the development team must strive to satisfy. This typically involves lengthy development cycles and a corresponding increase in resource allocation to deliver on the project. Often, the scope and complexity of the projects delay or even preclude their completion. Based on the progress made on projects during COVID, there has been a dynamic shift in development within Biomed toward identifying and prioritizing the most critical characteristics of the project and in evaluating whether additional deliverables are feasible. By more carefully focusing their scope, we have been able to bring more impactful projects to fruition.

Procurement Optimization

The efficiency with which the institution enabled us to source needed supplies during the pandemic was critical to our success. Without the fast turnaround and support in procuring needed supplies, many of our clinical deliverables would have been significantly delayed. When days make a difference, the acquisition of needed materials and equipment is significant and the response from our institution was without exception, exemplary. While the need for prudence during normal operation is clearly important, it is equally important that hospitals have the ability to quickly adapt in times of crisis. We would have been unable to respond to the needs of the hospital through the standard procurement process.

Community/Global Focus

Getting developmental ideas through administrative pathways is often a long and convoluted process. Things like patent protection, legal review, inter-institutional collaboration, academic publication, and community outreach are all areas with their own dedicated and developed processes. The efficiency with which these respective operations were streamlined and fast-tracked during COVID was remarkable. The time from completed concept to patent protection, clinical deployment, submission to academic journals, and posting for community outreach was exponentially faster; sometimes completing in 24 hours what previously took months. In particular, the willingness to share with outside institutions and easily collaborate with the global community was an excellent model of MSKCC's goal to serve the public good. While some of this efficiency and openness was a direct response to the crisis, we are hopeful that much of this momentum will continue to carry forward.

Public Relations and Community Outreach

The ability of our team to rapidly disseminate our work and help the broader community—locally, nationally, and internationally—was facilitated by the team dynamics associated with our institutional response to this crisis. Our Marketing and Communications group worked with us to make the narrative for our projects clear, efficient, and accessible to the broader community via the Crisis Innovation Hub on the MSK website. They also provided the appropriate pathway to legal review for dissemination of these projects. This pathway was important to highlight projects and allowed outside institutions and caregivers to learn from our experiences and streamline their own operations to best help people dealing with COVID-19.

References

1. L. Rosenbaum, "Facing Covid-19 in Italy—Ethics, Logistics, and Therapeutics on the Epidemic's Front Line," *N Engl J Med*, vol. 382, pp. 1873–1875, 2020.
2. J. Horowitz, "Italy's Health Care System Groans Under Coronavirus—A Warning to the World," *New York Times*, 12 March 2020.
3. G. Neyman and C. Irvin, "A Single Ventilator for Multiple Simulated Patients to Meet Disaster Surge," *Acad Emerg Med*, vol. 13, no. 11, pp. 1246–1249, 2006.
4. L. Paladino, M. Silverberg, J. G. Charchaflieh, J. K. Eason, B. J. Wright, N. Palamidessi, B. Arquilla, R. Sinert and S. Manoach, "Increasing Ventilator Surge Capacity in Disasters: Ventilation of Four Adult-Human-Sized Sheep on a Single Ventilator with a Modified Circuit," *Resuscitation*, vol. 77, no. 1, pp. 121–126, 2008.
5. K. Menes, J. Tintinalli and L. Plaster, "How One Las Vegas ED Saved Hundreds of Lives after the Worst Mass Shooting in U.S. History," *Emergency Physicians Monthly*, 3 November 2017.
6. Society of Critical Care Medicine, American association for respiratory care, Anesthesia Patient Safety Foundation, American Association of Critical-Care Nurses, American College of Chest Physicians. "Joint Statement on Multiple Patients Per Ventilator." American Society of Anesthesiologists; March 26, 2020. Available: https://www.asahq.org/about-asa/newsroom/news-releases/2020/03/joint-statement-on-multiple-patients-per-ventilator. [Accessed 10 August 2022].
7. D. Hazard, K. Kaier, M. V. Cube, M. Grodd, L. Bugiera, J. Lambert and M. Wolkewitz, "Joint Analysis of Duration of Ventilation, Length of Intensive Care, and Mortality of COVID-19 Patients: A Multistate Approach," *BMC Med Res Methodol*, vol. 20, 2020.
8. A. Cuomo, *New York State Governor's Daily Coronavirus Press Briefing*, New York City, 2020.

9. G. H. Chen, S. Hellman, T. Irie, R. J. Downey and G. Fischer, "Regulating Inspiratory Pressure to Individualise Tidal Volumes in a Simulated Two-Patient, One-Ventilator System," *Br J Anaesth*, vol. 125, no. 4, pp. 366–368, 2020.

10. Q. J. Leclerc, N. M. Fuller, L. E. Knight, S. Funk and G. M. Knight, "What Settings Have Been Linked to SARS-CoV-2 Transmission Clusters?," *Wellcome Open Res*, vol. 5, no. 83, 2020.

11. T. C. Bulfone, M. Malekinejad, G. W. Rutherford and N. Razani, "Outdoor Transmission of SARS-CoV-2 and Other Respiratory Viruses: A Systematic Review," *The Journal of Infectious Diseases*, vol. 223, no. 4, pp. 550–561, 2020.

12. K. Everington, "Taiwanese Doctor Invents Device to Protect US Doctors against Coronavirus," *Taiwan News,* 23 March 2020.

13. S. Hellman, G. H. Chen and T. Irie, "Rapid Clearing of Aerosol in an Intubation Box by Vacuum Filtration," *British Journal of Anesthesia*, vol. 125, no. 3, pp. 296–299, 2020.

14. Memorial Sloan Kettering Cancer Center, "MSK COVID-19 Innovation Hub," [Online]. Available: https://www.mskcc.org/clinical-trials-updates/msk-covid-19-innovation-hub. [Accessed 3 August 2021].

15. Prusa Research, "3D Printed Face Shields for Medics and Professionals," [Online]. Available: https://www.prusa3d.com/covid19/. [Accessed 20 March 2020].

16. Stratasys Ltd., *Biocompatible MED610, Material Specification Sheet*, Rehovot, 2020.

17. Formlabs, Inc., "3D Printed Test Swabs for COVID-19 Testing," [Online]. Available: https://formlabs.com/covid-19-response/covid-test-swabs/. [Accessed 28 March 2020].

Chapter 8

Combating COVID-19 with Germicidal Ultraviolet "C" Light

Arthur Krietenberg

Contents

DOI: 10.4324/b23264-8

What Is Germicidal UVC?

Ultraviolet germicidal irradiation (UVGI) has been known for nearly one century.[1] It was described as a medical tool in the fight against tuberculosis and measles as early as the 1940s. In recent decades, it has found use as an adjunct to disinfection of healthcare surfaces. SARS-CoV-2 brought germicidal ultraviolet "C" (UVC) to the forefront as a means of disinfection outside of the healthcare environment.

Ultraviolet (UV) light lies between visible light and X-ray in the electromagnetic spectrum (Figure 8.1). UV light spans a wavelength from about 100 nm to about 400 nm. UVA and UVB, with wavelengths from about 280 nm to about 400 nm, can pass through the Earth's atmosphere. Plant and animal species benefit from UVA and UVB wavelengths of light. UVC, with wavelengths from about 200 to 280 nm is readily absorbed by air in the atmosphere and does not reach the Earth's surface. From a teleological viewpoint, living organisms and viruses do not utilize UVC nor do they possess mechanisms to protect themselves from UVC.

UVC has specific adverse effects on biological molecules including nucleic acids that comprise DNA and RNA. When exposed to UVC, the nucleic acids form bonds known as "dimers." Dimers within DNA and RNA preclude normal cell physiology and replication, effectively killing the cell. Because viruses such as SARS-CoV-2 are technically not living, the term deactivation rather than killing is preferred.

Unlike antibiotics and some disinfecting chemicals, there are no known microbes resistant to UVC. However, in some bacterial cases, repair

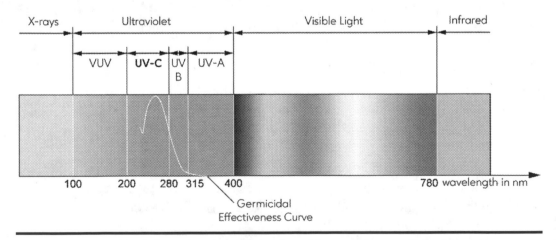

Figure 8.1 Germicidal UV is primarily in the "C" range from 200 to 280 nm. (Courtesy Dimer UV, LLC.)

mechanisms can overcome the damage caused by UVC, allowing some survival to occur. Virus particles do not have repair mechanisms.

Mode of COVID-19 Transmission Affects UVC Disinfection Strategies

In April 2021, more than one year after the World Health Organization (WHO) designated COVID-19 as a pandemic, the CDC issued a "Science Brief"[2] regarding COVID-19 transmission. Without supporting experimental data, the report indicated that "each contact with a contaminated surface has less than a 1 in 10,000 chance of causing an infection." Within the very same document the CDC states an opposite conclusion that "disinfection is recommended in indoor community settings where there has been a suspected or confirmed case of Covid-19 within the last 24 hours." Even trained medical practitioners cannot suspect COVID-19 in an asymptomatic yet viral shedding individual. This self-contradictory "Science Brief" may be interpreted as a recommendation to abandon or to continue routine surface disinfection.

To further complicate the recommendations, the document also references "disturbance of air and surfaces" as another method in which the virus may become suspended in the air and transmitted to potentially cause disease. As SARS-CoV-2 virus survives on surfaces up to three days,[3] this mode of "re-launch" or "secondary aerosolization" can be eliminated by routine surface disinfection, particularly with a "no-touch" technology such as UVC that does not disturb the surface.

In order to comply with COVID-19 CDC recommendations, it is prudent to employ disinfection protocols including UVC as it readily disinfects both air and surfaces.

Types of UVC Disinfection Equipment Used against COVID-19

COVID-19 UVC technologies may be divided into air disinfection and surface disinfection with the understanding that UVC will disinfect both nearby air and surfaces.

UVC has been deployed to disinfect air via strategies including placing UVC sources within HVAC ducting that relies on relatively frequent room air exchanges for effectiveness. Plug-in freestanding air filtration units with supplemental UVC have also become popular during COVID-19. Upper room air disinfection systems have been deployed that can selectively treat the air above room occupants with systems that preferentially circulate the air into the UVC rays for effective disinfection of the room air.

"Whole-room" surface disinfection units have been utilized in healthcare for decades. These units intend to disinfect multiple surfaces in the room. UVC treatment requires the room to be cleared of all personnel unless shielded from UVC exposure. With COVID-19, these units have found their way into non-healthcare facilities including gyms, schools, restaurants, hotels, entertainment venues, and prisons. Public transportation, including aviation, trains, subways, and buses present both challenges and opportunities for effective UVC disinfection that may profoundly affect public health.

Enclosed chambers and tunnels utilizing UVC have been deployed for the disinfection of surfaces for diverse applications including luggage, packaging, foodstuffs, and personal protective equipment (PPE).

Current UVC Generation Technologies

On Earth, UVC is human derived. The peak germicidal effectiveness within the UVC range occurs at about 262 nm.[4] Mercury-based fluorescent lamps are the oldest and most commonly used UVC source and produce peak irradiation at approximately 254 nm. Pulsed xenon emits multiple wavelengths of UV light within the germicidal UVC range as well as outside the germicidal range. "Far UV" produced with Excimer lamps produce peak wavelengths at approximately 222 nm and may be "safer" for humans. UVC generated from light emitting diodes (LEDs) is a rapidly evolving technology. Very recent advances promise to produce economically viable LED modules in the 265–275 nm range. Each of these sources has advantages and disadvantages that are beyond the scope of this chapter.

Just outside the UVC spectrum are emitters of light at 405 nm. This wavelength disrupts porphyrin, a molecule found within the cell membrane. Because viruses lack porphyrins, these devices have no specific utility in the fight against SARS-CoV-2.

UVC Measurement and SARS-CoV-2 Susceptibility

Units of UVC Measurement

The power of a UVC source may be measured in watts, similar to a household light bulb. A single light bulb is less effective in a large room than in a small room because the same amount of light produced must spread out over a larger volume and surface areas. Light is therefore measured in power per area of surface illuminated. For UVC, this is measured in watts per square meter or most commonly in milliwatts per square centimeter, abbreviated as mW/cm². This may be considered the intensity of the UVC exposure onto the target surface.

The germicidal UVC dose delivered onto a target surface is determined by the intensity and the number of seconds the target surface is exposed. This is expressed as mW sec/cm² or more commonly as millijoules per square centimeter, abbreviated as mJ/cm². This may be considered the cumulative or total dose of UVC exposure onto the target surface. For example, a UVC source producing 1 mW/cm² powered on for ten seconds delivers a cumulative dose of 10 mJ/cm².

UVC Measurement Devices

Dedicated UVC light meters can measure mW/cm² output in real time as well as the cumulative mJ/cm² for the duration the UVC light remains on (Figure 8.2). These meters tend to be expensive and require regular calibration to maintain accuracy.

One-time use economical photosensitive paper indicators are also commercially available but lack precision and may mislead as they change color with non-germicidal wavelengths of light such as ambient sunlight.

Figure 8.2   UVC cumulative dose is measured in mJ/cm² with available dedicated UVC meters. Photochromic indicators are widely used to measure approximate delivered dose.

Measurement devices are wavelength specific so a meter that is tuned for a fluorescent lamp at 254 nm may be useless for measuring the dose of Far UVC at 222 nm.

To accurately estimate germicidal activity on a horizontal surface, the meter or indicator must be placed horizontally on the surface and not stood up vertically to face the UVC source.

UVC Susceptibility of SARS-CoV-2 Relative to Other Microbes

UVC dosing, usually measured in mJ/cm^2, is an approximate guideline of germicidal effectiveness. An excellent compilation of the susceptibilities of multiple microbial species to UVC is available through the International Ultraviolet Association (IUVA).[5] However, these studies were performed in a variety of environments including air, water, and surface, with differing UVC wavelengths and experimental techniques that may or may not be applicable to real-world situations. Although cultures remain the gold-standard for efficacy, valuable guidance and relative susceptibilities can be gleaned from such data.

For example, to achieve a 99% reduction of Staphylococcus, the required UVC cumulative dose is approximately 6 mJ/cm^2 at 254 nm. Ebola,[6] a double-stranded DNA virus, has a susceptibility similar to Staphylococcus.

SARS-CoV-2 is a single-stranded RNA virus and appears to be more easily deactivated at lower doses than most microbes. At 254 nm UVC, a 99% reduction of SARS-CoV-2 was achieved[7] at less than 4 mJ/cm^2.

UVC Safety

UVC, like UVA and UVB, can damage human skin and eyes. The equivalent of sunburn can occur when unprotected skin is exposed to UVC. While there are no known cases of skin cancer caused by prolonged or repeated UVC exposure, deployment of the technology should take this possibility into consideration.

UV photokeratitis can occur with relatively low doses of UVC exposure. This is similar to a condition known as "welder's-flash" or "snow-blindness." Affected eyes become symptomatic 12–24 hours after UVC exposure. The discomfort may prompt an ER visit, but the treatment is symptomatic and resolves in 12–24 hours.

"Far UV" at 222 nm, particularly with filters designed to narrow the band of emission, holds great promise as this wavelength appears to be safer for human exposure than other UVC wavelengths. Preliminary studies on mice have been encouraging.[8] As of the time of this writing, within the COVID era, Far UV has not been sufficiently studied to determine safe dose thresholds for human exposure at 222 nm.

The Physics of UVC Drives Optimal Device Design

While the application of UVC disinfection is quite widespread and variable, the inviolable principles of UVC must be understood and designed into a UVC system to effect actual disinfection. Too many UVC systems provide only the appearance of disinfection due to a lack of understanding the subtleties of the technology.

UVC Distance to Target

The distance between the UVC source and the target surface is critical primarily due to the inverse square law (Figure 8.3). Moving the UVC source half the distance to the target surface causes the intensity to increase 4× and the required cumulative dose can be achieved in 1/4 of the time. Similarly,

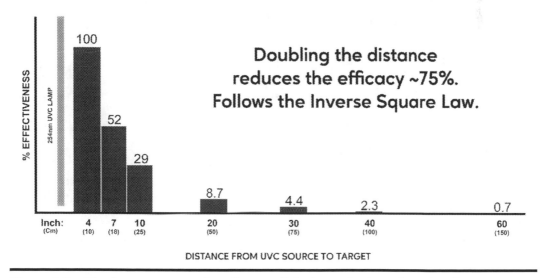

Figure 8.3 The inverse square law dictates light intensity based on the distance between the UVC lamp and the target surface. (From https://john-iovine.medium. com/red-light-therapy-power-density-exposure-time-and-dosage-bff1c94fa9e7.)

moving the UVC source 3× farther from the target surface will require 9× as long to reach the required dose.

A stationary UVC device will necessarily deliver UVC to objects in a room at varying distances, so nearby objects receive doses far higher than objects further away. Using multiple stationary devices simultaneously or using a stationary device positioned at multiple locations can help mitigate this limitation. A fully mobile device has an infinite number of positions and is most effective at minimizing distances to surfaces in a room.

UVC Angle of Incidence

The rays of UVC light emanating from the UVC source can strike the target surface at directly perpendicular (90°), tangential to the surface (0°), or at an intermediate angle known as the angle of incidence (Figure 8.4). Stand-up vertical tower UVC devices emit rays predominantly horizontally, parallel to the floor and tables. Such devices deliver seven times the dose to vertical surfaces as horizontal surfaces. This results in approximately 100-fold difference in the germicidal effectiveness between vertical and horizontal surfaces with such devices.[9] Like dust, pathogens such as SARS-CoV-2 are far more likely to land onto horizontal than vertical surfaces, placing stand-up tower units at a distinct disadvantage for whole-room disinfection.

Combining the effects of distance and angle of incidence means that lamps placed vertically 1 m from a horizontal surface will require time intervals approximately 1,000 times longer than the same lamps placed horizontally 10 cm from the surface to achieve the same germicidal effect. A UVC device that can optimally vary the height and orientation of its UVC lamps relative to the surface orientation is therefore far more efficient at dose delivery and disinfection.

Line of Sight, Shadows, and Poor Reflection

A significant limitation of UVC disinfection is that it is only effective when applied in direct line of sight. In areas shadowed from the UVC source, doses drop to nearly 0 with effectively no ability to reduce deposited *Clostridiodes difficile*.[9] This is likely true for SARS-CoV-2 as well.

Unlike visible light's ability to reflect off walls, UVC reflects very poorly, on the order of 1%–3%, off a typical interior wall. This has practical implications. For example, if an IV pole or rail car stanchion is to be

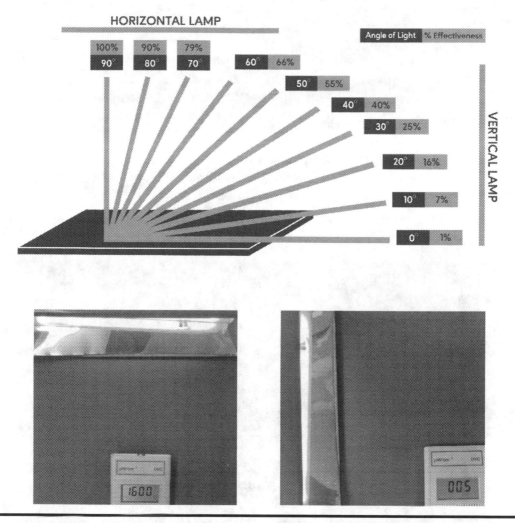

Figure 8.4 **The "angle of incidence" is formed between the UVC rays and the target surface. Horizontal lamps are far more efficient than vertical lamps in disinfecting horizontal surfaces. A horizontal aperture UVC meter reads 1,600 µW/cm² with the lamp in the horizontal position and only 5 µW/cm² with the same lamp at the same distance in the vertical position.**

effectively disinfected with UVC, one cannot depend upon reflection of UVC off the walls to reach the entire circumference of the pole where it is typically grasped. Rather, the UVC device must be placed in at least 2, and preferably 3 positions around the pole. Similarly, the underside of the surface of a table or chair, which is commonly touched, must be specifically and directly targeted by the UVC device without reliance on floor reflection.

The Canyon Wall Effect

Jaffe[10] observed and confirmed with microbiological experimental data, the UVC shadow phenomenon of textured surfaces at a microscopic level, termed the "canyon wall effect" (Figure 8.5). Textured surfaces include ubiquitous wood, vinyl, Formica, and stainless steel. These surfaces contain "pits and valleys" with depths of approximately 50–100 µm, similar to a human fingerprint and smaller than the diameter of a human hair. Relative to the size of a SARS-CoV-2 virus particle at 0.1 µm, these pits and valleys are the equivalent of a human standing in a several hundred-meter-deep canyon.

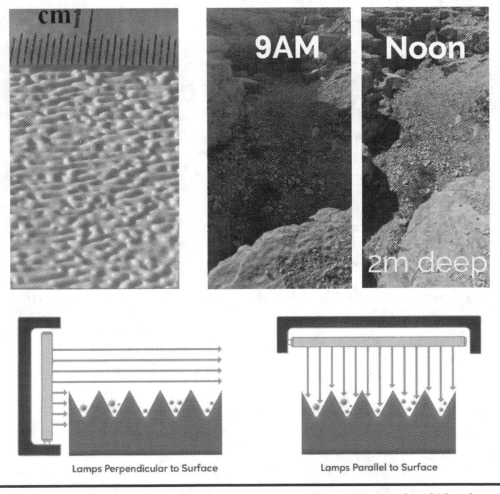

Figure 8.5   The "Canyon Wall Effect" occurs when SARS-CoV-2 particles "hide" deep in a canyon of a textured surface as the light is projected from the side. Smooth Formica has "valleys" about 100 µm deep, with walls 1,000× the height of the virus at 0.1 µm.

Applying a vertically oriented UVC source to a horizontal textured surface is analogous to standing in a canyon at sunrise. The lack of direct line of sight downward into the canyon allows virus particles within the canyon to survive. In contrast, placing the UVC source above the textured surface, like the sun at high noon, allows the germicidal rays to penetrate to the canyon floor and deactivate the viral particles.

UVC Transmission and Absorption by Common Materials

Clear or transparent glass and polymers are so-called because they allow transmission of visible light. However, like the Earth's atmosphere, UVC is very effectively blocked by most of these window-type materials. Therefore, a seemingly clear window is like a block wall to UVC rays. Surfaces and air beyond these materials cannot be disinfected with UVC. Similarly, these same materials serve as protective barriers for humans from the potentially harmful effects of UVC which were described above. Some quartz glass transmit both visible and UVC wavelengths.

Effect of UVC on Materials

Prolonged and repeated exposure to UVC can degrade some materials and paints causing color changes and surface damage. These effects are effectively mitigated by manufacturers including available UVC stabilizers and special UVC resistant coatings. Stationary UVC devices necessarily overexpose near objects in order to adequately expose distant objects and are more prone to cause damage than mobile UVC devices that provide a more uniform exposure pattern.

To fairly assess damage and color change caused by UVC, it is important to consider factors such as the frequency and dosing of UVC disinfection, as well as the normal aging wear and tear of surfaces in the specific environment. For perspective, effects of UVC on materials must be compared to the effects of repeated application of chemical disinfectants used properly with wet/dwell times and wet/dry cycling.

A Demonstrative Failure of UVC to Disinfect Public Transportation

In 2021, the Environmental Protection Agency (EPA),[11] in conjunction with the Los Angeles County Metropolitan Transport Authority conducted a field test on railcars using MS2, an innocuous viral surrogate of SARS-CoV-2. The tested devices were stationary vertically oriented pulsed-xenon UVC sources (Figure 8.6). A railcar is a complex environment with shadows, horizontal, and vertical textured surfaces. The researchers found "no significant reduction in MS2."

This was not a failure of UVC, but simply a vindication of the previously described inviolable physical properties of UVC including distance, angle of incidence, line of sight, shadowing, and the canyon wall effect.

In contrast, a UVC device, named to Time Magazine's Best Inventions of 2020, incorporating mobility, horizontal and vertical lamps can easily disinfect a railcar, similar to an aircraft cabin (Figure 8.7).

UVC versus Chemical Disinfection

The EPA has published the "N-list" of chemical disinfectants[12] that are likely effective against the SARS-CoV-2 virus but has remained on the sidelines regarding the use of UVC. Emphasis must be placed on following the manufacturer's instructions for use of these chemicals, which are rarely adhered to. This includes proper storage, dilutions, and wet/dwell times that vary from two to ten minutes. It is important that the end-user follow the directions explicitly keeping the surface wet for the required duration which usually involves multiple applications, particularly on vertical or inverted horizontal surfaces. Additionally, a potable water rinse is often required for surfaces that may come into contact with food.

UVC requires no wet/dwell time. Deactivation is instantaneous once the required UVC dose is achieved. Depending upon the UVC equipment deployed, this may take less than one second (Figure 8.8) or more than ten minutes for a surface to become disinfected.

The EPA approves the N-list chemical disinfectants only for "hard nonporous surfaces." Most environments present a variety of surfaces and many are not hard nonporous surfaces. For example only, in a typical hospital patient room there can be privacy curtains, soft textiles for bedding, upholstered seating, wood surfaces, and various plastics, metals, and glass. Properly applied UVC excels in disinfecting all such surfaces, potentially supplanting rather than supplementing chemical disinfectant use in some circumstances. When there is a spill, debris, or soiling of an environment, a mechanical wipe with an approved chemical disinfectant, followed by appropriate UVC disinfection may produce optimal results.

Figure 8.6 The EPA attempted to disinfect surfaces of a rail car with multiple station-ary-vertical-only UVC sources. They reported "no significant reduction" of virus. This was predictable based on UVC physics of distance, angle-of-incidence, shadowing, lack of reflection, and the canyon wall effect.

Figure 8.7 Beginning in 2020, UV has been successfully implemented and proven effective with a device that traverses an aircraft aisle with vertical and horizontal lamps overcoming distance, angle-of-incidence, lack of reflection, and the canyon wall effect. (Courtesy Honeywell, Inc.)

Control (No UVC)
Staphylococcus aureus

$5\log_{10}$ (99.999%) reduction
Distance: 21 cm
Dose: 6.54 mJ/cm^2
Duration: 0.95 seconds

Figure 8.8   UVHammer 21 cm above carriers, control and exposed culture plates. (Courtesy Dimer UV, LLC.)

The EPA requirements for chemical hospital disinfectants[13] specify a 6 $\log_{10}$ (99.9999%) reduction of the subject pathogen. Outside of healthcare, there is no consensus as to what level of disinfection is broadly accepted in the community. Based on accepted COVID-19 vaccine success rates, a 2 $\log_{10}$ (99%) reduction is likely satisfactory. This is easily achieved against SARS-CoV-2 with minimal UVC dosing.

Unlike chemicals effective for surface disinfection, UVC is effective for both surface and air disinfection. Whole-room UVC disinfection units, while directing their energy at target surfaces, have the added benefit of disinfecting the air between the UVC lamps and the target surface.

Lessons Learned on the Application of UVC to Mitigate Future Outbreaks

As of the time of this writing, we remain in the midst of the COVID-19 pandemic and we have not yet gained the vantage point of long-term experience. However, some insight "on the fly" is worthy as a framework for preventing and mitigating the next inevitable pandemic.

Early in the next pandemic, the mode of transmission, whether aerosol/droplet, food/water contamination, commonly touched fomites or fecal-oral routes should be determined. If the primary mode is unknown, strategies including UVC, should be deployed with inclusion of all routes. All known infectious disease-causing microbes are DNA/RNA based and all will be UVC sensitive, and dosing is relatively predictable.

Rapidly diminishing the viral load in public spaces should be part of the plan going forward the next time a pandemic occurs. This may mitigate disease transmission, decrease the need for lock-downs, and restore public confidence in return to work and travel.

UVC devices should be integral to the US Strategic National Stockpile just as are PPE and vaccines. Although UVC technology is rapidly improving, currently available devices are effective and have indefinite shelf-lives. Stockpiling will allow deployment of effective UVC disinfection devices early in a pandemic or severe influenza season.

Commercial air travel plays a special role in transmitting people and the germs they carry rapidly across the globe. As COVID-19 emerged, travel from China was suspended; and as the pandemic unfolded, international travel was largely halted. The airline industry unsuccessfully attempted to convince passengers that the risk of contracting COVID-19 on an airplane was minimal.

For the first time in nearly 100 years of commercial air travel, airlines attempted to disinfect their aircraft. However, no standards exist for aircraft disinfection efficacy so many airlines deployed visually attractive but ineffective disinfection techniques. A specific recommendation is made for certifying disinfection methods so the airlines may implement safe, efficient, and effective disinfection.

There is an overdue need for regulation of UVC devices and sanctions for false claims to protect the public. The IUVA is actively working on certification programs for UVC devices.

Even within healthcare, there are neither standards nor regulations for whole-room UVC emitters. The FDA and EPA exclude these devices from their oversight. In 2021, the *Journal of the National Institute of Standards and Technology* (NIST) published physician[14] authored patient-centric recommendations for these devices that can serve as the basis for meaningful standards by the appropriate organizations. Once implemented for healthcare, similar albeit less stringent, standards and certifications can be modified for community environments at risk.

Standards, regulations and certifications of UVC emitters can establish the credibility of UVC disinfection as a tool in the prevention and mitigation of future outbreaks and pandemics.

References

1. Reed, NG, The history of ultraviolet germicidal irradiation for air disinfection, *Public Health Rep*, 2010; 125(1): 15–27.
2. Science Brief: SARS-CoV-2 and Surface (Fomite) Transmission for Indoor Community Environments, https://www.cdc.gov/coronavirus/2019-ncov/more/science-and-research/surface-transmission.html, April 2021.
3. Van Doremalen, N, Bushmaker, T, Morris, DH, Myndi, NJ, Holbrook, G, Gamble, A, Branki, CA, Williamson, BN, Tamin, A, Harcourt, JL, Thornburg, NJ, Gerber, SI, Lloyd-Smith, JO, deWit, E, Munster, VJ, Aerosol and surface stability of SARS-CoV-2 as compared with SARS-CoV-1, *N Engl J Med*, 2020; 382.
4. Dai, T, Vrahas, MS, Murray, CK, Hamblin, MR, Ultraviolet C irradiation: an alternative antimicrobial approach to localized infections? *Expert Rev Anti Infect Ther*, 2012; 10(2): 185–195.
5. Malayeri, AH, Mohseni, M, Cairns, B, Bolton, JR, Chevrefils, G, Caron, E, Barbeau, B, Wright, H, Linden, KG, Fluence (UV-C dose) required to achieve incremental log inactivation of bacteria, protozoa, viruses and algae, *International Ultraviolet Association News*, 2016; 18(3). Available at https://iuva.org/resources/covid-19/UV%20101%20-%20Overview%20of%20Ultraviolet%20Disinfection%20-%20White%20Paper.pdf.
6. Sagrapanti, JL, Lytle, CD, Sensitivity to ultraviolet radiation of Lassa, vaccinia, and Ebola viruses dried on surfaces, *Arch Virol*, 2011; 156: 489–494, doi: 10.1007/s00705-010-0847-1.
7. Storm, N, McKay, LG, Downs, SN, Johnson, RI, Birru, D, deSamber, M, Willaert, W, Cennini, G, Griffiths, A, Rapid and complete inactivation of SARS-CoV-2 by ultraviolet-C irradiation, *Sci Rep*, 2020; 10: 22421, doi: 10.1038/s41598-020-79600-8.
8. Buonanno, M, Ponnaiya, B, Welch, D, Stanislauskas, M, Randers-Pehrson, G, Smilenov, L, Lowy, FD, Owens, DM, Brenner, DJ, Germicidal efficacy and mammalian skin safety of 222-nm UV light, *Radiat Res*, 2017; 187(4): 483–491.
9. Boyce JM, Donskey CJ, Understanding ultraviolet light surface decontamination in hospital rooms: a primer, *Infection Control & Hospital Epidemiology*, 2019, doi: 10.1017/ice.2019.161.
10. Jaffe, M, UV-C effectiveness and the "canyon wall effect" of textured healthcare environment surfaces, *UV-C Solutions Quarter*, 2019; 4: 14–16, available at https://UV-C solutionsmag.com/article-archive/digital-archive/.

11. Reducing environmental exposure to SARS-CoV-2: an overview of results, Environmental Protection Agency, June 29, 2021 available at https://www.youtube.com/watch?v=IvAHTmZATjE.
12. List N: products with emerging viral pathogens and human coronavirus claims for use against SARS-CoV-2. Date Accessed: 6 December 2020, Environmental Protection Agency, available at https://www.epa.gov/sites/default/files/2020-06/documents/sars-cov2_listn_06122020.pdf.
13. Product Performance Test Guidelines. OCSPP 810.2200: Disinfectants for Use on Environmental Surfaces. Guidance for Efficacy Testing. US Environmental Protection Agency, Office of Chemical Safety and Pollution Prevention (7510P) 712-C-17-004, February 2018.
14. Kreitenberg, A and Martinello, RA, Perspectives and recommendations regarding standards for ultraviolet-C whole-room disinfection in healthcare, *Journal of Research of the National Institute of Standards and Technology*, 2021; 126(126015), doi: 10.6028/jres.126.015.

Chapter 9

Optimizing Infection Control and Hand Hygiene during COVID

Matus Knoblich

Contents

The COVID-19 global pandemic changed people's lives in ways that cannot be overstated. Industries were forever changed, with healthcare policies and procedures being the most directly impacted. As the pandemic swept throughout the world and patients overwhelmed facilities, everyone looked to healthcare to be the savior of lives. With much of the focus on availability of hospital beds and ventilators, not much of the media focused on what was occurring within healthcare—infection control compliance. Infection control within healthcare effectively started in the late 1840s with

DOI: 10.4324/b23264-9

Hungarian physician Ignaz Semmelweis, who conducted observational studies and advanced the idea of hand hygiene in medical settings. He proposed the practice of using a chlorinated lime solution to wash hands in Vienna General Hospital's First Obstetrical Clinic, where mortality rates in the midwives' wards fell to three times lesser than those in the doctors' wards.

Over the years, the practice of hand washing further increased, and in the late twentieth century, healthcare began enacting many of the broader infection control policies we continue to use today. However, the COVID-19 pandemic demanded a re-examination at all levels of infection control to devise new practices and policies to combat the virus in healthcare settings. Despite the mainstream media focusing on hand washing in general, more drastic measures were implemented within healthcare regarding infection control compliance. This chapter examines the additional infection control measures taken in healthcare settings in response to the COVID-19 pandemic, largely reflected via personal experiences gathered over the past two years as a hands-on biomedical services provider in major healthcare networks.

Hand Hygiene

To understand the overall changes to infection control in healthcare environments during the COVID-19 pandemic, it helps to first review the hand hygiene compliance protocols for infection control implemented by healthcare facilities to combat the COVID-19 pandemic, which put a major focus on hand hygiene. The virus is easily transmitted, hence hands are a major contributing factor in viral transmission, as patients who touch their faces and other surfaces often can quickly transmit the virus from their mouth, nose, or eye area to various surfaces. Though the concept of hand washing in healthcare has been present for over 170 years as discussed earlier, compliance rates vary. Research has shown that, despite having easy access to hand washing stations and wall-mounted sanitizer dispensers, very few healthcare professionals adhere to proper hand washing and sanitizing practices as dictated by the World Health Organization (WHO)'s "5 moments of hand hygiene":

1. Before touching a patient,
2. Before clean/aseptic procedures,
3. After body fluid exposure/risk,
4. After touching a patient, and
5. After touching patient's surroundings.

To combat the lack of compliance with hand hygiene during COVID-19, hospitals started by installing additional wall-mounted dispensers. These were installed inside patient rooms, inside the entry when not already present, and outside in hallway corridors and areas that normally would be only presented with visitors. The emphasis was to encourage hand hygiene compliance not only with healthcare staff but also with any visitors to the facility across all areas. Despite the additional installation of these devices throughout facilities, their implementation came with problems. Maintenance of the large volume of devices was problematic, as these devices need to have the pouches containing sanitizer replaced when empty. Most of these devices do not notify users via any sort of messaging, lighting, or alarming when they are empty; therefore, staff must notify facilities to be changed when they are empty. Unless checked regularly, this creates a deficiency in maintenance. Furthermore, handless versions of these units require regular battery changes to operate properly. When the batteries are not changed in a timely manner, the devices do not operate. The issues of changing sanitizer bladders and batteries were further compounded by staff deficiencies during COVID-19, and an increase in work from additional devices installed to support patient care during the pandemic. As a result, there is a large gap between the number of items needing servicing and the staff available to service them.

And yet, the largest issue facing these devices may have been simply supplying them with hand sanitizer. The pandemic has resulted in a serious strain on supply chains. Lack of employees coming to work due to illness or fear of the illness have resulted in shorter production output. COVID-19 outbreaks within staff at facilities have resulted in shuttering of operations at sites entirely. This has been an issue across industries due to COVID-19, and especially in the healthcare industry, notably during 2020. High demands on hand sanitizer coupled with a strained supply chain leaves healthcare facilities with shortfalls in hand sanitizer for wall-mounted dispensers.

To counter the shortfalls, facilities looked to local and upstart manufacturers of sanitizer, whose products often did not function the same as standard sanitizers regarding hand feel, texture (often very soapy and slick), and smell. Concerns arose about counterfeit sanitizers without the correct alcohol content. Sanitizer needs to be at least 65% alcohol content for efficacy, with 75% being the standard alcohol content to guarantee killing of all bacteria and viruses. For example, bottled Purell has 70% alcohol content, and the Orbel personal hand sanitizer has 72%. Counterfeit products were found to contain below 50% alcohol content while claiming to contain 75% alcohol. Concerns were also raised that the alcohol used in some counterfeits was not (safe) ethyl alcohol, but methanol, which is toxic and can be absorbed through the skin. The FDA issued warnings and notices alerting users of issues with these sorts of products.

During the pandemic, high demand and low supply led to unsustainable price inflation. Industrial and independent suppliers raised prices on hand sanitizer to unseen levels, peaking at upward of 15 times their pre-pandemic pricing as demand greatly outstripped supply. With demand coming from commercial, industrial, and consumer sectors, manufacturing was unable to keep up, and pricing became quite volatile. As the pandemic went on, and supply chains were re-established, production returned and even increased with many new market players. To a degree, pricing and supply stabilized; however, 18 months into the pandemic, supply chains remain stressed and supply somewhat limited.

Masks

In addition to hand hygiene, facilities also put a major focus on wearing masks in healthcare facilities. Staff, patients, and visitors were and still are required to wear masks at all times while onsite, regardless of vaccination status. As the virus is easily transmitted through droplets carried by human breath, wearing a mask acts to prevent droplet transmission from a mask wearer to others. The mask, when worn properly, must cover both the nose and the mouth. When breathing, speaking, sneezing, coughing, or otherwise projecting, the droplets will be captured by the mask and prevent transmission from one person to another. When both parties wear masks, this protection is drastically increased, as masks help prevent both the expulsion and inhalation of those droplets.

Healthcare facilities encountered major obstacles with masks from the onset of the COVID-19 pandemic. The first was availability. As with hand sanitizer, demand for masks came from every sector. Individuals were advised to wear them in the streets, at work, even at home under certain circumstances. Again, there was huge demand and limited supply.

This was compounded in healthcare facilities, where masks needed to be frequently changed. Should someone be in contact or the vicinity of a COVID-19 patient, as has become very common in healthcare settings, masks need to be discarded and changed when moving between patient rooms in line with contact isolation requirements; this resulted in additional mask demand. Similar supply chain issues that created supply shortfalls for hand sanitizer also affected masks. For example, a majority of mask production was based in China at the onset of the pandemic. With border closings, production shortages, and limited shipping viability from China, supply from main channel factories was limited and at times impossible.

And again, counterfeit products created issues in mainstream supply channels. The Centers for Disease Control (CDC) initially promoted N-95 masks as those necessary for COVID-19 settings; however, due to shortfalls of these masks, many healthcare facilities resorted to three-ply surgical masks. Supply shortfalls often resulted in healthcare departments purchasing as many masks as possible, wherever possible. Many startup manufacturers seized the opportunity, manufacturing masks that were labeled as N-95 but were not legally certified as such. Significant mask counterfeiting taking place during the pandemic has exposed users to false infection control safety.

Changing CDC guidelines for mask wearing also created issues with mask compliance. When the CDC recommended moving from one mask to double-masking—wearing one mask over another—the rationale was to reduce droplet transmission by increasing layers that droplets would have to pass through to exit into free air. The more layers present, the fewer droplets that can get in or out. Also, due to the propensity of human beings to touch their face and in turn the masks, whether as a habit or to readjust the mask, having a second mask can protect the primary mask from contamination. The outer mask can be replaced more often, protecting the user from direct mask contamination. Minimum two-mask policies were instituted and followed at healthcare facilities in the hardest-hit pandemic regions.

User error with masks presented another major issue in healthcare. The mask must properly cover the user's face over their nose and mouth to provide the greatest efficacy. Unfortunately, many users wear the masks below their noses or below their chin. Whether due to a comfort issue or just plain forgetfulness, this issue of user error allowed transmission of droplets and caused virus transmission within healthcare.

Room Cleaning

With the major focus being on infection control of the virus via hand hygiene and mask wearing, an area not much talked about outside of healthcare was the implementation of new and updated processes and procedures for room and hallway sanitizing. The virus is easily transmittable through droplets and bodily fluids (sweat, saliva, etc.), which are in turn transmitted through contact with surfaces. Gloves protected the wearer but did not prevent transmission of the virus across surfaces. Therefore, having clean surfaces significantly reduces viral transmission. To combat this, Environmental Services (EVS) departments had to implement additional stringent measures to clean rooms, hallways, and surfaces to keep with changing and tightening infection control measures designed to protect patients, staff, and visitors.

For direct cleaning of surfaces, EVS staff used PDI germicidal disposable wipes to clean all surfaces more frequently than before. Where, in the past, such items would only be used on mattresses and equipment after patient use, new policies implemented the use of PDI Purple and PDI Gray wipes by EVS staff on all surfaces at all times. All medical equipment and items in patient rooms were wiped prior to use, in between procedures, after use, prior to servicing, after servicing, and then finally again prior to patient use. Nurse stations were regularly wiped down, and anything touched by anyone was to be wiped down immediately. The early days of the pandemic resulted in EVS policies that were perhaps overzealousness, wiping every possible surface at any possible time to prevent cross-contamination. As the pandemic entered its second year and COVID-19 transmission was better understood, policies were modified to meet refined CDC and hospital guidelines.

EVS staff implemented a more stringent floor cleaning policy. Hallways and rooms were scrubbed, burnished, vacuumed, and waxed with greater frequency, sometimes every few hours when possible, versus once every cycle as before. Electrostatic sprayers were introduced into much higher use. Demand grew well beyond supply for this equipment, which was very limited; production times became unsustainable. Electrostatic sprayers were rushed to production and broke easily, resulting in additional equipment shortfalls.

At the onset of the pandemic, ultraviolet light devices were mandated for use in all patient rooms after a COVID patient had left. It was eventually determined that these devices were over-utilized and not needed. While in use, they were very taxing on EVS staff. Prior to the pandemic, a typical 600-bed facility might utilize these devices for 200 UV room cleans per month; during the pandemic this surged to 800–900 UV room cleans per month. Overuse of these devices resulted in frequent burnouts of their lamps, which, due to supply chain shortfalls, were often on back order and difficult to attain, resulting in long repair times for equipment.

Air purification became a greater focus during the pandemic, attracting new manufacturers and new products to the healthcare market. Air purification offered both open- and closed-loop systems. Closed systems were preferred because they could be installed in COVID-19 patient rooms and run on a continuous closed-loop system to prevent any air from entering other rooms or sites. However, closed systems were almost impossible to obtain during the first year of the pandemic due to high demand and limited supply. Open systems that existed in the hospital relied heavily on filters, which were quickly in short supply. HEPA filters and vents were overall in such short supply that many were overused past their recommended lifespan, resulting in reduced efficacy in removing harmful agents such as COVID-19 particles from the air.

Overall, EVS and Facilities departments within healthcare were limited in their capacity to increase infection control due to a series of pandemic-related shortages. Supply chain shortfalls had a heavy negative impact on the ability of these departments to meet recommended guidelines set forth (and often changing) by the CDC, other governing bodies, and their own health-care facilities. Equipment maintenance was also an issue, as repair companies were unable to have their staff come onsite to service broken equipment. Staff shortages due to illness and fear of illness, along with limited access due to changing facility guidelines, meant that some companies that would normally come onsite to fix infection control compliance equipment were unable to do so. This resulted in additional downtime to critical cleaning equipment in those instances where replacement parts were available.

Staff

Healthcare staff compliance with infection control measures was perhaps the most important aspect to address during the pandemic. As information on the COVID-19 virus was continuously coming to light, CDC and healthcare facility guidelines reacted. Healthcare staff learned, adhered to, and complied with these infection control protocols. Mask wearing—including how many masks to wear—patient room cleaning, and additional cleaning procedures were just a few aspects of that compliance.

Staff education on the new policies and guidelines was key to compliance. Regular training sessions, webinars, emails, fliers, and posters were used as methods to continuously keep the staff apprised of the newest guidelines. However, guidelines often changed so frequently that it created confusion and misunderstanding as to what the most current infection control guidelines were. This situation created infection control compliance shortfalls.

Staff error within guidelines was another major shortfall for infection control compliance. Incorrect hand washing and sanitizing, incorrect mask wearing, not changing gloves often enough, and not cleaning rooms properly all resulted in infection control compliance shortfalls.

COVID-19 infection, of course, created one of the largest issues for healthcare staff. Many healthcare staff were infected and missed work. Others opted out of work or left their jobs due to fear of contracting the virus. This created staff shortages and resulted in overworked staff. Overworked and tired staff were more likely to suffer user error in regard to infection control, allowing for greater risk of transmission of the virus.

Conclusion

The COVID-19 pandemic created serious challenges to infection control in healthcare facilities during the pandemic. While a long overdue reassessment revealed insights like the primacy of hand hygiene to combat infection in healthcare environments, real-life supply chain and staff shortfalls created by the virus resulted in ever-greater risks of transmission. Equipment has been and remains short supply, and PPE items are in low supply and at risk of counterfeit. Staff are overworked, and guidelines for increased infection control are changing frequently. Despite all this, there has been significant innovation in both equipment and PPE to counter this virus, and the human spirit to persevere through this pandemic has not been deterred.

Case Study: Orbel—Improving the Habit of Hand Hygiene

According to the WHO, there are an estimated two million hospital acquired infections (HAIs) per year globally, affecting 10% of hospital patients. In Europe alone, the European Center for Disease Prevention and Control estimates that on any given day, 80,000 patients have at least one healthcare-associated infection, that is, 1 in every 18 patients in a European hospital. Practicing hand hygiene is a simple and effective way to prevent infection, however high workloads and poor accessibility can often result in complainace shortfalls.

It has been well established that when hand washing compliance can be increased, HAI rates can be reduced. The challenge has been finding ways to effectively increase compliance rates. The idea for the Orbel arose out of this necessity for hand hygiene, coming to market just months before the outbreak of COVID-19 in the United States as a frontline solution for infection control compliance.

Orbel is a patented, wearable hand sanitizer unit purpose-built to increase compliance rates. The orb-shaped unit clips onto your person (i.e., pocket or belt). By gently rolling a hand across its rollerball system, the proper amount of a premium 72% ethyl alcohol gel is released. When rubbed on hands, that gel kills 99.9% of germs within 15 seconds.

Orbel reinforces the habit of hand hygiene via intuitive hand sanitization movement and provides immediate access to compliance in a simple, easy, and cost-effective manner. In turn, Orbel saves lives through improved hand hygiene, reducing the spread of bacteria, viruses, and infection. Orbel won a European innovative product design award (iF DESIGN AWARD 2016, Discipline Product), being called the most innovative creation for hand hygiene in decades.

Glo-Med Networks, Inc., one of Orbel's leading distributors, is teaming up with the Orbel team to bring their product to various global markets. Glo-Med's current distribution footprint includes the Americas, Western Africa, Europe, and the Middle East, where current customers include hospitals, restaurants, hotels, banks, schools, professional sports leagues, and law enforcement. Glo-Med has sold this product globally, commencing sales prior to the COVID-19 pandemic, but garnering global attention during the pandemic with a focus on hand hygiene compliance.

> Orbel has actually been in development for quite a while. There's a lot of work that goes into launching a new product like this, a lot of research and development, logistics, certifications, etc. it wasn't developed specifically in response to COVID,

says Matus Knoblich, CEO of Glo-Med Networks and Managing Director of Med-Stat Consulting Services.

> Hospitals always saw the value of the product because of how easily it helps increase compliance rates, which is a continual problem they face. In today's COVID climate though, the general public is increasingly conscious of hand hygiene. Orbel is really an invaluable tool for anyone that comes into contact with the public or potentially contaminated surfaces, disinfecting with a simple swipe of the hand. We feel very fortunate that we're in a position to be able to help and continue to expand Orbel's footprint around the globe.

Increasing Compliance at Hospitals

For US hospitals and healthcare facilities, just three words, "The Joint Commission" (TJC), can send waves of panic through the halls. Regulatory compliance is always front of mind, but never more so than during a Joint Commission review, a deep audit performed approximately every three years, during which third-party inspections are performed of the normal daily operations of a hospital unit. Instead of focusing just on paperwork, TJC inspectors scrutinize the delivery of care, treatments, and other services provided by staff, for example, examining Infection Control, Competence, and Environment of Care. TJC's goal is to improve standards across the healthcare industry, including strategies to improve safety and quality of patient care, which is one reason hospitals elect to participate in their reviews.

The most challenging part of the process, perhaps, is that hospitals are provided with little advance warning that an inspection is coming. At most, they are given a seven days' notice, though sometimes it is a last-minute phone call from the lobby, so facilities find it imperative to have their affairs in order to avoid making last-minute improvements.

Orbel is designed to save hospitals and medical facilities significant effort in providing a hand hygiene solution to their staff, doctors, and visitors. The WHO's "five movements of hand hygiene" are widely acknowledged as the best method for preventing healthcare-associated infections. Yet in the critical situations you often find in hospitals, every second counts, and hand hygiene can be de-prioritized.

> That's what's most compelling about the Orbel—it provides a point-of-care hand hygiene tool for hospital staff that's literally at their fingertips when they need it. In hospitals, it's important to be able to focus attention on patients, not how they're going to sanitize their hands,

states Knoblich. "Hospitals today remain our core customer thanks to the perfect union of efficiency and effectiveness that Orbel provides."

Restaurants, Retail, Hospitality

The hospitality, retail, and food and beverage industries have been hit hard by the COVID-19 pandemic, subject to increased regulations for cleanliness.

These locations face extra scrutiny as crossroads for the transfer of the virus, as a high concentration of people come into close contact with one another, and quite simply, because people often do not take the care to clean their hands enough in these spaces. Bars, restaurants, cafes, hotels, offices, and workshops tend to be ill-prepared when it comes to preventing the spread of infections. Ordinary people (non-healthcare workers), while probably never more conscientious of germs and hand hygiene than they are now, still are not programmed to think about hand hygiene the way a hospital worker is.

In a hospital setting, healthcare workers are constantly reminded of the need to be clean. It is drummed into their daily practice, yet hand hygiene compliance typically hovers around just 50%–60%. Where the issue has yet to be examined, one can suspect even less compliance. Even with a well-trained staff, hand hygiene is not likely to be front of mind. Orbel seeks to address that challenge in any environment where people work together, whether they are serving customers, meeting clients, or just in the same space as other people. In the United States, Orbel intends to meet that need at grocery stores, restaurants, sporting events, and office settings, to provide just a few examples.

Today, infection control is no longer relegated to the realm of hospitals. Rather, it's something that the likes of McDonald's, Yum restaurants, and even Amazon are taking very seriously, presenting dynamic, multifaceted environments where people work together. Whether they are serving customers, meeting clients, or just performing in the same shared space, Orbel represents a solution to personal hand hygiene.

Orbel's shift into a consumer-facing product has revealed a wider audience for that solution. "While hand sanitizer usage has become fairly commonplace, especially this last year, there's nothing on the market that compares to the ease of use and versatility that the Orbel wearable unit provides," said Knoblich, "We're thrilled that we can now offer a direct to consumer option and bring more convenient hand hygiene into more environments."

Spreading the Solution: Orbel Distribution Grows

COVID-19 infection rates are still rising throughout the world, pushing advances in Orbel to from its conception, from reducing packaging to experimenting with different gel formulations to expanding into and navigating regulations in new locales in Europe, Latin America, the Middle East, and Africa.

The Middle East, for example, produced unique challenges to ensuring the premium aspect of the Orbel can be maintained globally, that is, high temperatures that might negatively impact the premium gel solution. Africa, which is set to be the most populous continent on the planet by 2050 and is seeing unprecedented rates of change and growth, presents a different set of challenges to provide Orbel in a cost-effective manner and make it as accessible as possible. Working with several businesses and NGOs, Glo-Med seeks to manufacture Orbel in Africa, fill it with a locally produced gel, and leverage existing distribution networks that might not always medically focused.

Getting Back to Normal

As we start returning to a "normal" way of life, it will be important to maintain a healthy respect of not only COVID-19, which is likely to be with us for many years to come, but also of virus transmission overall. We have a responsibility to keep each other safe that demands solutions, and Orbel hand hygiene can be extremely effective in infection control.

If you would like to know how Orbel came into existence, here is a great overview: https://www.youtube.com/watch?v=wpHbZBfmlbM.

Chapter 10

How COVID-19 Catalyzed Community-Driven AI in the Metaverse of Medical Data

Dexter Hadley, Cynthia Kyin, Rachna Sannegowda,
Jennifer Nedimyer Horner, Elena Cyrus, and David Metcalf

Contents

Background

By the time Facebook (FB) changed its name to Meta[1] earlier this year, an unprecedented virtualization of society had already taken place. COVID-19 forced communities to displace physical interactions with more digital ones to be able to navigate a new pandemic reality. The physical reality of going to work, school, or place of worship had become a shared virtual one for public health and wellness. This successful social experiment paved the way for the so-called Metaverse that encompasses a shared digital reality built on data that may be as disruptive to society as the original Internet was before it. For effective purposes, *the Metaverse spans the persistent digital representation of anything.* It now exists because of an implicit trust that is engineered by cryptographic data structures distributed by algorithms that define the security, privacy, and permanence of transactions over a network. Whereas the first Bitcoin community leveraged these, so-called "trustless," algorithms to digitize currency,[2] the Metaverse dictates an even larger community to support an alternative reality that includes cryptocurrency and everything else that it can be exchanged for.[3] This alternative reality may be purely virtual, like FB's vision and accessible through a 3D VR headset, or it might augment existing reality like Bitcoin did for a virtual global community that values real money.

The *Metaverse is built on trustless algorithms* that maintain a permanent ledger of transactions broadcast over a network such that no single node can easily corrupt the distributed ledger technology (DLT).[4] Just as the nascent consumer Internet of the early 1990s was built on mature TCP/IP networking protocols from the 1960s, this consumer Metaverse is being built on mature DLTs conceived since the 1990s.[5] The most valuable DLT is the original Blockchain that serves the Bitcoin community since the first one was mined in 2009.[6] This Blockchain technology facilitated a fundamental shift for the offline world by allowing the transfer of value across the World Wide Web without the need for a centralized authority.[7] However, this original Blockchain was computationally taxing across the network and thus the environment, and it was not programmable and therefore could only serve the Bitcoin community.[8] More sophisticated cryptographic algorithms have yielded a diversity of programmable DLTs that all feature significant energy savings over the original Blockchain and have thus commanded significant community support. Algorithms like Ethereum,[9] Algorand,[10] and Hedera Hashgraph[11] represent next-generation programmable DLTs that are supporting the nascent Metaverse.[12-14] These DLTs underlie a variety of applications including their own cryptocurrencies to support causes that community may share in a persistent digital reality.

As with the original consumer Internet and its exponential expansion, the Metaverse is evolving so quickly that society is racing to catch up. Next-generation DLTs support non-fungible tokens (NFTs) which are unique digital serial numbers programmed to track digital assets. It was by auctioning NFTs that the cryptocurrency community was able to covertly evacuate Sharbat Gula safely from Afghanistan to Italy after the Taliban takeover that followed US departure from her homeland.[15] The Complutense University in Madrid, Spain, one of the oldest and most reputable Universities in Europe, is teaching new business models based on NFTs in the Metaverse from 2022.[16] Seva.love is building a Metaverse for good and auctioning NFTs to help survivors of acquired brain injury (ABI).[17] Lasting communities are being built into the nascent Metaverse of digital assets that may fundamentally change our society as the original Bitcoin did based on the original Blockchain before it, and as the Blockchain did based on the original Internet before it. As humans have longed reaped the benefits of working together, the *Metaverse is the latest epoch of technological innovation that is bringing communities together* around shared and enforceable ideals.

Metaverse of Medical Data

Much like the rest of society, COVID-19 forced the virtualization of the practice of medicine into a new shared public health reality. Whereas patients used to physically go to the doctor, there are now digital portals to return ubiquitous testing results as well as to facilitate virtual visits including access to the electronic health records (EHR) data for both doctors and their patients. When defined as a persistent digital representation, therefore, the *Metaverse already exists for patient data* because of laws that maintain the security, privacy, and permanence of their health records. Board certification used to give clinicians almost the sole privilege to access this Metaverse of data for the patients they treat. Moreover, Health Insurance Portability and Accountability Act (HIPAA) regulation has long guaranteed every patient the right to access their own medical data and prescribes how to de-identify it with appropriate informed consent and medical release for research.[18] Therefore, with maturing DLTs, physicians and scientists can already begin to stake out the Metaverse of medical EHR data by engaging their patients to appropriately share it for machine learning and artificial intelligence (ML/AI) research.

While research in the Metaverse can be used to deliver better healthcare in theory, the reality of the data suggests that the most vulnerable patients will currently be left behind. National longitudinal data sourced from the 'How We Feel' (HWF) app[19,20] at the beginning of the pandemic demonstrates how online surveys can quickly recruit up to 500,000 individuals to share both clinical and behavioral data regarding how they feel about COVID-19. However, their response was over-represented by white females which is an expected bias reported by a systematic literature review that found the over-representation of young white women as a significant limitation to FB recruitment of participants for health research purposes.[21] This *ethnical bias in data disparities remains a longstanding problem in biomedical research* that will translate into any Metaverse of medical data. As recently as 2011, an analysis of open genomics datasets found 96% of samples derived from populations of European descent[22] (Figure 10.1a). Either knowingly or not, this data collection was largely funded by the National Institutes of Health (NIH) and directed by a few large academic centers. Consequently, the dearth of data from more diverse patient populations results in less useful medicine that may paradoxically worsen the existing healthcare disparities across the disease spectrum[23–28] (Figure 10.1b).

The disparate reality of US healthcare that must be reflected in the Metaverse of medical data is that people of color (POC) experience overall higher morbidities, earlier onset of morbidities, and higher mortality rates when compared to non-Hispanic whites (NHW)[29,30] (Figure 10.1b). Vulnerable/marginalized

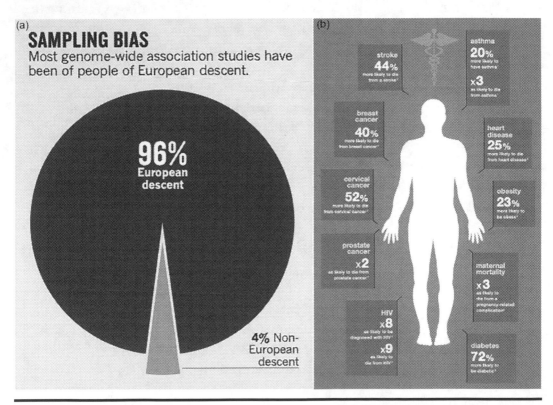

Figure 10.1   Significant disparities persist in Big Data research that contribute to significant health disparities. Panel (a) shows significant sampling bias of 96% in genetics research studies highlighted by Bustamante *et al.*,[22] while panel (b) shows significant inequities reported by the CDC in African American adults relative to their white counterparts.[23]

populations suffer higher rates of chronic and co-morbid conditions[31] that compound their risks of contracting and dying from COVID-19.[32–34] These patterns hold across the spectrum of disease because when compared to NHW, African Americans (AA) have significantly more morbidity and mortality from diabetes,[35] heart disease,[36] asthma,[37] obesity,[38] and HIV,[39] despite comprising only 13% of the population. Similar trends hold for Latino/Latina (Latinx)[40–42] and American Indian/Alaska Native (AIAN)[43–45] when compared to NHW controls. Therefore, to ethically leverage medical data in the Metaverse and to develop digital interventions that may improve these disparate outcomes, digital communities must actively incentivize a diverse recruitment of patients from the most vulnerable communities to identify this implicit bias across the healthcare data and ultimately correct for it with finely tuned ML/AI.

The national response to COVID-19 further exposed stark inadequacies in the US health system that further exponentiated these morbidity and mortality statistics that plague the most underserved patient populations.[46,47] The Centers for Disease Control (CDC) data on race and ethnicity showed systemic effects of deaths across ethnicity disproportionately affecting non-white, black, and Hispanic minorities while white patients were paradoxically protected (Figure 10.2). Underlying causes for these disparities often

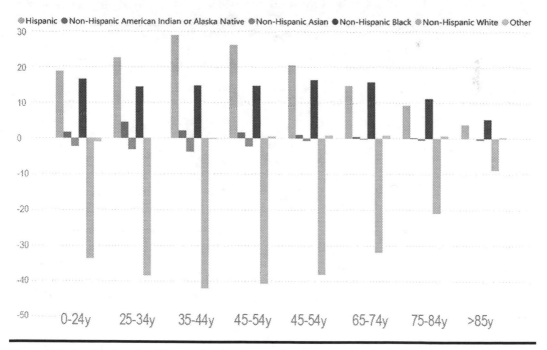

Figure 10.2 Systemic effects of COVID-19 deaths across ethnicity. Bar chart shows the relative proportion of COVID-19 deaths scaled by the total population size across ethnicity grouped by age as reported by the CDC as of writing.[47]

are misattributed to primarily biological predispositions, at the expense of understanding critical social determinants of health (SDH), such as race and ethnicity, that may interact with biological factors to determine an individual's level of vulnerability to COVID-19 infection and death.

When the pandemic first hit, race and ethnicity were not even mandated reportable factors making SDH difficult to track. As early as April 2020 and long before CDC publicly released its ethnicity data,[48,49] we developed indirect methods to understand the impact of COVID-19 on black populations at the start of the pandemic[50] by triangulating the AA density versus COVID-19 death rates across counties (Figure 10.3). Our results were among the first to show that communities with a high AA density have been disproportionately burdened with COVID-19 and motivated a further characterization of SDH that may be enriched in members of these communities that explain the significantly worse COVID-19 outcomes.

Indeed, we have now learned how POC have a significantly increased risk of COVID-19 exposure and worse outcomes due to many SDH such as occupation,[53,54] insurance status, and resource availability[55,56] or any combination of factors[57,58] (Figure 10.4). Moreover, common outcomes such as

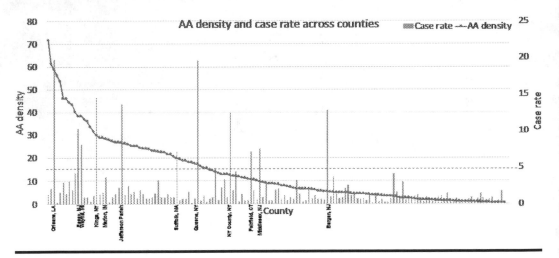

Figure 10.3 The impact of COVID-19 on African American (AA) communities from Cyrus *et al.* 2020.[46] Counties (x-axis) are sorted by decreasing AA density (primary y-axis) shown by a blue line. Orange bar chart shows computed AA incidence spikes (secondary y-axis). Data were analyzed for cases collected between January 22, 2020 and April 12, 2020. The data were sourced from USA Facts[48] and population estimates were derived from the US Census[49] with analyses conducted using SPSS 22.0.[51] Inset: State COVID-19 Data by Race. This CDC map shows that only two US states had released COVID-19 testing data by race[52] for the same period we analyzed.

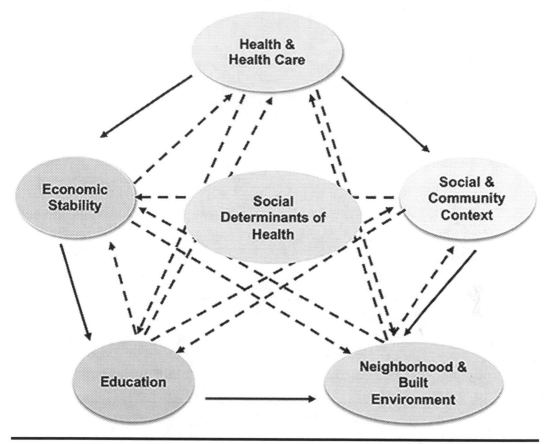

Figure 10.4 The social determinants of health (SDH) are social and economic conditions that are categorized into five interacting key determinants across health and healthcare, social and community context, neighborhood and built environment, education, and economic stability.[63]

asymptomatic cases represent over 40%–50%[59–62] of cases that are the main drivers of community spread in the United States but are not a reportable outcome for testing protocols. This regulatory oversight manifests as missing data for deep ML/AI algorithms whose performance to identify symptomatic cases early on will be doubtless boosted by training on asymptomatic cases as well.

The root cause of this significant and well-documented bias in research data from underserved populations is doubtless influenced by the initial anonymization process that de-identifies the data to be shared with the data science and bioinformatics community in the first place. Commercial aggregators lawfully capture EHR data *en masse* from healthcare providers without informed consent for human subject research, or

HIPAA medical release to share protected health information (PHI). The Institutional Review Boards (IRB) approve anonymization and de-identification protocols are intended to maintain privacy, but they also largely break re-contact with the patient in so doing. As such, once this de-identified data is released to the larger research community, it is almost impossible to interactively probe the patient population on a large scale to understand the SDH that are often more predictive of ethnic disparities than genetic factors alone. Therefore, there are no standardized large-scale mechanisms to directly recruit patients and/or to interactively follow them to probe conceptual models that explain SDH. Moreover, when large-scale data repositories do gather informed consent as often required for genomics sequencing studies, there is no incentivization or hardly any active efforts in the first place to improve diversity in the data collected which results in the stark ethnic data disparities that exist today.

Now reactive to this data disparity that it helped to perpetuate, the NIH has actively begun to assemble more diverse datasets for MI through building consortia like AIM-AHEAD and Bridge2AI with over $150M allocated in budget already.[64,65] However, the SDH that are so critical to explaining diseases with disparate outcomes are unlikely to even be present in the EHR data that these consortia will combine. Without informed consent for interactive human subject research, or HIPAA medical release to share PHI, there is no lawful mechanism to directly recruit patients and interactively follow them to fine-tune deep learning (DL) AI algorithms for clinical grade performance. Moreover, without online recruitment and digital community building, these biases will be further compounded for EHR data when large-scale repositories capture it *en masse* among consortia members. Therefore, without the ability to enrich for vulnerable populations and engage them to donate their clinical data, biased and/or incomplete small data sets causes MI to discriminate against large groups at scale[66] and may even worsen already significant disparities in healthcare outcomes for patients.

To ethically leverage the Metaverse and to collect useful and diverse data from communities of patients, we need to engineer transparent ecosystems that incentivize patients to share their data more equitably. These ecosystems must serve the communities of patients, doctors, and scientists pioneering work of mapping this Metaverse of medical data that will serve as the substrate for more useful AI to be developed. As evidenced by the lack of ethnicity data mandated by government for COVID-19 testing at the beginning of the pandemic (Figure 10.3 inset), the clinical data should not be centralized, politicized, or obfuscated, but must rather be supported by an open community providing diverse patient data to serve AI research. To achieve those goals and ideals, medical data in the Metaverse must be interactive and personal to patients, albeit anonymized and accessible, so that data scientists may begin to understand SDH and model their effects on health outcomes. Therefore, the promise of the Metaverse of medical data is that it can be used to (1) measure, (2) control for, and (3) reduce existing disparities in outcomes of the current health system.

Community-Driven AI

Community-driven AI is made possible by a Metaverse that can doubtless generate useful and interactive AI for patients willing to share their medical data. In this scenario, patients can share their clinical EHR data via trustless algorithms in IRB-approved research that contributes toward our shared clinical intelligence. For the current state-of-the-art DL frameworks that have come to dominate AI, generalized models must be pre-trained on massive, labeled datasets that require fine-tuning on smaller more curated datasets for accurate performance across more specialized applications. This fine-tuning or so-called "transfer learning" of a specialized models allows for SDH and other drivers of the existing disparities in health outcomes to be directly incorporated into MI and as part of the experimental design. Medical education at our University of Central Florida College of Medicine incorporates a Student Focused Inquiry Research Experience (FIRE) program that puts medical students into the community to do biomedical research as a requirement for graduation. *Community-Driven AI is to build interactive digital communities that can be more finely curated* and we can leverage medical students to curate SDH and other features from patients directly "in the loop" of the MI by simply extending existing IRB protocols to allow them to do so (Figure 10.5) as a requirement for graduation.

As such, community-driven AI is a paradigm of digital medicine, a term which emerged since 2007 when the iPhone was introduced as the first smartphone[67] and is now used to describe any kind of mobile app-based intervention that serves patients via smartphones or wearables. Since then, programs like the Patient-Centered Outcomes Research Institute (PCORI) have supported online patient engagement to recruit patients to share data and improve healthcare outcomes.[68–77] In perhaps one of the most impactful instances of digital health innovation, the Apple Heart Study[78] recruited

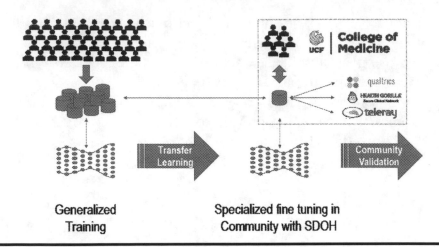

Figure 10.5   Community-driven AI extends existing IRB protocols to adapt FIRE to AI (FIRE-AI) research to engage digital members of diverse communities to share their imaging and EHR data.

419,297 participants over eight months to eventually develop an FDA approved real-time algorithm for Apple Watch to detect atrial fibrillation through its integrated EKG. The massive NIH-sponsored AllOfUs[79] research program plans to enroll at least 1M participants to track medical records in order to accelerate research and improve health. However, none of these studies are intended to access and return EHR data to the patient, to keep the patient "in the loop" of active ML, or to build interactive diverse communities of patients to better understand SDH, therefore their results run the risk of propagating the existing data disparities that mirror disparate health-care outcomes in underserved populations.

CovidImaging.US Pilot Study

The adage of a picture is worth a thousand words is most true in AI where DL models require massive labeled imagesets to achieve state-of-the-art for image classification.[80–96] The ImageNet Large Scale Visual Recognition Challenge (ILSVRC) evaluated various algorithms for image classification at large scale in an annual competition, and *DL has surpassed human performance* at >97%[97–100] accuracy in image classification since 2015.[89,97–99,101–107] The final ISLVRC competition was last held in 2018 because the DL algorithms had become so expert in image classification there was little challenge left. Therefore, ISLVRC effectively proved that for AI and specifically DL in image classification, *bigger data leads to better decisions* (Figure 10.6).

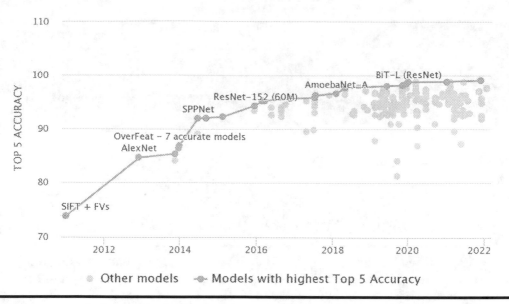

Figure 10.6 Relative performance improvement in accuracy rates on ImageNet's classification of the top-5 error rate. Top-5 is the fraction of test images for which the correct label is not among the five labels considered most probable.

Despite the United States leading the world in COVID-19 cases based on testing volume, and likely radiology imaging based on hospitalizations, a *lack of accessible clinical imaging for AI research* has obstructed our ability to follow suit. Much like the extremely biased data available for training AI, health information blocking *(HIB) is a growing concern* as the rise of AI in the United States where market conditions create business incentives for some persons and entities to exercise control over EHR data in ways that unreasonably limit its availability and use.[108] Indeed, this panned out early in the pandemic where at least three high-profile COVID-19 studies[109–111] were being investigated[112,113] and retracted for using unreliable EHR data that was blocked from peer-review, which means the effects of HIB have incorrectly influenced global government responses to the pandemic.

As early as February 2020, China reportedly trained DL models using training imageset from 1,136 patients with analytical sensitivity of 97% and specificity of 92% on computerized tomography (CT) scans across a variety of pulmonary diseases and deployed them across five hospitals to effectively predict 96% of cases.[114] At the time of initial publication, the COVIDx dataset[115] is the largest accessible repository of COVID imaging in the United States with ONLY 76 radiology images from 53 COVID-19 patient cases – far too few to train clinical grade AI models. It has since

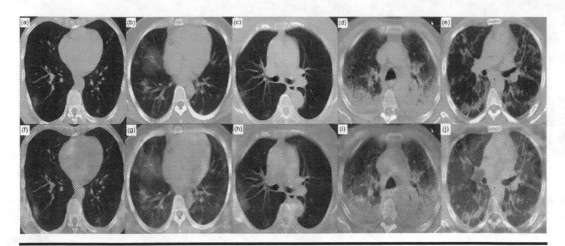

Figure 10.7 Deep learning prediction in diverse multinational patients. Original CT images are shown in the first row and DL generated heat maps with COVID-19 prediction are shown below. (a, b) Images and (f, g) associated maps from Hubei, China cohort. (c) Image and (h) associated map from Tokyo, Japan cohort. (d) Image and (i) associated map from an advanced case in Milan, Italy.

expanded to thousands of images derived from various other smaller studies without much rigor for assembling a rigorous and less biased dataset for AI/ML. Moreover, none of these images are tied to digital patients that are currently accessible in the United States to probe SDH. However, outside of the United States, our colleagues trained DL models on the first multinational imaging cohort of 1,280 patients to achieve up to 91% accuracy, with 84% sensitivity and 93% specificity to localize parietal pleura/lung parenchyma followed by classification of COVID-19 pneumonia[116] across populations from China, Japan, and Europe (Figure 10.7). Therefore, the clinical utility of these models remains unproven in a diverse US population without diverse data to validate their findings. Moreover, none of them even attempt to model SDH that are so critical to predicting outcomes in underserved populations in the United States, thereby exponentiating their marginalization in the age of AI.

Introduction

We are engineering CovidImaging.US as an interactive radiology imaging repository to reduce COVID-19 disparities in AI. This is because when deployed at scale, AI can predict COVID-19 outcomes and can triage cases more quickly. In the absence of PCR tests, AI can predict patient outcomes such as survival and ventilator utilization, as well as help health systems to standardize clinical

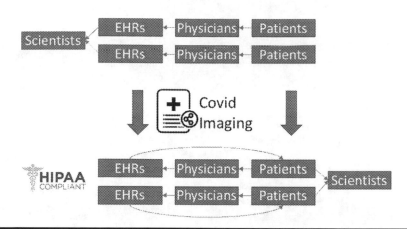

Figure 10.8   CovidImaging.US will combat health information blocking by EHR developers to allow patients to interactively share that information with scientists and researchers.

workflows to optimally allocate limited resources.[117] Building a community-driven platform for patients to share their medical data will combat HIB by EHR developers and data administrators to allow patients to directly share that information with scientists and researchers (Figure 10.8).

Methods

When compared with traditional recruitment methods (print, radio, television, and email), benefits of social media recruitment include reduced costs, shorter recruitment periods, better representation, and improved participant selection in young and hard to reach demographics.[118] We designed an IRB-approved study as part of the Student FIRE program at UCF College of Medicine (Figure 10.5) to investigate the use of FB to recruit a digital community of patients necessary to develop AI models of radiographic imaging to accurately predict patient's clinical outcomes (such as asymptomatic, oxygen flow, ICU admission, intubation, or even death). We leveraged our NIH-funded methods for capture and curation of imaging data for breast cancer mammography[119,120] and partnered with the HIPAA-approved TeleRay platform (Figure 10.9) to transfer, store, and ultimately return DICOM imaging for COVID-19 patients.

FB pixel is a tracking technology that developers embed in their landing pages to allow FB's proprietary AI algorithms to optimize ad placement that maximized targeted exposure that minimized the cost per click. We

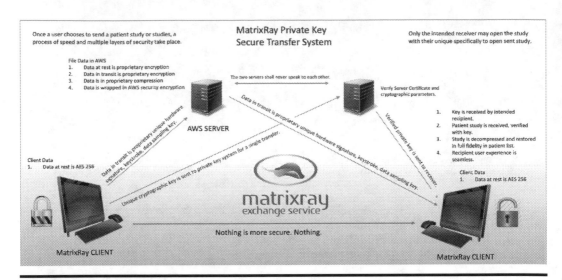

Figure 10.9   TeleRay's secure transfer peer-to-peer technology system. A combination of hardware signatures, key strokes, and mouse movements to create unique private keys that ensure foolproof data security in order to manage, collect, and redistribute patient imaging and related information, and we will use to directly transfer patient imaging through a secure cloud storage intermediate.

designed a landing page at http://CovidImaging.US and embedded FB pixel to anonymously select patients that met enrollment criteria before deploying Qualtrics questionnaires to capture PHI.

We deployed four linked Qualtrics interactive surveys via email to affirm (1) enrollment criteria, and to collect (2) informed consent, (3) medical release, and the (4) imaging sites that may hold any imaging (Table 10.1). We manually deployed a fifth unlinked survey to all subjects who shared their email address (i.e., PHI) to gauge their experience or difficulties with completing the study and to collect their COVID-19 clinical course including their general demographics and other socioeconomic factors and potential SDH that may predict their outcomes.

Results

To measure the inherent social media bias in recruiting human subjects over the Internet to access their clinical imaging for AI research, we specifically administered generic FB ads to identify patients with a history of hospitalization for COVID-19 without specifically targeting any ethnic groups or populations by design (Figure 10.10). Moreover, we employed only automated

Table 10.1 Qualtrics Surveys Were Used to Identify Imaging Sites That Hold Patient Clinical Imaging and COVID-19 Clinical Course

#	Name	Description
1	Enrollment criteria	Patient identifiable information (PII) and confirms • at least 18 years old • has been diagnosed with COVID-19 • has had chest imaging (X-ray, MRI, etc.)
2	Informed consent	Patient digitally signs to confirm they understand the risks and benefits of participation in the study
3	HIPAA release	Patient digitally signs to give access to their clinical data
4	Imaging sites	All locations that may hold their clinical imaging
N/A	COVID-19	The patient's clinical course of COVID-19 including outcomes, and any motivations or reservations in participating in the study, demographics, and socioeconomic factors including potential SDH.

The table shows the order of serial deployment, the name of the Qualtrics survey, and the description of the survey. The patient must serially complete all numbered surveys in order to release their imaging for use in the study. We designed a fifth independent study to capture the patient's clinical course of COVID-19 and other relevant factors we think are necessary to better predict outcomes from the imaging we received.

study coordination via Qualtrics email reminders every week for up to 60 days to assess attrition in the enrollment process without any human intervention or other study coordination.

We ran the study from March 2021 to November 2021, and we identified 48 distinct imaging sites we could map from 44 patients (Figure 10.11) who completed the full series of linked Qualtrics forms (Table 10.1). The geographic distribution of these imaging sites clustered locally in Central Florida, and it showed a gradual decline with increasing geographic distance from that Central Florida centroid.

To identify these 48 imaging sites, we spent just over $7K to enroll 44 patients at an average cost of $163 in FB advertisement cost per patient. The monthly distribution of Qualtrics responses (Figure 10.12) showed a sharp decline in the completion of the linked series of surveys once the initial Enrollment Criteria form was completed. On the cumulative distribution of recruitment (Table 10.2), we found the most dramatic attrition and only a

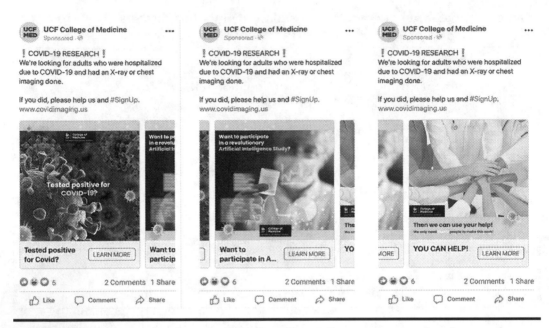

Figure 10.10   FB recruitment ad campaign. Figure shows an example ad campaign we used for recruitment of patients. By design the ad campaign was intended to target.

20% yield (104/508) of patients progressing to the Informed Consent form from the initial Enrollment Criteria one. We found the least dramatic attrition with 77% yield (80/104) of patients progressing to HIPAA Release from Informed Consent. We found a 54% yield (43/80) of patients progressing to the Imaging Sites from the HIPAA Release form.

Beyond these four serially linked Qualtrics surveys, we manually deployed a fifth COVID-19 Qualtrics survey by email (Table 10.1) to all 508 respondents that completed the initial Enrollment Criteria form, and we had 63 complete responses for gender and ethnicity (Figure 10.13). We found 55 women responded versus only 8 men which represents an almost seven-fold increase among female subjects we recruited. The 55 respondent females were dominated by 49 white women (89%), followed by 4 Latinas (7%), only one black woman (2%), and one native American female (2%). The eight respondent males were also dominated by four white men (50%), three native Americans (38%), and one black man (13%).

Given the paucity of data for men, we calculated the ethno-specific economics of FB recruitment for women (Figure 10.14). White women had the lowest recruitment costs of $183 followed by dramatic increases for more diverse ethnic subjects. We spent over $2,000 to recruit Latina respondents and this cost jumped to almost $9,000 for black women or for native American women.

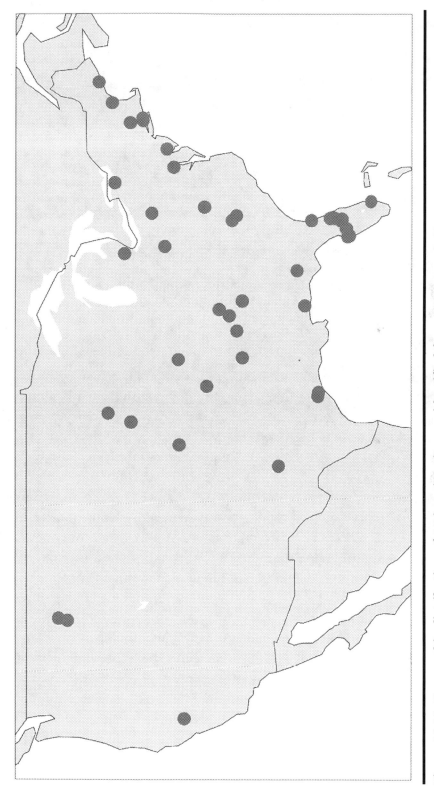

Figure 10.11 Geographic distribution of 48 imaging sites we identified from 44 respondents.

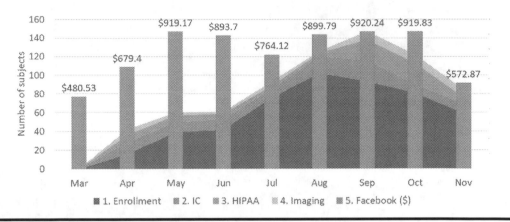

Figure 10.12   Monthly distribution of Qualtrics responses and FB costs.

Discussion

We investigated using FB to recruit adult patients with a history of COVID-19 that were willing to share their data for AI research. Our FB recruitment campaign was automated by design without any human intervention, and our attrition rate was high with over 80% subjects failing to complete the series of linked Qualtrics surveys required to share their data with us. This high attrition rate could likely be overcome with human intervention where a study coordinator could call participants to walk them through the process to complete enrollment. However, we also confirmed a significant and expected over-representation of females which means that FB would be more suited for recruitment of diseases enriched in women such as breast cancer. Moreover, Qualtrics does not allow for FB pixel embedding in their surveys, so FB pixel could only optimize for conversion at our CovidImaging.US landing page and not for subjects likely to complete the entire series which likely exaggerated our high attrition rate. We also found respondent white females on FB dominated the study population which represents a significant limitation as others have shown.[21] The costs to overcome this disparity is significant at an almost 50-fold increase in FB advertising costs alone to recruit a single black or Latina woman ($9,000) versus a single white female ($183). We may likely decrease these estimated costs with ethno-specific ads that target minority populations or by hiring ethno-specific influencers to help with recruitment.

Table 10.2 Cumulative Distribution of Facebook Adverting Costs across Qualtrics Survey Yields

Month	Enrollment		IC		HIPAA		Imaging		Total
	Average FB costs = $164/complete response								
March	N/A	(0)	N/A	(0)	N/A	(0)	N/A*	(0)	$480.53
April	$72.50	(16)	$96.66	(12)	$144.99	(8)	$193.32	(6)	$1,159.93
May	$37.80	(55)	$90.40	(23)	$138.61	(15)	$231.01	(9)	$2,079.10
June	$30.65	(97)	$87.44	(34)	$141.56	(21)	$270.25	(11)	$2,972.80
July	$21.60	(173)	$84.93	(44)	$155.71	(24)	$249.13	(15)	$3,736.92
August	$16.86	(275)	$74.79	(62)	$165.60	(28)	$272.75	(17)	$4,636.71
September	$15.10	(368)	$65.38	(85)	$111.14	(50)	$213.73	(26)	$5,556.95
October	$14.42	(449)	$68.90	(94)	$88.72	(73)	$185.05	(35)	$6,476.78
November	$13.88	(508)	$67.79	(104)	$88.12	(80)	$163.95	(43)	$7,049.65

The table shows the cumulative cost and corresponding yield of respondents in parenthesis for sequential completion of Qualtrics forms distributed by email for (1) Enrollment Criteria, (2) Informed Consent (IC), (3) HIPAA Release authorization, and (4) Imaging sites. At the end of the study, we recruited 43 individuals who shared their imaging sites with us at a cost of $163.95 in FB advertising costs.

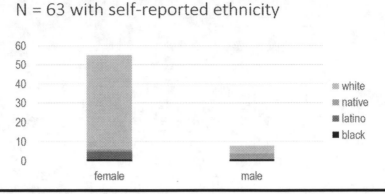

N = 63 with self-reported ethnicity

Figure 10.13 **Ethno-specific distribution of 63 respondents across gender. The stacked bar chart segregates males versus females and counts the number of respondents that are colored by their self-described ethnicity.** •

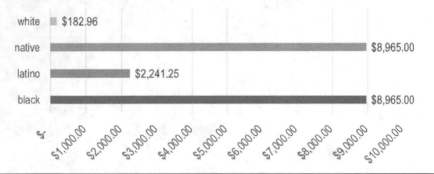

Estimated ethno-specific FB recruitment costs for women. 9x higher for men.

Figure 10.14 **Ethno-specific economics of FB recruitment of women. The bar chart shows the estimated cost of FB recruitment of women based on ethno-specific yield of FB recruitment (Figure 10.13). Anticipated costs for men are expected to be nine times higher.**

Regardless of the approach, increasing the diversity of online recruitment of patients becomes unsustainable for AI and MI where thousands of subjects are usually required to train models to achieve clinical grade performance. The meteoric rise of the Metaverse and the permanence of the data that comprise it suggests that failure to measure and correct for the lack of diverse data now will forever persist in perpetuity making AI exponentiate the existing disparities in healthcare and disease outcomes with likely unintended consequences. The transparency of the trustless algorithms that underlie this budding Metaverse, however, makes it now possible to differentially incentivize diverse patients to share their data as well as interactively probe these patients to better understand critical SDH in terms of their influence on disparate disease outcomes. In fact, the same secure cryptographic trustless algorithms underlying trillions of dollars in value in the original non-programmable Bitcoin, and now Ethereum and a host of other programmable cryptocurrencies allows us to develop ecosystems of data donation programmed to differentially reimburse for more diverse patient recruitment automatically. The Metaverse of medical data, therefore, may represent one of the best chances to develop community-driven AI that can be trained to eventually reduce disparities in disease outcomes.

Conclusion

The unparalleled rate of development of the Metaverse suggests that blockchain and subsequent DLTs are poised to revolutionize more than just the payment and finance industries. Given the existing inadequacies of the US healthcare system that COVID-19 laid bare, healthcare may be among the greatest opportunities for meaningful use of these technologies. While early pioneers have explored some of the first use cases for medical payments, EHR, HIPAA/data privacy, drug counterfeiting, and credentialing of healthcare professionals,[121] the future can be far brighter if we build patients and their data into a Metaverse with new systems that focus on trust, transparency, and most importantly the alignment of incentives to make available the patient data needed to be able to automate the complexities of today's healthcare system in the United States with AI. Therefore, the nascent Metaverse may represent among the best opportunities for a new reality of community-driven AI that is more just, equitable, diverse, and inclusive toward precision medicine for all.

References

1. The Facebook Company Is Now Meta|Meta. Accessed January 22, 2022. https://about.fb.com/news/2021/10/facebook-company-is-now-meta/
2. Nakamoto S. Bitcoin: A Peer-to-Peer Electronic Cash System. *Decentralized Business Review*. 2008. Published online October 31, 2008. Accessed October 18, 2022. https://www.debr.io/article/21260-bitcoin-a-peer-to-peer-electronic-cash-system

3. Jeon H, Youn H, Ko S, Kim T. Blockchain and AI Meet in the Metaverse. In: *Blockchain Potential in AI [Working Title]*. IntechOpen; 2021. doi:10.5772/intechopen.99114

4. Rauchs M, Glidden A, Gordon B, et al. Distributed Ledger Technology Systems: A Conceptual Framework. *SSRN Electronic Journal*. 2018. Published online August 13, 2018. doi:10.2139/SSRN.3230013

5. Townes M. The Spread of TCP/IP: How the Internet Became the Internet. *Millennium: Journal of International Studies*. 2012;41(1):43–64. doi:10.1177/0305829812449195

6. Goldenfein J, Hunter D. Blockchains, Orphan Works, and the Public Domain. *The Columbia Journal of Law & the Arts*. 2018;41(1):1–43. doi:10.7916/JLA.V41I1.2037

7. Dhillon V, Metcalf D, Hooper M. *Blockchain Enabled Applications : Understand the Blockchain Ecosystem and How to Make It Work for You*. Apress; 2021.

8. Bonneau J, Miller A, Clark J, Narayanan A, Kroll JA, Felten EW. SoK: Research Perspectives and Challenges for Bitcoin and Cryptocurrencies. *Proceedings of the IEEE Symposium on Security and Privacy*. 2015;July:104–121. doi:10.1109/SP.2015.14

9. Home|ethereum.org. Accessed January 24, 2022. https://ethereum.org/en/

10. Algorand|The Blockchain for FutureFi|Algorand. Accessed January 24, 2022. https://www.algorand.com/

11. Hello Future|Hedera. Accessed January 24, 2022. https://hedera.com/

12. Buterin V. *Ethereum: A Next-Generation Smart Contract and Decentralized Application Platform*. 2014. Accessed October 18, 2022. https://ethereum.org/669c9e2e2027310b6b3cdce6e1c52962/Ethereum_Whitepaper_-_Buterin_2014.pdf

13. Chen J, Micali S. Algorand. Published online July 5, 2016. doi:10.48550/arxiv.1607.01341

14. Baird L, Harmon M, Madsen P. *Hedera: A Public Hashgraph Network & Governing Council*. 2018. Accessed October 18, 2022. https://hedera.com/hh_whitepaper_v2.1-20200815.pdf

15. "Afghan Girl" Sharbat Gula Safely Evacuated to Italy Via Efforts of Photographer Steve McCurry, Metagood/OnChainMonkey Crypto Community & Future Brilliance Charity|Business Wire. Accessed December 22, 2021. https://www.businesswire.com/news/home/20211126005556/en/Afghan-Girl-Sharbat-Gula-Safely-Evacuated-to-Italy-Via-Efforts-of-Photographer-Steve-McCurry-MetagoodOnChainMonkey-Crypto-Community-Future-Brilliance-Charity

16. The Complutense University Presents Two Specific Training Courses in the Metaverse – Kiratas. Accessed January 24, 2022. https://www.kiratas.com/the-complutense-university-presents-two-specific-training-courses-in-the-metaverse/

17. SEVA.LOVE. Accessed December 22, 2021. https://nft.seva.love/

18. Individuals' Right under HIPAA to Access their Health Information|HHS.gov. Accessed November 12, 2017. https://www.hhs.gov/hipaa/for-professionals/privacy/guidance/access/index.html

19. Home|How We Feel. Accessed September 7, 2020. https://howwefeel.org/

20. Allen WE, Altae-Tran H, Briggs J, et al. Population-Scale Longitudinal Mapping of COVID-19 Symptoms, Behaviour and Testing. *Nat Hum Behav.* 2020:1–11. Published online August 26. doi:10.1038/s41562-020-00944-2

21. Whitaker C, Stevelink S, Fear N. The Use of Facebook in Recruiting Participants for Health Research Purposes: A Systematic Review. *Journal of Medical Internet Research.* 2017;19(8):e290. doi:10.2196/jmir.7071

22. Bustamante CDC, Francisco M, Burchard EGE, De la Vega FM. Genomics for the world. *Nature.* 2011;475(7355):163–165. doi:10.1038/475163a.Genomics

23. African American Health Inequities Compared to Non-Hispanic Whites. Accessed January 27, 2019. https://familiesusa.org/sites/default/files/product_documents/HSI-Health-disparities_african-americans-infographic.pdf

24. Schiller JS, Lucas JW, Peregoy JA. Summary health statistics for U.S. adults: National Health Interview Survey, 2011. *National Center for Health Statistics.* Published online 2012. doi:10.1037/e403882008-001

25. Moorman JE, Akinbami LJ, Bailey CM, et al. *National Surveillance of Asthma: United States, 2001-2010.* 2012. doi:10.1016/j.jpowsour.2014.10.117

26. 2012 National Healthcare Quality and Disparities Reports. Accessed January 28, 2019. https://archive.ahrq.gov/research/findings/nhqrdr/nhqrdr12/7_mental-healthsubstanceabuse/T2_7_1_1-2a.html

27. Murphy SL, Xu J, Kochanek KD. Deaths: Final Data for 2010. *National Vital Statistics Reports.* 2013;61(4):1–117. http://www.ncbi.nlm.nih.gov/pubmed/24979972

28. Heron M, Hoyert DL, Murphy SL, Xu J, Kochanek KD, Tejada-Vera B. Deaths: Final Data for 2006. *National Vital Statistics Report.* 2009;57(14):1–134. http://www.ncbi.nlm.nih.gov/pubmed/19788058

29. Anderson KM. *Roundtable on the Promotion of Health Equity and the Elimination of Health Disparities Board on Population Health and Public Health Practice.* National Academies Press; 2012.

30. Cunningham TJ, Croft JB, Liu Y, Lu H, Eke PI, Giles WH. Vital Signs: Racial Disparities in Age-Specific Mortality among Blacks or African Americans – United States, 1999–2015. *Morbidity and Mortality Weekly Report.* 2017. Published online 2017. doi:10.15585/mmwr.mm6617e1

31. Disparities Report. *2016 National Healthcare Quality and Disparities Report|Agency for Healthcare Research; Quality.* Rockville, MD: Agency for Healthcare Research and Quality. Published online 2017.

32. Williams DR. Stress and the Mental Health of Populations of Color: Advancing Our Understanding of Race-related Stressors. *Journal of Health and Social Behavior.* 2018. Published online 2018. doi:10.1177/0022146518814251

33. CDC Updates, Expands List of People at Risk of Severe COVID-19 Illness. Centers for Disease Control and Prevention. Accessed October 18, 2022. https://www.cdc.gov/media/releases/2020/p0625-update-expands-covid-19.html

34. People with Certain Medical Conditions|CDC. Accessed October 18, 2022. https://www.cdc.gov/coronavirus/2019-ncov/need-extra-precautions/people-with-medical-conditions.html

35. Diabetes and African Americans – The Office of Minority Health. Accessed October 18, 2022. https://minorityhealth.hhs.gov/omh/browse.aspx?lvl=4&lvlid=18

36. Heart Disease and African Americans – The Office of Minority Health. Accessed October 18, 2022. https://minorityhealth.hhs.gov/omh/browse.aspx?lvl=4&lvlid=19

37. Asthma and African Americans – The Office of Minority Health. Accessed October 18, 2022. https://minorityhealth.hhs.gov/omh/browse.aspx?lvl=4&lvlid=15

38. Obesity and African Americans – The Office of Minority Health. Accessed October 18, 2022. https://minorityhealth.hhs.gov/omh/browse.aspx?lvl=4&lvlid=25

39. US COVID-19 cases and deaths by state|USAFacts.

40. Bandi P, Goldmann E, Parikh NS, Farsi P, Boden-Albala B. Age-Related Differences in Antihypertensive Medication Adherence in Hispanics: A Cross-Sectional Community-Based Survey in New York City, 2011–2012. *Preventing Chronic Disease*. 2017. Published online 2017. doi:10.5888/pcd14.160512

41. Foti K, Wang D, Appel LJ, Selvin E. Hypertension Awareness, Treatment, and Control in US Adults: Trends in the Hypertension Control Cascade by Population Subgroup (National Health and Nutrition Examination Survey, 1999–2016). *American Journal of Epidemiology*. 2019. Published online 2019. doi:10.1093/aje/kwz177

42. Hales CM, Carroll MD, Fryar CD, Ogden CL. *Prevalence of Obesity and Severe Obesity among Adults: United States, 2017–2018 Key Findings Data from the National Health and Nutrition Examination Survey*. 2017. Accessed October 19, 2022. https://www.cdc.gov/nchs/data/databriefs/db360-h.pdf

43. Heart Disease and American Indians/Alaska Natives – The Office of Minority Health. Accessed October 18, 2022. https://minorityhealth.hhs.gov/omh/browse.aspx?lvl=4&lvlid=34

44. Obesity and American Indians/Alaska Natives – The Office of Minority Health. Accessed October 18, 2022. https://minorityhealth.hhs.gov/omh/browse.aspx?lvl=4&lvlid=40

45. Diabetes and American Indians/Alaska Natives – The Office of Minority Health. Accessed October 18, 2022. https://minorityhealth.hhs.gov/omh/browse.aspx?lvl=4&lvlid=33

46. Cyrus E, Clarke R, Hadley D, et al. The Impact of COVID-19 on African American Communities in the United States. *Health Equity*. 2020;4(1):476–483. doi:10.1089/heq.2020.0030

47. COVID-19 Provisional Counts - Health Disparities. Accessed October 7, 2020. https://www.cdc.gov/nchs/nvss/vsrr/covid19/health_disparities.htm

48. US COVID-19 cases and deaths by state. Accessed October 19, 2022. https://usafacts.org/visualizations/coronavirus-covid-19-spread-map

49. U.S. Census Bureau Releases 2013-2017 ACS 5-Year Estimates. https://www.census.gov/programs-surveys/acs/news/updates/2018.html

50. Cyrus E, Clarke R, Hadley D, et al. The impact of COVID-19 on African American communities in the United States. *medRxiv*. 2020. Published online May 19, 2020. doi:10.1101/2020.05.15.20096552

51. IBM Corp. Released. IBM SPSS Statistics for Windows, Version 22.0. 2011. Published online 2011.

52. CDC. Information for Healthcare Professionals about Coronavirus (COVID-19). Center for Disease Control and Prevention. Published online 2020. Accessed April 24, 2020. https://www.cdc.gov/coronavirus/2019-nCoV/hcp/index.html

53. National Center for Immunization and Respiratory Diseases (U.S.). Division of Viral Diseases. United States. Department of Homeland Security. Cybersecurity and Infrastructure Security Agency. COVID-19 in Racial and Ethnic Minority Groups. Published online 2020. Accessed October 19, 2022. https://stacks.cdc.gov/view/cdc/89820

54. Artiga S, Garfield R, Orgera K. Communities of Color at Higher Risk for Health and Economic Challenges due to COVID-19|KFF. Published 2020. Accessed October 19, 2022. https://www.kff.org/coronavirus-covid-19/issue-brief/communities-of-color-at-higher-risk-for-health-and-economic-challenges-due-to-covid-19/

55. Sohn H. Racial and Ethnic Disparities in Health Insurance Coverage: Dynamics of Gaining and Losing Coverage over the Life-Course. *Population Research and Policy Review*. 2017. Published online 2017. doi:10.1007/s11113-016-9416-y

56. Anderson KM. *Roundtable on the Promotion of Health Equity and the Elimination of Health Disparities Board on Population Health and Public Health Practice*. National Academies Press; 2012.

57. Noonan AS, Velasco-Mondragon HE, Wagner FA. Improving the Health of African Americans in the USA: An Overdue Opportunity for Social Justice. *Public Health Rev*. 2016;37(1):1–20. doi:10.1186/s40985-016-0025-4

58. Cunningham TJ, Croft JB, Liu Y, Lu H, Eke PI, Giles WH. Vital signs: Racial Disparities in Age-Specific Mortality among Blacks or African Americans – United States, 1999–2015. *Morbidity and Mortality Weekly Report*. 2017. Published online 2017. doi:10.15585/mmwr.mm6617e1

59. Mizumoto K, Kagaya K, Zarebski A, Chowell G. Estimating the Asymptomatic Proportion of Coronavirus Disease 2019 (COVID-19) Cases on Board the Diamond Princess Cruise Ship, Yokohama, Japan, 2020. *Eurosurveillance*. 2020;25(10). doi:10.2807/1560-7917.ES.2020.25.10.2000180

60. Qian G, Yang N, Ma AHY, et al. A COVID-19 Transmission within a Family Cluster by Presymptomatic Infectors in China. *Clinical Infectious Diseases*. 2020. Published online March 23, 2020. doi:10.1093/cid/ciaa316

61. Bai Y, Yao L, Wei T, et al. Presumed Asymptomatic Carrier Transmission of COVID-19. *JAMA – Journal of the American Medical Association.* 2020;323(14):1406–1407. doi:10.1001/jama.2020.2565

62. Hu Z, Song C, Xu C, et al. Clinical Characteristics of 24 Asymptomatic Infections with COVID-19 Screened among Close Contacts in Nanjing, China. *Science China Life Sciences.* 2020;63(5):706–711. doi:10.1007/s11427-020-1661-4

63. Singu S, Acharya A, Challagundla K, Byrareddy SN. Impact of Social Determinants of Health on the Emerging COVID-19 Pandemic in the United States. *Front Public Health.* 2020;8:406. doi:10.3389/fpubh.2020.00406

64. NIH Funds New Consortium Aimed at Advancing Health Equity and Researcher Diversity|Data Science at NIH. Accessed January 22, 2022. https://datascience.nih.gov/news/nih-funds-new-consortium-aimed-at-advancing-health-equity-and-researcher-diversity

65. Data Generation Projects for the NIH Bridge to Artificial Intelligence (Bridge2AI) Program (OT2). Accessed October 19, 2022. https://commonfund.nih.gov/sites/default/files/OT2-Data-Generation-Projects-B2AI-051321-508.pdf

66. Crawford K. The Trouble with Bias NIPS 2017 Keynote Kate Crawford # NIPS 2017 fMym_BKWQzk. Published 2017. Accessed October 19, 2022. https://archive.org/details/the-trouble-with-bias-nips-2017-keynote-kate-crawford-nips-2017-f-mym-bkwqzk

67. Topol EJ. A decade of digital medicine innovation. *Science Translational Medicine.* 2019;11(498). doi:10.1126/scitranslmed.aaw7610

68. Manchikanti L, Falco FJE, Benyamin R, Helm S, Parr AT, Hirsch JA. The Impact of Comparative Effectiveness Research on Interventional Pain Management: Evolution from Medicare Modernization Act to Patient Protection and Affordable Care Act and the Patient-Centered Outcomes Research Institute. *Pain Physician.* 2011;14(3):E249-82.

69. Franck LS, McLemore MR, Williams S, et al. Research priorities of women at risk for preterm birth: Findings and a call to action. *BMC Pregnancy Childbirth.* 2020;20(1):10. doi:10.1186/s12884-019-2664-1

70. Lo B, Zhang T, Leung K, et al. Identifying Best Approaches for Engaging Patients and Family Members in Health Informatics Initiatives: A Case Study of the Group Priority Sort Technique. *Research Involvement and Engagement.* 2020;6(1):25. doi:10.1186/s40900-020-00203-8

71. Andress L, Hall T, Davis S, Levine J, Cripps K, Guinn D. Addressing Power Dynamics in Community-Engaged Research Partnerships. *Journal of Patient Reported Outcomes.* 2020;4(1):24. doi:10.1186/s41687-020-00191-z

72. Esmail L, Moore E, Rein A. Evaluating Patient and Stakeholder Engagement in Research: Moving from Theory to Practice. *Journal of Comparative Effectiveness Research.* 2015;4(2):133–145. doi:10.2217/cer.14.79

73. Forsythe L, Heckert A, Margolis MK, Schrandt S, Frank L. Methods and Impact of Engagement in Research, from Theory to Practice and Back Again: Early Findings from the Patient-Centered Outcomes Research Institute. *Quality of Life Research.* 2018;27(1):17–31. doi:10.1007/s11136-017-1581-x

74. Kraft SA, McMullen C, Lindberg NM, et al. Integrating Stakeholder Feedback in Translational Genomics Research: An Ethnographic Analysis of a Study Protocol's Evolution. *Genetics in Medicine*. 2020;22(6):1094–1101. doi:10.1038/s41436-020-0763-z

75. Forsythe LP, Ellis LE, Edmundson L, et al. Patient and Stakeholder Engagement in the PCORI Pilot Projects: Description and Lessons Learned. *Journal of General Internal Medicine*. 2016;31(1):13–21. doi:10.1007/s11606-015-3450-z

76. Hemphill R, Forsythe LP, Heckert AL, et al. What Motivates Patients and Caregivers to Engage in Health Research and How Engagement Affects Their Lives: Qualitative Survey Findings. *Health Expectations*. 2020;23(2):328–336. doi:10.1111/hex.12979

77. Forsythe LP, Carman KL, Szydlowski V, et al. Patient Engagement in Research: Early Findings from the Patient-Centered Outcomes Research Institute. *Health Affairs*. 2019;38(3):359–367. doi:10.1377/hlthaff.2018.05067

78. Turakhia MP, Desai M, Hedlin H, et al. Rationale and Design of a Large-Scale, App-Based Study to Identify Cardiac Arrhythmias Using a Smartwatch: The Apple Heart Study. *American Heart Journal*. 2019;207:66–75. doi:10.1016/J.AHJ.2018.09.002

79. Murray J. The "All of Us" Research Program. *The New England Journal of Medicine*. 2019;381(19):1884. doi:10.1056/NEJMc1912496

80. Ba J, Mnih V, Kavukcuoglu K. Multiple Object Recognition with Visual Attention. *International Conference on Learning Representations*. 2014. Published online December 24, 2014:1–10. doi:10.48550/arXiv.1412.7755

81. The Three Breakthroughs That Have Finally Unleashed AI on the World|WIRED. Accessed October 5, 2015. http://www.wired.com/2014/10/future-of-artificial-intelligence/

82. Gonzalez-Dominguez J, Lopez-Moreno I, Moreno PJ, Gonzalez-Rodriguez J. Frame-by-Frame Language Identification in Short Utterances Using Deep Neural Networks. *Neural Networks*. 2015;64:49–58. doi:10.1016/j.neunet.2014.08.006

83. Nair A, Srinivasan P, Blackwell S, et al. Massively Parallel Methods for Deep Reinforcement Learning. 2015:14. Published online 2015. *arXiv:150704296.*84. Angelova A, Krizhevsky A, Vanhoucke V. Pedestrian Detection with a Large-Field-of-View Deep Network. *Proceedings – IEEE International Conference on Robotics and Automation*. Vol 2015-June. 2015:704–711. doi:10.1109/ICRA.2015.7139256

85. Heigold G, Vanhoucke V, Senior A, et al. Multilingual Acoustic Models Using Distributed Deep Neural Networks. *The International Conference on Acoustics, Speech, & Signal Processing*. 2013:8619–8623. doi:10.1109/ICASSP.2013.6639348

86. Hinton G, Deng L, Yu D, et al. Deep Neural Networks for Acoustic Modeling in Speech Recognition. *IEEE Signal Processing Magazine*. 2012;(November):82–97. doi:10.1109/MSP.2012.2205597

87. Zeiler MD, Ranzato M, Monga R, et al. On Rectified Linear Units for Speech Processing. *IEEE International Conference on Acoustics, Speech and Signal Processing – Proceedings*. 2013:3517–3521. doi:10.1109/ICASSP.2013.6638312

88. Karpathy A, Toderici G, Shetty S, Leung T, Sukthankar R, Li FF. Large-scale video classification with convolutional neural networks. *Proceedings of the IEEE Computer Society Conference on Computer Vision and Pattern Recognition*. 2014:1725–1732. doi:10.1109/CVPR.2014.223

89. Szegedy C, Liu W, Jia Y, et al. Going Deeper with Convolutions. *Proceedings of the IEEE Computer Society Conference on Computer Vision and Pattern Recognition*. 2014:1–9. doi:10.1109/CVPR.2015.7298594

90. Frome A, Corrado G, Shlens J. Devise: A Deep Visual-Semantic Embedding Model. *Advances in Neural Information Processing Systems*. 2013:1–11. Published online 2013.

91. Vinyals O, Kaiser L, Koo T, Petrov S, Sutskever I, Hinton G. Grammar as a Foreign Language. 2014:1–10. Published online 2014. doi:10.1146/annurev. neuro.26.041002.131047

92. Mikolov T, Corrado G, Chen K, Dean J. Efficient Estimation of Word Representations in Vector Space. *Proceedings of the International Conference on Learning Representations (ICLR 2013)*. 2013:1–12. Published online 2013. doi:10.1162/153244303322533223

93. Le QV, Ranzato M, Monga R, et al. Building High-Level Features Using Large Scale Unsupervised Learning. *International Conference in Machine Learning*. 2011:38115. Published online 2011. doi:10.1109/MSP.2011.940881

94. Ramsundar B, Kearnes S, Riley P, Webster D, Konerding D, Pande V. Massively Multitask Networks for Drug Discovery. 2015. Published online February 6.

95. Lusci A, Pollastri G, Baldi P. Deep Architectures and Deep Learning in Chemoinformatics: The Prediction of Aqueous Solubility for Drug-Like Molecules. *Journal of Chemical Information and Modeling*. 2013;53(7):1563–1575. doi:10.1021/ci400187y

96. Alipanahi B, Delong A, Weirauch MT, Frey BJ. Predicting the Sequence Specificities of DNA- and RNA-Binding Proteins by Deep Learning. *Nature Biotechnology*. 2015;33(8):831–838. doi:10.1038/nbt.3300

97. Deng J, Dong W, Socher R, Li L-J, Li K, Li Fi-F. ImageNet: A Large-Scale Hierarchical Image Database. *2009 IEEE Conference on Computer Vision and Pattern Recognition*. 2009:2–9. Published online 2009. doi:10.1109/CVPR.2009.5206848

98. Russakovsky O, Deng J, Su H, et al. ImageNet Large Scale Visual Recognition Challenge. *International Journal of Computer Vision*. 2015;115(3):211–252. doi:10.1007/s11263-015-0816-y

99. Krizhevsky A, Sutskever I, Hinton GE. ImageNet Classification with Deep Convolutional Neural Networks. *Advances in Neural Information Processing Systems*. 2012:1097–1105.

100. Google AI Blog: Using Machine Learning to Explore Neural Network Architecture. Accessed January 24, 2019. https://ai.googleblog.com/2017/05/using-machine-learning-to-explore.html

101. He K, Zhang X, Ren S, Sun J. Delving Deep into Rectifiers: Surpassing Human-Level Performance on ImageNet Classification.

102. Huang G, Liu Z, Van Der Maaten L, Weinberger KQ. Densely Connected Convolutional Networks. In: *Proceedings – 30th IEEE Conference on Computer Vision and Pattern Recognition, CVPR 2017*. Vol 2017-January; 2017:2261–2269. doi:10.1109/CVPR.2017.243

103. Shin HCC, Roth HR, Gao M, et al. Deep Convolutional Neural Networks for Computer-Aided Detection: CNN Architectures, Dataset Characteristics and Transfer Learning. *IEEE Trans Med Imaging*. 2016;35(5):1285–1298. doi:10.1109/TMI.2016.2528162

104. Simonyan K, Zisserman A. Very Deep Convolutional Networks for Large-Scale Image Recognition. In: *3rd International Conference on Learning Representations, ICLR 2015 – Conference Track Proceedings*. 2015.

105. Cao C, Liu X, Yang Y, et al. Look and Think Twice: Capturing Top-Down Visual Attention with Feedback Convolutional Neural Networks. *Proceedings of the IEEE International Conference on Computer Vision*. 2015:2956–2964. doi:10.1109/ICCV.2015.338

106. Canziani A, Paszke A, Culurciello E. An Analysis of Deep Neural Network Models for Practical Applications. 2016:1–17. Published online May 24, 2016. doi:10.48550/arXiv.1605.07678

107. Szegedy C, Ioffe S, Vanhoucke V, Alemi AA. Inception-v4, inception-ResNet and the impact of residual connections on learning. In: *31st AAAI Conference on Artificial Intelligence, AAAI 2017*. 2017. Accessed November 16, 2016. http://arxiv.org/abs/1602.07261

108. (ONC) O of the NC for HIT. Report on Health Information Blocking. 2015:1–39. Published online 2015.

109. Patel A, Desai S. Ivermectin in COVID-19 Related Critical Illness. 2020. *SSRN Electronic Journal*. Published online 2020. doi:10.2139/ssrn.3570270

110. Mehra MR, Desai SS, Kuy S, Henry TD, Patel AN. Cardiovascular Disease, Drug Therapy, and Mortality in Covid-19. *New England Journal of Medicine*. Published online May 1, 2020:NEJMoa2007621. doi:10.1056/nejmoa2007621

111. Mehra MR, Desai SS, Ruschitzka F, Patel AN, The Lancet Editors TL. Hydroxychloroquine or chloroquine with or without a macrolide for treatment of COVID-19: a multinational registry analysis. *The Lancet*. 2020;0(0). doi:10.1016/S0140-6736(20)31180-6

112. Rubin EJ. Expression of Concern: Mehra MR et al. Cardiovascular Disease, Drug Therapy, and Mortality in Covid-19. *New England Journal of Medicine*. doi:10.1056/NEJMoa2007621. *New England Journal of Medicine*. Published online June 2, 2020. doi:10.1056/nejme2020822

113. The Lancet Editors TL. Expression of Concern: Hydroxychloroquine or Chloroquine with or without a Macrolide for Treatment of COVID-19: A Multinational Registry Analysis. *The Lancet*. 2020. doi:10.1016/S0140-6736(20)31290-3

114. Jin S, Wang B, Xu H, et al. AI-Assisted CT Imaging Analysis for COVID-19 Screening: Building and Deploying a Medical AI System in Four Weeks. *medRxiv*. 2020. Published online March 23, 2020. doi:10.1101/2020.03.19.20039354

115. Wang L, Wong A. COVID-Net: A Tailored Deep Convolutional Neural Network Design for Detection of COVID-19 Cases from Chest X-Ray Images. 2020. Published online 2020.
116. Harmon SA, Sanford TH, Xu S, et al. Artificial Intelligence for the Detection of COVID-19 Pneumonia on Chest CT Using Multinational Datasets. *Nature Communications*. 2020;11(1):4080. doi:10.1038/s41467-020-17971-2
117. Cohen JP, Morrison P, Dao L. COVID-19 Image Data Collection. 2020. Published online March 25.
118. Betsch C. Social Media Targeting of Health Messages: A Promising Approach for Research and Practice. *Human Vaccines and Immunotherapeutics*. 2014;10(9):2636–2637. doi:10.4161/hv.32234
119. Lituiev DS, Trivedi H, Panahiazar M, et al. Automatic Labeling of Special Diagnostic Mammography Views from Images and DICOM Headers. *Journal of Digital Imaging*. 2019;32(2):228–233. doi:10.1007/s10278-018-0154-z
120. Trivedi HM, Panahiazar M, Liang A, et al. Large Scale Semi-Automated Labeling of Routine Free-Text Clinical Records for Deep Learning. *Journal of Digital Imaging*. 2019;32(1):30–37. doi:10.1007/s10278-018-0105-8
121. Metcalf D (David S), Bass J (Founder and C of HH, Hooper M (CEO of MT, Cahana A, Dhillon V (Research fellow). *Blockchain in Healthcare : Innovations That Empower Patients, Connect Professionals and Improve Care.*

Chapter 11

Remote Respiratory Care for Rural Asia— Impetus for the World

Chris Landon and Vinay Joshi

Contents

Introduction

COVID-19 has and will deepen economic and social inequalities: jobs—people who are unable to work from home have lost their income/have greater risk of infection; digital divide—countries lacking the digital capabilities for workers to work from home; gender gap—women are more likely to take care of children and domestic chores, leading to an unequal distribution of household duties within the family; increasing protectionism—greater

DOI: 10.4324/b23264-11

protectionism in developed countries shuts developing countries out of their richer markets, leaving limited opportunities to gain from world trade; vaccine access—low-income countries will bear heavy costs, both human and economic, if the advanced economies reserve essential medical supplies for their own citizens and if they cut, rather than expand, aid, and other concessional financial support.

Access to Healthcare

The combination of ventilator shortages, lack of healthcare workers, and the challenges of rural area vaccination highlight the importance of remote respiratory care as a current solution in rural areas. Tele-ventilators will require fewer healthcare workers to manage along with fewer bedside visits, hence also reducing infection risk.

Ventilator shortages in 2020 were magnified in developed nations. Countries in Asia faced shortages in ventilators, including rural Malaysia, India, and Indonesia. By March of 2020 garbage bags were used by nurses as personal protective equipment (PPE), single ventilators in hospitals with global demand for ventilators ten times what was available. By July of 2020 the rush to produce ventilators in India non-invasive features were skipped.

Country case studies published by the United Nations Children's Fund (UNICEF) on the topic of immunization and related health services for the urban poor in Cambodia, Indonesia, Mongolia, Myanmar, the Philippines, and Vietnam, found that in urban areas, low immunization coverage is associated with lower socio-economic status. This could be due to lack of legal status, living in areas where there is limited public health infrastructure and services. This is especially acute in rural areas. According to the World Bank, in 2019, 65.6% of the population in South Asia and 40.1% of the population in East Asia and the Pacific live in rural areas. In Asia's rural areas with poor infrastructure, there are challenges to conquer for COVID-19 vaccines including education. There is also a lack of healthcare workers— the world's poorest populations are located mainly in Southeast Asia, with the largest shortfall of healthcare workers, and in Asia Pacific, the migration of healthcare workers from Philippines, Bangladesh, and Indonesia to the Middle East further compounds the problem. WHO predicts that by 2030, worldwide demand for health workers will increase to 80 million, but only

65 million will be supplied, amounting to a shortage 15 million workers. WHO Southeast Asia region needs to increase nurses and midwives by 1.9 million to achieve health for all by 2030.

Solutions

With the vaccination challenges in rural areas, the importance of remote healthcare cannot be overlooked. This led to start-ups accelerating projects mid-pandemic. Resmetrix is developing a wearable sensor to detect respiratory inconsistencies and is wirelessly connected to a smartphone app that provides real-time access to respiratory and vital signs for the patient and clinicians; enables health systems to monitor quarantined or mildly ill COVID-19 patients, avoiding unnecessary hospital trips and preventing exposure to the coronavirus. ResApp Health has developed a smartphone application that can accurately diagnose disease from cough and respiratory sounds. COVID-19 is a respiratory disease, with symptoms akin to other respiratory diseases. Apps like these enable patients to receive medical examinations at home, eliminating the risk of spreading the virus in overcrowded hospitals.

ABM Respiratory Care has developed the world's first tele-ventilator which includes advanced ventilator modes as well as key safety and alarm features as per international regulatory standards. Healthcare professionals can securely monitor and adjust ventilator settings through their online portal from any location. The tele-ventilator allows healthcare professionals the ability to monitor and program numerous ventilators from anywhere in the world, with real-time response. By utilizing the telehealth connection, they can reduce the number of bedside visits they perform to check the ventilator and reduce their exposure to infected patients.

The first ventilator was completed in June 2020 in Singapore, at a time of great need and severe shortage. When set up in rural areas with a lack of healthcare workers, with numerous patients with respiratory conditions, the Alpha ventilators reduce the strain on the healthcare system, as they require less healthcare professionals to operate. Additionally, the Alpha ventilators will reduce exposure and hence infection risk, reducing the potential spread of COVID-19.

Produced at less than half the cost of normal ventilators, the price point makes it more accessible to hospitals or care centers in rural areas. The

Alpha ventilator can help patients with both the invasive and non-invasive ventilating options, providing care for patients that need either option.

In the Pandemic and Beyond: Tele-ventilation Opens the Way for Respiratory Care Everywhere

Across the world, mechanical ventilation enables patients to breathe easier. However, each time a setting needs to change, a trained healthcare provider needs to make that adjustment. In the pandemic, that means donning a new full set of PPE each time the provider enters the patient's room—risking disease transmission. Even beyond the pandemic, ventilators require trained staff close at hand to continually monitor and optimize each patient's therapy as their condition changes.

In locations where PPE supplies and/or trained staff may be scarce, a way to mitigate these barriers to care is with the use of a tele-ventilator such as Alpha from ABM Respiratory Care. The Alpha ventilator gives healthcare professionals the flexibility to program and monitor the device from anywhere in the world—with real-time response. This telehealth connection effectively reduces the: volume of PPE needed; number of bedside visits required to check the ventilator; risk of healthcare staff exposure to infected patients; and need to travel by expanding a provider's reach and ability to deliver immediate support.

A Novel Way to Address a Critical Shortage

Demand for ventilators has exponentially increased during the COVID-19 pandemic. This unforeseen burden has created a significant shortage not only in the life-saving devices, but also the trained healthcare professionals to program and manage them.

The pandemic revealed how vital remote management of healthcare is, particularly in geographies with limited access to medical infrastructure. Even areas with highly developed healthcare systems have quickly become overwhelmed with people needing emergency and ongoing care. These new realities reinforce the need for an innovation like the Alpha ventilator: As the world's first tele-ventilator, Alpha is ideally suited for treating patients globally with infectious diseases.

Alpha uses an advanced turbine technology to implement several therapy modes for invasive and non-invasive ventilation. The ventilator can be used with both pediatric and adult patients in the hospital, skilled nursing facilities and home care environments. The large touchscreen and simplified navigation enable users to quickly master the skills needed to operate Alpha. The user interface was created based upon months of clinician feedback on the navigation menus and monitoring functions to provide an optimal clinical experience—without extensive training.

Cutting-Edge Security

As with any remote monitor device, data security has to be at the highest level to guard against malicious breaches. This includes employing certification-based authentication mechanisms and other advanced means of ensuring cybersecurity.

Multi-Encounter Longitudinal in Situ Simulation with Alpha Ventilator ("MERIT")

The Department of Respiratory & Critical Care Medicine Dr Sewa Duu Wen, Senior Consultant Dr Chai Hui Zhong, Consultant Ms. Constance Teo, Principal Respiratory Therapist Dr Michelle Koh, Senior Resident Dr Tan Hui Li, Advanced Practice Nurse Ms. Huang Ching-Feng, Respiratory Therapist were engaged by ABM Respiratory Care to conduct an evaluation of the onboarding in the face of COVID-19 infectiousness.

The COVID-19 pandemic has placed enormous strain on healthcare systems around the world, especially when there are large numbers of patients with respiratory failure who may require ventilator support in the intensive care unit (ICU). This has not only created a worldwide shortage of ventilators for patients with severe COVID-19 but also a shortage of ICU-trained healthcare professionals ("intensivists") to manage the large number of mechanically ventilated patients. The demand for intensivists exceeds available supply in many regions, and exposed disparities in distribution of access to critical care expertise across hospitals. The highly infectious nature of this disease also requires changes in peacetime ICU workflows to limit contact time between the healthcare professionals and infected patients so as to minimize the risk of healthcare transmission of the disease.

The potential impact of a tele-ventilator on productivity, infection control, safety of healthcare professionals and patients in the pandemic ICU is tremendous. The delay in response time in negative pressure isolation rooms and meeting infection control requirements for healthcare staff and patient safety have had an impact on productivity in the pandemic ICUs. In Singapore General Hospital, all COVID-19 ICU patients had only been admitted to negative pressure isolation rooms. A negative pressure isolation room is designed to contain airborne pathogens within the patient's room with the addition of an anteroom and ventilation systems to keep the patient's room and anteroom negatively pressured relative to adjacent spaces. Compared to normal pressure rooms, a significantly longer time is required for healthcare professionals to don PPE and wait for the anteroom to be negatively pressured before they can enter the patient's room. This delay may be mitigated with the use of the tele-ventilator, as remote troubleshooting and changing of ventilator settings may be initiated before entering the patient's room.

Patients infected with COVID-19 are kept under airborne and contact isolation precautions to prevent disease transmission. Healthcare professionals need to don a N95 respirator and face shield or powered air purifying respirator (PAPR), isolation gown, and gloves to perform patient care. The global surge in demand for PPE had prompted resource conservation in hospitals. To reduce the number of times that Restricted, Sensitive (Normal) healthcare professionals don a new set of PPE, patient care activities are consolidated and remote monitoring can help to meet this shortage.

During a pandemic, surges in ICU utilization may require hospitals to rapidly expand capacity and implement tiered staffing models where physicians without formal critical care training have to care for severely ill patients. Although the physical ICU bed capacity may not be exceeded, the increased number and acuity of patients due to COVID-19 will create strain in pre-existing staffing models and among teams that are unaccustomed to caring for such a combination of patient volume and acuity. It is usually not possible to just deploy more intensivists on the ground, so innovative solutions are needed to expand the reach of physicians with critical care expertise. Tele-ventilation allows respiratory care providers, including intensivists and respiratory therapists (RT), to remotely participate in the care of mechanically ventilated patients and provide advice to a less experienced team on the ground. Combined with the use of other technologies, the tele-ventilator can provide the best environment for a virtual meeting coordinated between the off-site intensivist and on-site team to discuss cases in a combined patient round. The off-site intensivist can assist the team in making changes on the ventilators or even effect changes himself, but this should be done with full knowledge of the on-site team. This can increase access to critical care expertise during the COVID-19 pandemic and also shorten the response time to alterations in patient's respiratory physiology. The ratio of respiratory care provider to patients can be potentially increased due to more efficient delivery of care. Multiple patients at different localities can be concurrently reviewed by a single respiratory care provider. This will increase the available ICU resources during a surge and help to reduce burnout due to lower manpower requirements. By using the tele-ventilator function coupled with other telemonitoring tools, the hospital can consider tapping on critical care trained staff who would otherwise be unable to care for patients during the pandemic (due to high risk factors, quarantined status, or retired doctors) using the remote function to expand the pool of ICU manpower available to contribute in a pandemic surge. In addition, peacetime teaching activities can continue as the senior staff can provide supervision to junior staff through the tele-ventilation function.

This all demands a new assessment of workflow in the pandemic ICU. We have identified a list of best practices that will help to increase the success of implementing a tele-ventilator system such as Alpha ventilator in ICUs. The list includes factors to maintain critical care quality standards while addressing concerns of healthcare safety and operational efficiencies in this process. Restricted, Sensitive (Normal). This begins with the identification of clinical champions to implement tele-ventilator management system. This is an important and crucial step to identify one or more clinical leaders to serve as champions at each institution and facilitate the implementation of such a system. These leaders should have explicit buy-in from hospital senior management for such an initiative. These champions will form the link between the vendor and the users on the ground and help to identify the optimal local care models, fine-tune workflows, and provide opportunity to troubleshoot any challenges during implementation.

Standards of care should improve and establishing pre-implementation benchmarks prior to rolling out new tele-ventilator management system is an essential part of this process. By gathering baseline data before initiating the tele-ventilator management system, users can better assess where improvements have been achieved post-tele-ventilator implementation and where more work is needed. Logistical and resource management benchmarks may include ventilator-related frequency of users' entry into the isolation room, time spent per entry, rate of PPE consumption, and man-hours per patient spent on work related to ventilator adjustment. Patient safety benchmarks may include response time to critical ventilator alarms, frequency of critical ventilator alarms, and compliance to evidence-based standards of mechanical ventilation care, for example, lung protective ventilation.

Additionally, this requires establishing protocols for ventilator-related activities which can benefit from remote monitoring and remote adjustment of settings. By providing protocol-based management and establishing activities which can be predominantly managed with remote adjustment of the tele-ventilators will allow maximizing the benefits and limiting patient safety issues.

These can include: (1) Daily assessment and titration of ventilator settings based on bedside physiological parameters or arterial blood gas result. (2) Troubleshooting and silencing non-critical alarms after assessment of patient's conditions remotely or based on input from ICU nurses who are already inside the room. (3) Daily screening and ensuring compliance to evidence-based lung protective mechanical ventilation measures on all ventilated patients using a dashboard function. (4) Transitioning between different modes of mechanical ventilation through remote adjustment. (5) Initiating and terminating spontaneous breathing trial (SBT) when patients fulfill institutional criteria for sedation break and SBT. (6) Rapidly switching to emergency ventilator settings while the healthcare professionals prepare to don the appropriate PPE to enter the isolation room to reduce the length of inadequate ventilator support during medical emergencies.

In this modern age of digitally driven record keeping patient's data confidentiality is key but also preventing unauthorized access to patient's ventilator control. Restricted, Sensitive (Normal) Innovative connected health technologies offer a promising solution to many of the challenges facing healthcare delivery. However, there are significant privacy and security risks in telehealth systems that can adversely affect patients' and clinicians' levels of trust and willingness to adopt and use the system. Tele-ventilator vendors need to work closely with the hospital's IT system provider to guard against potential security loopholes and backdoors that can lead to breaches in patient's data confidentiality or even allow malicious changes in the patient's ventilator settings. There must be robust safeguards in place to avoid human as well as systemic errors.

What becomes clear is that continued evaluation, experience, and adoption will lead to adoption outside the ICU. Within the ICU, the current version of the Alpha ventilator used in the simulation study is suitable for COVID-19 patients who require stable ventilator settings and are being gradually weaned off mechanical ventilation. As oxygen is supplied via a low flow device like a flow meter, the Alpha ventilator can also be used for patient transport or chronic home ventilation in patients' homes or long-term care facilities. The tele-ventilation function would allow a chronic ventilation specialist in the specialist hospital to remotely monitor ventilated patients in the community. This is analogous to wearable ECG monitors and blood pressure monitors that encourage patients to manage personal health better and enable clinicians to better understand their patients' conditions. In healthcare systems where chronic ventilation specialists work with geographic networks of community healthcare professionals to care for patients spread over large distances, the specialists may use the tele-ventilation function to guide community healthcare professionals to monitor and change ventilator settings. This would save significant time and costs as ventilated patients have to travel in an ambulance or specialized wheelchair van. In the absence of a healthcare professional, most changes in ventilator settings should not be performed remotely as a thorough physical examination of the patient and close observation of the patient's reaction(s) are required for patient safety.

Summary

When combined with vital signs monitoring from the ICU's central physiological monitor, a well-documented recent physical examination and clinical management guidelines, the Alpha ventilator is suitable for use in the COVID-19 pandemic ICU. It has the necessary ventilation modes to provide invasive and non-invasive ventilator support for patients on stable ventilator support and its tele-ventilation function allows remote monitoring of patient's ventilation parameters and quick ventilator setting changes before entering the patient's room in the event of a medical emergency. To maintain limited contact time with patients and increase the hospital's capacity in the event of a surge, non-specialists can make ventilator setting changes within the patient's room under the remote supervision of intensivists and respiratory care providers.

Chapter 12

High-Throughput Antibody Discovery Comes of Age in Response to COVID-19

Tim Germann

Contents

The Carterra LSA and how biologics discovery will never be the same.

How Carterra's LSA platform has changed biologics discovery for this pandemic and the next.

"Do you know why I'm here?"

I had just interrupted the Chief Executive Officer of Carterra, a little-known biotech company in Salt Lake City, Utah. Josh Eckman was barely 40 years old but had been a co-founder of the company and CEO for about 15 years. I was only a few minutes into my first visit and Josh was already a chapter or so into his talk track on how the business came to be when I could tell he wasn't sure what I was doing there.

"Uh, no," he replied, a bit surprised that his confusion was so obvious.

DOI: 10.4324/b23264-12

We were suddenly in a stand-off there in the exceptionally wide hallway of what was originally St. Mark's Episcopal hospital-turnedoffice building. Josh had been a tenant there as the co-founder of Carterra for a decade.

The building had a glorious pedigree as a hospital but more recently as a place of world-changing experiments and discoveries. Shortly after aging out of its original charter as a hospital, it became the home of the University of Utah's Institute for Biomedical Engineering and its Artificial Heart Research Laboratory which conducted experiments there with implanted artificial hearts in calves and sheep.[1]

Josh knew that history when he leased his first office there in 2007. The spirit of discovery was strong in that building and he wanted his company to follow the lead of Dr. Willem Kolff and Dr. Don Olsen who both used their experience in that building to eventually develop and implant the first artificial heart in one Barney Clark.[2]

I had been consulting for a few years helping technology companies get sea legs in their respective markets. The process of early stage commercialization is not intuitive to folks who have never scaled a business and I had begun to leverage about 25 years of experience as a commercial operator into a nice living as a consultant.

In the summer of 2017, a long-time friend who had made his fortunes in venture capital called to let me know that his firm had made an equity investment in a small life science company in Salt Lake City. Indeed, they had acquired a majority interest.[3]

Having gone to college in Utah many years prior, I was aware of biotech and life science companies spinning out of the fertile research community at the University of Utah and, to a lesser degree, Brigham Young University.

"What did you buy in Salt Lake?" I asked my friend.

"Wasatch Microfluidics. They're not yet commercial but we think there's some real potential there. Would you take a look at it?"

That's how I ended up in that stand-off with Josh. I eventually explained to him how I had come to know about Wasatch (eventually renamed Carterra) and that I was excited to not only meet his acquaintance but also to learn more about what they were doing.

The Origins of Wasatch

Wasatch Microfluidics was a product of the University of Utah's Lassonde Entrepreneur Institute, one of the nation's top-10 programs for founding businesses per *U.S. News and World Report*.[4] At Lassonde, both graduates and undergraduates are instructed, funded, and even housed as they learn how to establish and run successful businesses.

Josh Eckman had been an enterprising business undergraduate but at the successful attainment of his degree, he felt the need to stretch his academic muscles and applied to several graduate engineering programs—a bit backward for most people but not for a guy this smart.

Admitted to the University of Utah's graduate engineering program, Josh teamed up with his advisor, Dr. Bruce Gale, who had a binder full of ideas and intellectual property. Through a few coincidences and a verifiable need from another department at the University, Josh and Bruce settled on a technology that included a silicone manifold that could move very small amounts of fluid around—microliters—and deposit them on a surface.

In 2004, Josh took the concept to the Lassonde Institute and made a presentation about how the device could be used to actually *print* certain types of molecules in solution onto a surface. Present for that presentation was a young doctoral student, Jim Smith, who had come to Lassonde from the Department of Materials Science to apply for a fellowship. Little did he know that he would become enamored with Josh's technology that day. As Jim tells the story, Josh had him at the word *silicone* ....

Jim would soon join Josh and Bruce in founding Wasatch Microfluidics based on developing and commercializing what became known as the Continuous Flow Microspotter (CFM). Wasatch was founded using funding from Lassonde and slowly but surely the CFM began to emerge as a real solution for highly parallelized analysis of biomolecules.

The CFM miniaturizes what researchers have been doing in larger quantities for decades. When you can accurately and precisely do those experiments using a fraction of the fluid or sample, your experiments are more efficient and a lot faster. You can begin to do dozens or hundreds of individual experiments at the same time (Figure 12.1).

While the CFM had a number of applications it found the most traction when combined with a detection technique called surface plasmon resonance, or SPR. SPR uses the diffraction of light directed at a surface to determine changes in mass on that surface. So, in the case of the CFM, researchers were able to print biomolecules like proteins—more specifically antibodies—on the sensor surface and then watch in real time as other molecules—like antigens—were washed over the antibodies to see how the molecules acted in each other's presence.

Figure 12.1 Proprietary fluidics are at the heart of Carterra's intellectual property. Shown here is the printhead which enables the bi-directional flow of proteins in microchannels to the surface of a biosensor. This type of printing under flow maintains sensitive proteins throughout immobilization.

Prior to the advent of Carterra's CFM, researchers could only watch this molecular dance a few samples at a time. Original versions of SPR devices could accommodate just two samples. Then, over 30 years, the technology advanced enough to be able to see eight of these interactions at a time. The CFM has shattered this arduous and low-throughput paradigm by allowing scientists to now evaluate almost 400 samples simultaneously in real time.

The promise of the CFM combined with SPR detection energized Wasatch's founders. They began developing a compelling business case which they eventually entered into several competitions. After a solid fourth-place finish at a competition in Oregon, they returned home and in 2005 entered Utah's well-regarded Entrepreneur Challenge … and won first place which netted them $70,000. That money then funded the move from Bruce's garage to their modest beginnings at that hospital-turned-office building.

Good Guys versus Bad Guys

Antibodies have become the topic of household conversations, endless newsreels, and water cooler chatter for the last couple of years. There is plenty of lay understanding of what antibodies are, where they come from, and why they are important, as both native to our bodies and also as drugs.

In biology, antibodies are the good guys. They circulate in the body looking to bind to an antigen which plays the role of the bad guy. Antibodies are derived from a special kind of white blood cell called B-cells. B-cells send out the good guys to put a stop to the bad guys.

Think about it this way: You wake up one morning to find that there is a rash of car break-ins in the neighborhood. You call the police station (B-cell) who dispatches a couple of cruisers. In one cruiser you have a very large, donut-fueled police officer (antibody) who is strong but not very light on his feet. It turns out that while his chance of catching a more-nimble perpetrator (antigen) is low, if and when he does encounter him he can not only bind him up, but he can also hold him like that for a long time.

In the other cruiser is a skinny cop who may be more likely to catch up to the vandal but is also more easily swatted away. This officer's ability to bind up the bad guy is weaker and lasts for a shorter time.

The relationship between antibodies and antigens is called *affinity*. It relates to how strong the bond is between them and how long they stay bound. These characteristics are oftentimes used as surrogates for how well an antibody might work as a drug and how often it may be dosed. For instance, if the antibody that binds to the target antigen which causes migraines is considered a tight binder, that usually means that the drug will (a) be effective at stopping migraines and (b) need only be administered once a month or even once every three months.

Another characteristic of the relationship between these good guys and bad guys is where the binding actually takes place. The landing spot on an antigen for antibodies is called the *epitope*. Going back to our analogy, if the police officer puts a headlock on the bad guy, that will neutralize the threat differently than if our cop is holding on to one foot as the bad guy tries to slither away.

Knowing where an antibody binds to its target is as important as describing the affinity. Both characteristics can determine a potential drug's efficacy, dosing regimen, immunogenicity, manufacturability, etc.

Antibodies as drugs—also called biologics—are more common and probably more successful than most people know. The most successful drug of all time, adalimumab (Humira), rakes in more than $20 billion a year; it's an antibody.[5] It's treatment of rheumatoid arthritis as well as several other indications is life changing for millions of people. Indeed, a majority of the best-selling drugs of all time are antibodies.[6] Companies like Biogen, Amgen, Genentech, and others have pioneered the use of biologics to improve the human condition.

Meaningfully Funded

Winning a few business case competitions certainly provided Carterra's founders with great expectations and hope. But $70,000 only goes so far with starving graduate students. Over the next ten years, Josh led the Herculean effort to keep the dream alive. Through government and university grants, friends and family, and angel investors, the promise of changing the way biologics would be discovered did—miraculously—live on.

In 2015, Wasatch Microfluidics got the attention of Pfizer's venture investing group. After the requisite diligence effort Pfizer reasoned that if they could provide some gas in the Wasatch tank that the prospect of not only improving biologics discovery but transforming it forever was within the reach of Wasatch and its CFM. So, Pfizer invested $1 million saying essentially, "Please make this happen."

It was only then that the broader investment community sat up and took notice. "What's going on in Salt Lake City?" was likely heard in board rooms throughout the venture world. Yes, Josh and the team at Wasatch had been knocking on doors for years looking for a meaningful amount of capital to get the CFM into a commercially viable format. But there is a big difference between the promise demonstrated by a fledgling technology and the person or firm who will actually write a seven or eight-figure check to back it.

Enter Telegraph Hill Partners (THP). Based in San Francisco, THP had been raising investment funds and putting capital to work in the life sciences and healthcare for more than 20 years. Their record of investing was stellar and they had been ranked in the top quartile of venture firms for return on investment after some strikingly prescient investments.

After an extensive diligence exercise in 2016, THP made the investment that Josh, Bruce, and Jim had been looking for more than a decade—enough money to scale the company and commercialize the CFM.[7] In the process, THP became Wasatch Microfluidics' majority investor. Shortly thereafter, they rebranded the company which included a name change to Carterra.

Since the original THP investment in Carterra, the company has executed almost exactly on the vision Josh presented to the Lassonde Entrepreneur Institute 15 years prior. An analytical instrument designed around the versatility and efficiency of the CFM, and using SPR for detection, was launched to the world by Carterra in early 2018. Named the Load Star Array (LSA), it is being used all over the world by scientists in pharmaceutical and biotech companies, contract research organizations

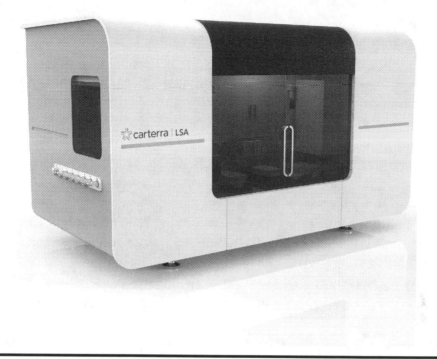

Figure 12.2   The Carterra LSA® instrument, used for antibody screening and char-acterization, employs the highest throughput, greatest assay sensitivity, and lowest sample requirement of any label-free biosensor. It is currently used throughout the world by pharmaceutical, biotech, academic, and government researchers to speed biologics and vaccine discovery.

(CROs), vaccine developers, antibody makers, as well as in the United States Food and Drug Administration (FDA) and the National Institutes of Health (NIH).[8] There are now greater than 100 of these devices all over the world, changing the method and the rate that biologics are being dis-covered (Figure 12.2).

A Global Pandemic—What Can We Do to Help?

In February of 2020 as the reality of a global pandemic settled in, I went to Josh and said,

> Hey, I know this looks bad for the world but I really think we can make a difference if we offer up some of our capacity. Are you OK if I volunteer some instrument and scientist time to see if we can help?

Without hesitation, Josh said, "Do it."

I immediately reached out to some of our contacts at the Bill & Melinda Gates Foundation and said, "What can we do to help?"

Our timing was good. Gates was in the process of announcing $125 million in seed funding for their COVID-19 Therapeutics Accelerator in conjunction with MasterCard and Wellcome.[9] As part of that effort they explained, a global consortium would be funded to try and discover antibodies that could be effective against COVID-19. "Hurry though," they said as the newly minted Coronavirus Immunotherapy Consortium (CoVIC) was putting out a press release to kick-off the effort the very next day.

We hustled to meet the principals at the La Jolla Institute for Immunology from which the consortium would be run and were able to join them in the press release.[10]

Since that introduction, the work that the consortium has accomplished is nothing short of astounding. Dr. Erica Ollmann Saphire was tapped by The Gates Foundation based on the very similar approach she led during the Ebola outbreak in 2013. As a result of that effort, several antibodies as therapeutic candidates were discovered and dozens of scientific papers were published.[11]

COVID-19 though was spreading fast and killing thousands and would only get worse. Rarely in science is there such an explicit need to go faster than ever before in the discovery of helpful medicines. The word then went out across the globe: send in your candidate antibodies and gain leverage in your research efforts by combining your work with other scientists from around the world.

While keeping intellectual property to themselves, the scientific community responded. Within a few months, more than 300 antibodies from dozens of labs far and wide began showing up at CoVIC. Governments, academic labs, and companies of every stripe began working together, sharing data, and trying to make sense of COVID-19 and the antibodies that could stop it.

Carterra's LSA was used as the principal engine to characterize the antibodies coming in from all over the world. Together with a lab at Duke University which also deployed the LSA, both affinity and epitope data was combined with other techniques to determine which antibodies had the best activity against COVID-19. Beyond that, there were also able to suggest which antibodies may be combined with each other in cocktails to make the therapeutic effect even more potent. All of this work was exquisitely presented in one of the most prestigious journals, *Science.*[12]

The First COVID-19 Therapeutic

In addition to the pro bono work done with CoVIC, Carterra's platform has been used by myriad other research teams to go faster than ever before in discovering and characterizing antibodies that will become effective drugs.

The fastest and most renown effort was conducted by Eli Lilly and Company along with their collaborator, AbCellera, a Canadian biotech based in British Columbia. While most commercial efforts by drug researchers are concealed until intellectual property can be protected and validating research is complete, Lilly and AbCellera announced to the world their intention to collaborate in order to find a potential therapeutic for the dreaded COVID-19. They would isolate 500 or more antibodies from the blood of one of the first COVID-19 survivors.[13]

From the time of their announcement to collaborate in March of 2020 to initiating a clinical trial for their candidate antibody was about 90 days. There had been no biologic discovered and characterized faster than that in the history of the planet. *Bamlanivimab* (nicknamed Bam-bam in the media) went through extensive testing and on November 9, 2020, was granted emergency use authorization by the FDA for use in mild to moderate COVID-19 patients with the risk of complications or hospitalization.[14]

At the time of this writing, a second therapeutic born from the Lilly-AbCellera collaboration named *Bebtelovimab* is being studied for its neutralizing activity across currently known and reported variants of concern, including Delta and Omicron.

Carterra's LSA played a significant role in the speed and efficiency that this record-breaking discovery demonstrated as explained in a webcast by one of Lilly's scientists in May 2021. And like CoVIC, Eli Lilly, and AbCellera published their work in the journal *Science* to help the world understand how such a transformation in biologics discovery was brought to bear at a time when it was never more important. They concluded, "The resulting speed at which this drug discovery and development effort proceeded, with progression to human treatment only 90 days after the initiation of antibody screening, was due to advanced discovery and characterization platforms …."[15]

Josh Eckman's dream to found a company that would not only be successful but also change the way in which humans do research has indeed been realized. From a garage to the hospital-turned-office building, Carterra has become one of the most important companies ever to be founded in Utah and the LSA will continue to help scientists improve the human condition.

References

1. Halverson, Dee. *St. Mark's Hospital, 1872–1997*. Salt Lake City: Heritage, 1997.
2. Horiuchi, Vincent. "Utah Artificial Heart Pioneer Dies." *UNews*. 7 August, 2018. U of Utah. <https://unews.utah.edu/utah-artificial-heart-pioneer-dies/>
3. Abery, Julian. "Carterra Inc. Raises $10M from Telegraph Hill Partners." *THPartners.net*. 17 January, 2018. Telegraph Hill Partners. <https://thpartners.net/carterra-inc-raises-10m-telegraph-hill-partners-develop-launch-next-generation-antibody-characterization-platform/>
4. Staff, Lassonde Institute. "U of Utah Ranked #8 Among Undergrad Entrepreneurship." *LEI*. 15 September, 2021. U of Utah. <https://lassonde.utah.edu/u-of-utah-ranked-no-8-for-undergraduate-entrepreneurship-no-5-among-public-schools-for-2022-by-u-s-news>
5. Dunleavy, Kevin. "Top 20 Drugs by Worldwide Sales in 2020." *Fierce Pharma*. 3 May, 2021. Special Reports. <https://www.fiercepharma.com/special-report/top-20-drugs-by-2020-sales-humira>
6. Brumley, James. "The 15 All-Time Best-Selling Prescription Drugs." *Kiplinger*. 5 December, 2017. Kiplinger/Investing. <https://www.kiplinger.com/slideshow/investing/t027-s001-the-15-all-time-best-selling-prescription-drugs/index.html>
7. Abery, Julian. "Carterra Inc. Raises $10M from Telegraph Hill Partners." *THPartners.net*. 17 January, 2018. Telegraph Hill Partners. <https://thpartners.net/carterra-inc-raises-10m-telegraph-hill-partners-develop-launch-next-generation-antibody-characterization-platform/>
8. Tan et al. "Bispecific Antibodies Targeting Distinct Regions of the Spike Protein Potently Neutralize SARS-CoV-2 Variants of Concern." *Science Translational Medicine*. 20 October, 2021. <https://www.science.org/doi/10.1126/scitranslmed.abj5413>
9. BMGF Media Contact. "Bill & Melinda Gates Foundation, Wellcome, and Mastercard Launch Initiative to Speed Development and Access to Therapies for COVID-19." *Gates Foundation*. 10 March, 2020. Gates/Media Center. <https://www.gatesfoundation.org/ideas/media-center/press-releases/2020/03/covid-19-therapeutics-accelerator>
10. McKinley, John. "Carterra, Inc. Selected by The La Jolla Institute for Immunology to Provide Antibody Screening and Characterization for the Coronavirus Immunotherapy Consortium (CoVIC)." *CISION-PRWeb*. 31 March, 2020. <https://www.prweb.com/releases/carterra_inc_selected_by_the_la_jolla_institute_of_immunology_to_provide_antibody_screening_and_characterization_for_the_coronavirus_immunotherapy_consortium_covic/prweb17016841.htm>
11. Saphire et al. "How to Turn Competitors into Collaborators." *Nature*. 19 January, 2017. Comment/article. <https://www.nature.com/articles/541283a>
12. Hastie et al. "Defining Variant-Resistant Epitopes Targeted by SARS-CoV-2 Antibodies: A Global Consortium Study." *Science*. 23 September, 2021. Report/coronavirus. <https://www.science.org/doi/10.1126/science.abh2315>

13. Hebert, Nicole. "AbCellera and Lilly to Co-Develop Antibody Therapies for the Treatment of COVID-19." *Eli Lilly.* 12 March, 2020. Investors/News Release. <https://investor.lilly.com/news-releases/news-release-details/abcellera-and-lilly-co-develop-antibody-therapies-treatment>

14. Jingling, Jessica. "AbCellera-Discovered Antibody Receives U.S. FDA Emergency Use Authorization as a Monotherapy for the Treatment of COVID-19." *AbCellera.* 9 November, 2020. News/Events. <https://investor.lilly.com/news-releases/news-release-details/abcellera-and-lilly-co-develop-antibody-therapies-treatment>

15. Jones et al. "The Neutralizing Antibody, LY-CoV555, Protects against SARS-CoV-2 Infection in Non-Human Primates." *Science.* 5 April, 2021. Research/coronavirus. <https://www.science.org/doi/10.1126/scitranslmed.abf1906>

Index

Note: **Bold** page numbers refer to tables; *italic* page numbers refer to figures.

Printed in the United States
by Baker & Taylor Publisher Services